Information Visualisation and Virtual Environments

Springer

London
Berlin
Heidelberg
New York
Barcelona
Hong Kong
Milan
Paris
Santa Clara
Singapore
Tokyo

Chaomei Chen

Information Visualisation and Virtual Environments

With 144 Figures

 Springer

Chaomei Chen, PhD, MSc, BSc
Department of Information Systems and Computing,
Brunel University, Uxbridge UB8 3PH, UK

ISBN 1-85233-136-4 Springer-Verlag London Berlin Heidelberg

British Library Cataloguing in Publication Data
Chen, Chomei
    Information visualisation and virtual environments
    1. Information display systems 2. Virtual reality 3. Computer
    Graphics Technological innovations
    I. Title
    006.7
ISBN 1852331364

Library of Congress Cataloging-in-Publication Data
Chen, Chomei, 1960-
    Information visualisation and virtual environments / Chaomei Chen.
    p. cm.
    Includes bibliographical references and index.
    ISBN 1-85233-136-4
    1. Information display systems. 2. Visualization. 3. Virtual
    reality. I. Title.
      TK7882.I6C477 1999   99-12444
      006—dc21   CIP

Typeset by Gray Publishing, Tunbridge Wells, Kent
Printed and bound at Kyodo Printing Co (S'pore) Pte Ltd
34/3830-543210 Printed on acid-free paper SPIN 10680991

To Baohuan, Calvin, and Steven

Contents

Preface

This book presents a comprehensive introduction to information visualisation and virtual environments. It not only provides a systematic overview of the two, but also reflects the latest research and development in the convergence of the two fields. It can be used as the main text, or a major source of references for courses in information visualisation, multimedia and virtual environments, human-computer interaction, hypertext/hypermedia, and information retrieval, and also provides a useful source of reference for consultants and practitioners.

During the course of the book, many significant, but so far isolated, research fronts are unified into a generic framework. As well as explaining underlying principles and details of a number of information visualisation techniques, it also highlights how these techniques can be adapted to meet specific requirements.

Information visualisation is growing fast, both as a field of research and as an industry with tremendous potential. Its interdisciplinary nature is becoming increasingly clear – the literature of information visualisation spans the spheres of computer graphics, electronic engineering, information systems, geography, and information science. Studies of information visualisation may focus on one or more aspects, including visual representation criteria, data structures and algorithms, rendering techniques, usability and evaluation, and work domain analysis. This makes a synthesis of such a diverse literature necessary for researchers and practitioners to identify and adapt the most suitable information visualisation solutions to their particular needs.

Virtual environments provide a unique medium for people to communicate and interact with each other across the boundary between geographical locations. Virtual environments are more than the technological infrastructure that enables users to communicate and interact. It is the experience of transcending geographical distance in the physical world, and constructing a mutual understanding and social dynamic that makes them particularly valuable. However, until recently, studies focusing on such experience have been relatively rare.

The focus of this book is not only on individual techniques, but also on the inspiration, extensibility, and adaptability resulting from a synthesis of these techniques and design principles. Special attention is paid to the role of information visualisation as an enabling technology in the design of new generations of virtual environments. The book is also intended to reflect the evolution of our own research in the areas of information visualisation, spatial hypertext, and semantically organised virtual environments.

The main topics are presented in each of six chapters:

Chapter 1: *Introduction*, introduces a number of intriguing examples of historical and geographic visualisations, including the loss of Napoleon's army, *ARPANET* maps, *NSFNET* traffic, and the *MBone* network. Information foraging and cognitive maps are highlighted as a major area of focus – visual navigation and information foraging in an abstract information space.

Chapter 2: *Finding Salient Structures*, introduces methods commonly used for extracting implicit structures, including automated construction of hypertext and the role of information retrieval models, especially the well-known *Vector Space* model and *Latent Semantic Indexing* model. The use of *WordNet*, structural analysis and modelling, and an introduction to *Generalised Similarity Analysis* (GSA) are also included.

Chapter 3: *Spatial Layout and Graph Drawing Algorithms*, focuses on aesthetic criteria and generation of spatial layouts and graph drawing. Clustering and scaling algorithms are introduced as a general background. Visualisation strategies for data structures such as hierarchies and networks are considered, and graph-drawing algorithms for general undirected graphs, especially the spring-embedder model and its variants, are discussed in detail.

Chapter 4: *Information Visualisation Systems and Applications*, the largest chapter in this book, classifies representative information visualisation systems into various categories, to clarify the rationale behind using particular information visualisation techniques. Categories include visualisation of search results, visualisation for exploration information spaces, and visualisation of the Web and the literature of a subject domain. The transition from visualising abstract information spaces to the concept of online communities and the social dynamics of a virtual environment is the focus of the last section of the chapter – 'The Web and online communities'.

Chapter 5: *Individual Differences in Visual Navigation*, focuses on the interrelationships between cognitive factors, such as spatial ability, associative memory, and visual memory, and the use of a user interface, in which a semantic space is visualised as an associative network. Three empirical studies incrementally investigate the interrelationships, based on factor-referenced tests of these cognitive abilities.

Chapter 6: *Virtual Environments*, explores the fundamental issues concerning the design of virtual environment and, especially, the role of abstract information spaces. It includes several examples of virtual environments, in particular, the design of *StarWalker*, a unique, three-dimensional virtual environment developed from our own research, and initial experience of its use on the Web. Dialogues in the *StarWalker* virtual environment are analysed with reference to theories on the duality of discourse structure and social context. In the final chapter, the notion of social navigation and its realisation in *StarWalker* raises a number of research issues concerning the integration of information visualisation and virtual environments.

Acknowledgements

This book draws heavily on the outcome of our research project funded by the British Engineering and Physical Sciences Research Council (EPSRC) under the Multimedia and Networking Applications Programme (MNA) (Grant Number GR/L61088). The research was also funded in part by the Brunel Research and Innovative Enterprise Fund (BRIEF).

I would like to thank Professor Ray Paul at Brunel University for his encouragement and support in writing this book, and Professor Bob O'Keefe for arranging a congenial environment for research at Brunel University. I would also like to express my gratitude to people who have helped to crystalise the ideas and thoughts that shape the book, and to those who have helped the research in general.

Thanks to my colleagues and students at Brunel University for participating in a series of empirical studies described in this book.

Special thanks to Linda Thomas of Brunel University, UK; Mary Czerwinski of Microsoft Research, USA; Wendy Hall and Les Carr of Southampton University, UK; Roy Rada of Rice University, USA; John Davies of BT Laboratories, UK; Terry Mayes of Glasgow Caledonian University, UK; Alistair Kilgour of Heriot-Watt University, UK; Mike Foryth of Calligrafix Ltd., UK; and Janet Cole of Brunel University, UK.

Special thanks also to Rebecca Moore for her efficient work at Springer-Verlag, London.

Chaomei Chen
Uxbridge, England

Chapter 1
Introduction

Information visualisation as a distinctive field of research has less than ten years of history, but has rapidly become a far-reaching, inter-disciplinary research field. Works on information visualisation are now found in the literature of a large number of subject domains, notably information retrieval (IR), hypertext and the world-wide web (WWW), digital libraries (DL), and human-computer interaction (HCI). The boundary between information visualisation and related fields such as scientific visualisation and simulation modelling is becoming increasingly blurred.

Information visualisation represents one of the latest streams in a long-established trend in the modern user interface design. The desire to manipulate objects on a computer screen has been the driving force behind many popular user interface design paradigms. Increasing layers of user interface are being added between the user and the computer, yet the interface between the two is becoming more transparent, more natural, and more intuitive, as, for example, the 'what-you-see-is-what-you-get' (WYSIWYG) user interfaces, 'point-and-click and drag-and-drop' direct manipulation user interfaces, and 'fly-through' in virtual reality worlds.

The fast advancing of information visualisation also highlights fundamental research issues. First, the *art* of information visualisation perhaps appropriately describes the state of the field. It is currently a challenging task for designers to find out the strategies and tools available to visualise a particular type of information. Information visualisation involves a large number of representational structures, some of them well understood, and many new. Furthermore, new ways of representing information are being invented all the time. Until recently, systematic integration of information visualisation techniques into the design of information-intensive systems has not occurred. An exceptional trend is the use of cone trees and fisheye views to visualise hierarchical structures. For example, cone trees are used in LyberWorld (Hemmje *et al.*, 1994), Cat-a-Cone (Hearst & Karadi, 1997), and Hyperbolic 3D (Munzner, 1998). The WWW has significantly pushed forward the visualisation of network structures and general graphs. Nevertheless, a taxonomy of information visualisation is needed so that designers can select appropriate techniques to meet given requirements. It is still difficult to compare information visualisation across different designs.

The second issue is the lack of generic criteria to assess the value of information visualisation, either independently, or in a wider context of user activities. This is a challenging issue, since most people develop their own criteria for what makes a good visual representation. The study of individual differences in the use of information visualisation systems is a potentially fruitful research avenue. Much attention has been paid to a considerable number of cognitive factors, such as spatial ability, associative memory, and visual memory. These cognitive factors, and various cognitive styles and learning styles, form a large part of individual differences, especially when visual representations are involved.

The third issue is the communicative role of information visualisation components in a shared, multi-user virtual environment. It is natural to combine information visualisation with virtual reality, and the use of virtual reality naturally leads to the construction and use of virtual environments. The transition from information visualisation to multi-user virtual environments marks a significant difference in user perspective. Individual perspectives are predominant in most information visualisation design, while social perspectives are inevitable in a virtual environment.

Individuals may respond with different interpretations of the same information visualisation. In a virtual environment, the behaviour of users and how they interact with each other is likely to be influenced by the way in which the virtual environment is constructed. So far, few virtual environments are designed using abstract information visualisation as an overall organisational principle. How do we ascertain the influence of information visualisation techniques on the construction of a virtual environment, on user behaviour, their understanding, interpretation, and experiences? Do people attach special meanings to these abstract information visualisation objects? And in what way will visualised information structures affect social interaction and intellectual work in a virtual environment? To answer these questions may open a new frontier to research in information visualisation. More fundamentally, appropriate theories and methodologies are needed to account for such cognitive and social activities in relation to information visualisation.

In this book, we use some representative examples of information visualisation to illustrate these issues and potential research areas in information visualisation and virtual environments. We aim to take a step towards a taxonomy of information visualisation, by highlighting and contrasting the commonality and uniqueness of existing information visualisation designs in terms of overall design rationale, interaction metaphors, criteria and algorithms, and evaluation. Three empirical studies are included, which concern the relationships between individual differences, namely three cognitive factors, and the use of a user interface design based on a visualised semantic space for information foraging. The studies provide the reader with some results of our latest research.

Each chapter in the book addresses one main topic. Chapter 2 introduces methods for finding or extracting backbone structures from a complex set of information. Chapter 3 focuses on techniques for generating spatial layouts and graph-drawing techniques. General criteria for visualising hierarchical and network structures are also highlighted. Chapter 4 collects and arranges representative information visualisation designs and systems into several broad categories, in order to highlight their similarities and distinctiveness of design. Chapter 5 presents three empirical studies, focusing on the interrelationships between individual differences, and the use of information visualisation techniques in user interface design. In particular, the three cognitive factors of spatial ability, associative memory, and visual memory, are examined. All these tests are based on the widely accessible factor-referenced tests prepared by the

Educational Testing Service (Eckstrom *et al.*, 1976). Finally, Chapter 6 looks beyond information visualisation *per se,* and focuses on its role in shaping social interactive behaviour in a virtual environment. StarWalker is introduced, as a unique 3D multi-user virtual environment, to explore the social and ecological dimensions of virtual environments.

We will start with examples of geographical visualisation, in which information is organised on a geographical framework. Information visualised in this way tends to be intuitive and easy to understand, and will provide a starting point for us to proceed to visualising more abstract information, where we may not be able to map information onto a geographic map, or a relief map of the earth. We must, therefore, find new ways to organise and accommodate such information, and create data structures capable of representing characteristics of an abstract information space. There will also be some discussion of optimal foraging theory and cognitive map theories, and their implications on information visualisation.

1.1 Geographic Visualisation

Information visualisation is rooted in a number of closely related areas, particularly in geographical information. When geographical mapping is possible, information can be organised in association with geographical positions in a very natural and intuitive way. The influence of geographical and spatial metaphors is so strong that they can be found in most information visualisation systems.

Spatial metaphors not only play a predominant role in information visualisation, but also become one of the most fundamental design models of virtual environments. The central theme of this book is to reveal the underlying connection between information visualisation and virtual environments, which are effectively brought together by spatial metaphors. Such integration sets information visualisation in the wider, richer context of social and ecological dynamics, provided by a virtual environment. At the same time, virtual environments are better able to fulfil their ambitions with the power of information visualisation.

1.1.1 The Loss of Napoleon's Army

One picture is worth a thousand words. A classic example is the compelling story-telling map by Charles Joseph Minard (1781–1870), which vividly reveals the losses of Napoleon's army in 1812 (Figure 1.1).

The size of Napoleon's army is shown as the width of the band in the map, starting on the Russian-Polish border with 422,000 men. By the time they reached Moscow in September, the size of the army had dropped to 100,000. Eventually, only a small fraction of Napoleon's original army survived the journey.

Recently, the map was re-drawn by a group of researchers at Carnegie Mellon University using an information visualisation system called SAGE (Roth *et al.*, 1997).[1] The new version of the map, shown in Fig. 1.2, and drawn using almost

---

[1] See Chapter 4 for more details about SAGE.

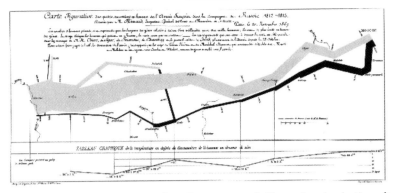

Figure 1.1   The paths of Napoleon's army (http://www.cs.cmu.edu/Groups/sage/project/samples/sage/
Minard-Tufte.html).

the same techniques as Minard's original ones, aims to reveal various details and their relationships more accurately. The steadily dropping temperature was a major factor during the retreat. The SAGE version is able to represent such change of temperature in different colours along with the shrinking size of Napoleon's army. This colour coding clearly shows the heat wave in the first few months, and the steady decline in temperature throughout the retreat. There was a spell of milder temperatures when the retreating army was between the cities of Krasnyj and Bobrsov.

Figure 1.3 is another map generated by SAGE, based on Minard's data. Here, time, place, and temperature are incorporated in the visual representation. The horizontal axis is the time line. Lengthy stays at particular places are shown as gaps between coloured blocks. and battlefields are shown as diamonds. These improvements show something that was not so obvious in Minard's map, i.e. what happened to the northern flank of Napoleon's army – it branched off from the main force, captured Polock in August, and remained there until after a

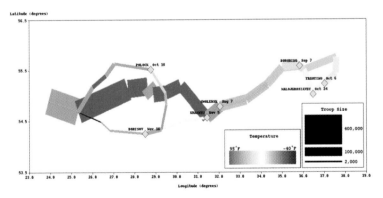

Figure 1.2   Napoleon's retreat, visualised by the SAGE system (http://www.cs.cmu.edu/Groups/sage/
project/samples/sage/napol-sage1.gif). (Reprinted with permission of Mark Derthick.)

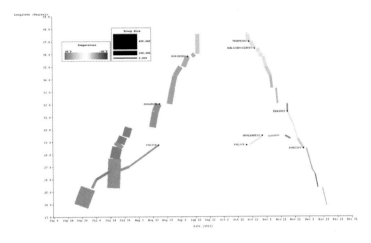

Figure 1.3 Time, place, and temperature are attributes of the movement (http://www.cs.cmu.edu/Groups/sage/project/samples/sage/napol-sage2.html). (Reprinted with permission of Mark Derthick.)

second battle in October. Later in November, they rejoined the main retreat, as the temperature dropped dramatically.

Information visualisation is often a powerful and effective tool for conveying a complex idea. However, as shown in the above example, one may often need to use a number of complimentary visualisation methods in order to reveal various relationships.

1.1.2 The Origins of the Internet

As we will see in later chapters, many information visualisation systems are based on organisational principles rooted in the geographical paradigm, which is closely related to the more generic use of spatial metaphors in information visualisation and virtual environments. Spatial metaphors are traditionally, and increasingly, popular in information visualisation and virtual environments. A fruitful way to explore their role is to examine the boundary conditions of when and where they would be an appropriate and adequate option.

The following examples represent some of the major developments in visualising the Internet and its predecessors. Special attention is drawn to the role of the geographical paradigm in information organisation and visualisation.

Where Wizards Stay Up Late: The Origins of the Internet, written by Hafner and Lyon (1996), provides a wonderful starting point to explore the early days of computer networks across universities, countries, and continents. It is a thought-provoking book to read, and to reflect upon today's widespread use of the WWW. There is a companion website, wizards,[2] aiming to establish a central repository for information concerning the origins of the Internet. Wizards

---

[2]http://www.fixe.com/wizards/

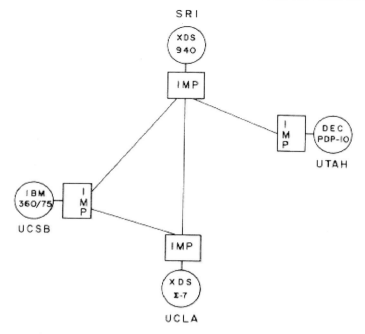

Figure 1.4   The initial four-node ARPANET (http://www.fixe.com/wizards/fournode.html).

website invites people to contribute and recommend new links to the site. (E-mail: wizards@construct.net.) Wizards contains dozens of diagrams, hand-drawn sketches and maps, photographs and technical papers, in particular, maps and drawings of the earliest networks.

In 1966, the U.S. Defense Department's Advanced Research Projects Agency (ARPA) funded a project to create computer communication among its university-based researchers. This multimillion-dollar network, known as the ARPANET, was launched in 1969 by ARPA, with the aim of linking dozens of major computer science labs throughout the country. An informative timeline of this part of its history is now available on the Web.[3]

The first four sites chosen to form the ARPANET were University of California Los Angles (UCLA), SRI, University of California Santa Barbara (UCSB), and the University of Utah. Figure 1.4 is the initial configuration of this ARPANET. IMP is the packet switch scheme used on it.

The network had grown to 34 IMP nodes by September 1972. The first ARPANET geographic map (Fig. 1.5) appeared in August 1977. Hubs at both the west and east coasts are clearly shown in the map, and links to Hawaii and London were based on satellite circuits.

Figure 1.6 is the geographic map of the ARPANET in October 1987, ten years later.

---

[3]http://www.bbn.com/timeline/

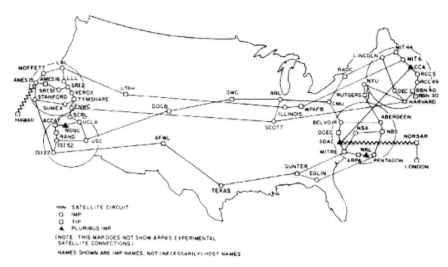

Figure 1.5   Geographical map of ARPANET (1977) (http://www.fixe.com/wizards/images/net77.gif).

NSFNET, commissioned by the National Science Foundation (USA), marks another historical stage in the development of global computer networks. The following section contains visualisations of NSFNET traffic in the 1990's. They are also based on geographical maps.

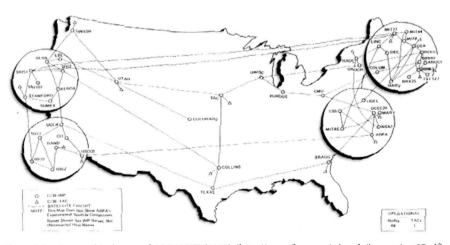

Figure 1.6   Geographical map of ARPANET (1987) (http://www.fixe.com/wizards/images/net87.gif).

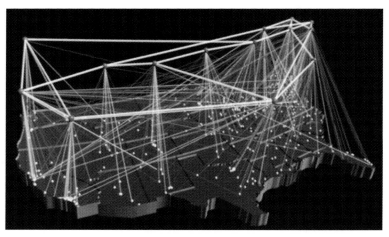

Figure 1.7   Billion-byte traffic into the NSFNET T1 backbone in 1991 (http://www.ncsa.uiuc.edu/SCMS/DigLib/stills/1452.cox.lg.gif).

1.1.3 Visualisation of the NSFNET

NSFNET was commissioned by National Science Foundation until April 1995. A number of commercial carriers have maintained the NSFNET backbone service. Donna Cox and Robert Patterson at the National Center for Supercomputing Applications (NCSA) visualised various traffics on the NSFNET, from 1991 until the NSFNET was decommissioned in 1995.[4]

Visualisations of the NSFNET include byte and billion-byte traffic into the NSFNET backbones at two levels: T1 backbone (up to 100 billion bytes) and T3 backbone (up to one trillion bytes from its client networks). The volume of the traffic is colour-coded, ranging from zero bytes (purple) to 100 billion bytes (white).

Figure 1.8 is a visualisation of inbound traffic measured in billions of bytes on the NSFNET T1 backbone in September 1991. The volume of the traffic is colour-coded, ranging from zero bytes (purple) to 100 billion bytes (white). Traffic on the NSFNET has been vividly characterised by these powerful geographic visualisations.

Figure 1.9 represents byte traffic into the ANS/NSFNET T3 backbone in November, 1993. The coloured lines represent virtual connections from the network sites to the backbone.

1.1.4 Geographical Visualisation of WWW Traffic

The WWW is by far the most predominant traffic on the Internet. There is a growing interest in understanding the geographical dispersion of access patterns

---

[4]http://www.ncsa.uiuc.edu/SCMS/DigLib/text/technology/Visualization-Study-NSFNET-Cox.html

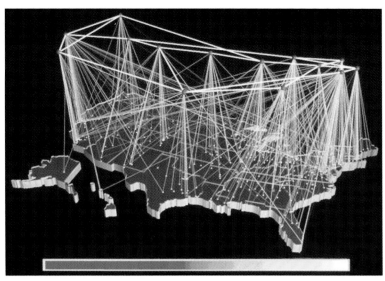

Figure 1.8   Billion-byte inbound traffic on the NSFNET T1 backbone (1991) (http://www.ncsa.uiu-c.edu/SCMS/DigLib/stills/1445.cox.lg.gif).

to the WWW, especially from electronic commerce and commercial Internet service providers. A geographical visualisation of the WWW traffic is presented by a group of researchers at the National Center for Supercomputing

Figure 1.9   Byte traffic into the ANS/NSFNET T3 backbone in November 1993 (http://www.ncsa.uiu-c.edu/SCMS/DigLib/stills/1678.cox.lg.jpg).

Table 1.1 File types and filename extensions

File types	Extension/format
text	txt, html, ps, doc, tex, pdf
graphics	gif, jpg, tif
audio	au, aiff, aifc, wav
video	mpeg
VRML worlds	wrl

Table 1.2 Domain name conversions

Domain name extension	Domain type
edu	U.S. education
com	U.S. commercial
ac.uk	UK academic
co.uk	UK commerical

Applications (NCSA) (Lamm *et al.*, 1995). Patterns of access requests received by the WWW server complex at the NCSA are mapped to geographic locations on the globe of the earth. Because the Mosaic WWW browser was developed at NCSA, the access load on the NCSA WWW server is always high, which makes the NCSA WWW server an ideal high-load test bed.

All the WWW servers run NCSA's Hypertext Transfer Protocol Daemon (httpd), which deals with access requests. It maintains four logs on the local disk: document accesses, agents, errors, and referers. NCSA's geographical map of the WWW traffic focuses on the document access logs, because they record interesting information about each access request. Nevertheless, other logs also provide potentially useful data. For instance, statistics of the use of Netscape or Internet Explorer can be obtained from the agent logs. More interestingly, one may identify how the user gets to the current link from the referer's logs.

Each entry of the access log includes seven fields, namely the IP address of the requesting client, the time of the request, the name of the requested document, and the number of bytes sent in response to the request. Particularly, the file name usually contains further information about the nature of the request; the extension of a filename may reveal whether the requested file is text, an image, audio, video or special types of files.

Geographic mapping particularly relies on the information encoded in the IP address field of server access logs. Each IP address can be converted to a domain name. It is this domain name that can be used to match each access request to a geographical location, although this matching scheme may break down in certain circumstances.

NCSA's geographical visualisation is based on IP addresses and domain names. The geographic mapping also relies on the InterNIC, *whois* database containing information on domains, hosts, networks, and other Internet administrators, and, more usefully for geographical mapping, a postal address. Each access request is mapped to a city, or the capital of a country if it is outside the US. The latitude and longitude of the city is then retrieved from a local database.

Initially, the geographical mapping must rely on the results of queries sent to the remote *whois* database, but a local database is gradually replacing the need for accessing to a remote database, as a greater number of matched IP addresses are accumulated in the local database.

Figure 1.10 shows two snapshots of the NCSA geographic visualisation. The surface of the earth is rendered according to altitude relief from the USGS

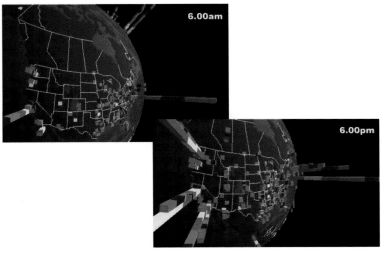

Figure 1.10   Access requests to NCSA's WWW server complex (Eastern Standard Time August 22, 1995, 6.00 a.m. and 6.00 p.m.) (http://www5conf.inria.fr/fich_html/papers/P49/Overview.html). (Reprinted with permission of Daniel Reed).

ETOP05 database,[5] and political boundaries are drawn from the CIA World Map database.

Arcs and stacked bars are two popular methods of visualising data on a sphere. Arcs are commonly used to display point-to-point communication traffic, for example, the visualisation of the topology of MBone (Munzner *et al.*, 1996).

Stacked bars are particularly useful for associating data to a geographical point, representing various data by position, height, and colour bands. In NCSA's geographic visualisation, each bar is placed on the geographic location of a WWW request to the NCSA's Web server. The height of a bar indicates the number of bytes, or the number of requests relative to other sites. The colour bands represent the distribution of document types, domain classes, or time intervals, between successive requests.

Figure 1.10 contains two snapshots of a single day, separated by twelve hours, on August 22, 1995. The first was in the morning Eastern Standard Time (6.00 a.m.), and the second was in the evening (6.00 p.m.). Europe is a major source of activity at the NCSA WWW server. The first snapshot shows some high stacked bars in Europe, while most of the US sites were quiet. In the evening, access requests from the US were in a full swing. Even now, one could still see a similar pattern as on the geographical map of the ARPANET twenty years ago – the west and east coasts generated by far the most access requests to NCSA's server. High population areas, such as New York and Los Angeles, are major sources of WWW traffic.

According to Lamm *et al.*, (1995), large corporations and commercial Internet service providers tend to appear as the originating point for the largest number

---

[5]http://www.usgs.gov/data/cartographic/

of accesses. Smaller sites, such as universities, government laboratories, and small companies, constitute a large portion of all accesses, but they are geographically distributed more uniformly. Based on NCSA's data in 1994 and 1995, government and commercial access is growing much more rapidly than that of educational institutions. Lamm *et al.* also found that requests for audio and video files are much more common during the normal business day than during the evening hours. They conjecture that this reflects both lower bandwidth links to Europe and Asia, and low speed modem-based access via commercial service providers. Such findings have profound implications for the design of WWW servers and browsers, as well as Internet services providers.

The NCSA group is working on a geographical visualisation that would allow users to zoom closer to selected regions, and gain a more detailed perspective than is presently possible with fixed region clustering. They are currently adding more detailed information to geographical databases for Canada and the UK.

1.1.5 Geographical Visualisation of the MBone

The MBone is the Internet's multicast backbone. Multicast distributes data from one source to multiple receivers, with minimal packet duplication. A visualisation of the global topology of the Internet MBone is presented by Munzner *et al.*, (1996), again illustrating the flexibility and extensibility of the geographical visualisation paradigm.

The MBone provides an efficient means of transmitting real-time video and audio streams across the Internet. It has been used for conferences, meetings, congressional sessions, and NASA shuttle launches. The MBone network is growing exponentially, without a central authority; visualising the topology of the MBone has profound implications for network providers and the multicast research community.

Munzner *et al.* maps the latitude and longitude of MBone routers on a 3D geographical information. The connections between MBone routers are represented as arcs. The geographical visualisation of the MBone is made as an interactive 3D map using VRML – Virtual Reality Modelling Language. The visualisation is shown in Fig. 1.11. In Fig. 1.12, the globe is wrapped with a satellite photograph of the earth surface.

1.1.6 Visualisation of Routing Dynamics

How long will it take for packets to travel from one point to another on the Internet? CAIDA's Skitter[6] is designed to measure and visualise routing dynamics (CAIDA, 1998; Huffaker *et al.*, 1998). The round-trip time taken from the source to the destination and back to the source is measured and visualised. Skitter measures the round-trip time by sending packets to a destination and recording the replies from routers along the way. Figure 1.13 shows a visualisation of paths from one source host to 23,000 destinations.

---

[6]http://www.caida.org/Tools/Skitter

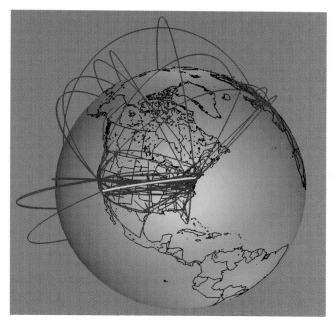

Figure 1.11 Geographical visualisation of the MBone (Munzer *et al.*, 1996). (© 1996 IEEE, reprinted with permission).

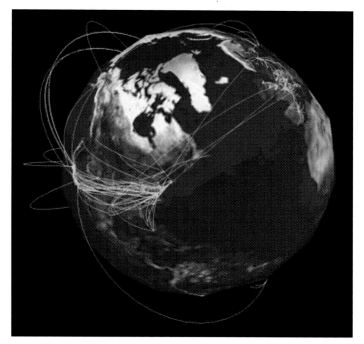

Figure 1.12 Geographical visualisation of the MBone on a satellite photograph of the earth surface (Munzer *et al.*, 1996). (© 1996 IEEE, reprinted with permission).

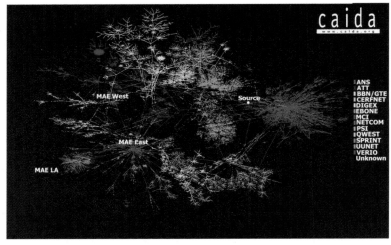

Figure 1.13 Skitter visualisation of top autonomous system (AS): a component of the network that controls its own routing within its infrastructure and uses an external routing protocol to communicate with other AS'es (http://www.caida.org/Tools/Otter/Skitter/Images/skitter.topas.gif). (Reprinted with permission from CAIDA).

Analysis of real-world trends in routing behaviour across the Internet has direct implications for the next generation of networking applications. The primary design goal of Skitter was to visualise the network connectivity from a

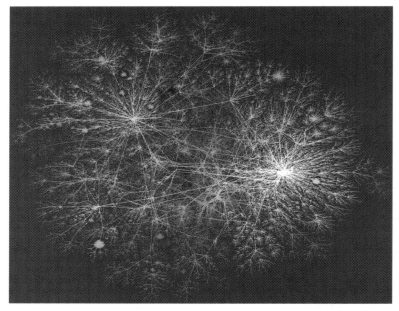

Figure 1.14 Another visualisation from Skitter. (Reprinted with permission from CAIDA.)

source host as a directed graph. Skitter probes destinations on the network. The results are represented as a spanning tree with its root node at the probing host, also known as the polling host. The data is then aggregated and shown as a top-down, macroscopic view of a cross-section of the Internet. Visualisation of macro-level traffic patterns can give insights into several areas; for example, mapping dynamic changes in Internet topology, tracking abnormal delays, and identifying bottleneck routers and critical paths in the Internet infrastructure.

Interestingly, CAIDA is planning to tap the Skitter output data with a geographical database of various crucial backbone networks on the Internet, the MBone and caching hierarchy topology. These data together can help engineers to pinpoint routing anomalies, and track round-trip times and packet loss.

CAIDA's short term plans include developing 3D visualisations of Skitter measurements, using additional active and passive measurement hosts throughout the Internet, and analysing trends in these traffic data.

Similar work has been done at Matrix Information Directory Services (MIDS) in mapping the Internet. MIDS produces an animated map known as the Internet Weather Report[7] (IWR), which updates network latencies on the Internet six times a day, probed from MIDS's Headquarters in Texas to over 4,000 domains around the world.

Martin Dodge, at University College of London, maintains a wonderful collection, called the Atlas of Cyberspace, of fascinating geographical visualisation images on the Web.[8] The original sources of some examples in this book were found via hyperlinks from the Atlas. The site also distributes a monthly newsletter on new updates on the gallery to subscribers. Subscription is free.

1.2 Abstract Information Visualisation

We have seen some fascinating visualisation works based on geographical maps. These visualisations appear to be simple, intuitive, and natural. They seem to break the barrier between a complex system and the knowledge of a specific subject domain.

This intuitiveness is largely due to the use of a geographical visualisation paradigm – information is essentially organised and matched to a geographical structure. The visualisations are based on the world map that we are all familiar with, and yet a large amount of information is made available for people to understand. Having seen the power of geographical visualisation paradigms, we will focus on some questions concerning information visualisation and virtual environments more generally.

- Are these geographic visualisation paradigms extensible to information that may not be geographical or astronomical in nature?
- How do we visualise abstract information spaces in general?
- What are the criteria for an informative and insightful visualisation of an abstract information space?

---

[7]http://www.mids.org/weather/
[8]http://www.atlascyberspace.org/geographic.html

● What are the human factor issues that must be taken into account?

The following sections will introduce optimal information foraging and cognitive maps, in order to understand the context in which information visualisation might be useful.

1.3 Optimal Information Foraging

Information visualisation often plays an integral part in more complex intellectual work. The value of specific information visualisation techniques can only be fully appreciated in such contexts. The design of information visualisation has produced numerous analogues and metaphors, navigating in information landscape and treasure hunting in digital information spaces being the most influential ones.

Information foraging theory is built on an ecological perspective to the study of information-seeking behaviour (Pirolli and Card., 1995).Optimal foraging theory was originally developed in biology and anthropology, being used to analyse various food-foraging strategies and how they are adapted to a specific situation. Information foraging theory is an adaptation of the optimal foraging theory, to provide an analytic methodology to assess information search strategies in a similar approach. Like the original optimal foraging theory, it focuses on the trade-off between information gains and the cost of retrieval for the user.

Information foraging is a broad term. A wide variety of activities associated with assessing, seeking, and handling information sources can be categorised as information foraging. Furthermore, the term 'foraging' refers both to the metaphor of browsing and searching for something valuable, and to the connection with the optimal foraging theory in biology and anthropology. In information foraging, one must make optimal use of knowledge about expected information value and expected costs of accessing and extracting the relevant information. Pirolli (1998) applies information foraging theory to the analysis of the use of Scatter/Gather browser (Pirolli *et al.*, 1996), and particularly explains the gains and losses from the user's point of view in accessing the relevance of document clusters. The Scatter/Gather interface presents users with a navigable, automatically computed overview of the contents of a document collection, represented as a hierarchy of document clusters.

Information foraging on the Web provides a good example of the types of decisions that one has to make. Here is a typical scenario: 'I have a meeting in half an hour. Should I spend 12 minutes downloading this big file? It seems interesting, but I am not sure how useful it is until I have read the contents.'

In hypertext, or on the Web, we may experience common navigational behaviour, known as branching, when we have to decide which thread of discussion we want to follow. Such decision making has been identified as one of the major sources of cognitive overload for hypertext readers. Users cannot simply read *on*. They must choose, or gamble in many situations, the path that is most likely to be informative and fruitful to them. The cost of such decision making is associated with how easy a user interface or the network connection allows users to *undo* their selected actions. Global overview maps are often used to help users make up their mind easily. Information visualisation in an abstract information space is largely playing a similar role: to guide users to find valuable information with the minimum cost.

1.4 Exploring Cyberspaces

The concept of a cognitive map plays an influential role in the study of navigation strategies, such as browsing in hyperspace and wayfinding in virtual environments (Darken and Sibert, 1996). A cognitive map could be seen as the internalised analogy in the human mind to the physical layout of the environment (Tversky, 1993; Thorndyke and Hayes-Roth, 1982; Tolman, 1948). The acquisition of navigational knowledge proceeds through several developmental stages, from the initial identification of landmarks in the environment to a fully formed mental map (Thorndyke and Hayes-Roth, 1982).

Landmark knowledge is often the basis for building our cognitive maps (Thorndyke and Hayes-Roth, 1982). The development of visual navigation knowledge may start with highly salient visual *landmarks* in the environment, such as unique and magnificent buildings, or natural landscapes. People associate their location in the environment with reference to these landmarks.

The acquisition of *route* knowledge is usually the next stage in developing a cognitive map. Route knowledge is characterised by the ability to navigate from one point to another using acquired landmark knowledge, without association to the surrounding areas. Route knowledge does not provide the navigator with enough information about the environment to enable the person to optimise their route for navigation. If someone with route knowledge wanders off the route, it would be very difficult for that person to backtrack to the right route.

The cognitive map is not considered fully developed until *survey* knowledge has been acquired (Thorndyke and Hayes-Roth, 1982). The physical layout of the environment has to be mentally transformed by the user to form a cognitive map.

Dillon *et al.* (1990) point out that when users navigate through an abstract structure such as a deep menu tree, if they select wrong options at a deep level they tend to return to the top of the tree altogether, rather than just take one step back. This strategy suggests the absence of survey knowledge about the structure of the environment, and a strong reliance on landmarks to guide navigation. Existing studies have suggested that there are ways to increase the likelihood that users will develop survey knowledge of an electronic space. For instance, intensive use of maps tends to increase survey knowledge in a relatively short period of time (Lokuge *et al.*,1996). Other studies have shown that strong visual cues indicating paths and regions can help users to understand the structure of a virtual space (Darken and Sibert, 1996).

By and large, visual information navigation relies on the construction of a cognitive map, and the extent to which users can easily connect the structure of their cognitive maps with the visual representations of an underlying information space. The concept of a cognitive map suggests that users need information about the structure of a complex, richly interconnected information space. However, if all the connectivity information were to be displayed, users would be unlikely to navigate effectively in spaghetti-like visual representations.

Give this conundrum, how do designers of complex hypertext visualisations optimise their user interfaces for navigation and retrieval?

One problem faced by designers is that detail concerning an explicit, logical structure may not be readily available in visualisation form. An explicit organising structure may not always naturally exist for a given data set, or the existing structure may simply be inappropriate for the specific tasks at hand. What methods are available for designers to derive and expose an appropriate structure in the user interface? How can we connect such designs with the user's cognitive map for improved learning and navigation?

1.5 Social Interaction in Online Communities

An example of a move from individualistic views of knowledge to socially constructed views has been found in the work of Barrett (1989), concerning the hypertext community. Most virtual environments on the Internet have a common goal of supporting social interaction in an electronic information space. Much attention has been devoted to the role of spatial metaphors in fostering social interaction in such environments. A powerful framework of navigation distinguishes three major paradigms: spatial, semantic, and social navigation (Dourish and Chalmers, 1994).

Spatial navigation mimics our experiences in the physical world. A virtual environment may be a geometric model of a part of the real world, such as a town hall, a bank, or a theatre. Users may navigate in the virtual world entirely based on their experiences in navigating through a city or a building in the real world.

Instead of following the geometric properties of a virtual world, in semantic navigation, navigation is driven by semantic relationships, or underlying logic. A good example of semantic navigation is navigation in hypertext. We follow a hypertext link from one part of the hyperspace to another because they are semantically related, rather than based on geometric properties. Finally, social navigation is an information browsing strategy that takes advantage of the behaviour of like-minded people.

The use of spatial models in attempts to support collaborative virtual environments has been criticised as over-simplifying the issue of structuring, or framing, interactive behaviour. Harrison and Dourish (1996) examine the notions of space and spatial organisation of virtual environments. They call for a re-examination of the role of spatial models in facilitating and structuring social interaction. They highlight the critical distinction between space and place by arguing that it is the notion of place, rather than that of space, which actually frames interactive behaviour.

According to Harrison and Dourish (1996), designers are looking for a critical property that can facilitate and shape interactive behaviour in a distributed working environment. This critical property, called appropriate behavioural framing, will provide users with a reference framework in which they can judge the appropriateness of their behaviour. They argue that spatial models are simply not enough for people to adapt their behaviour accordingly. Rather, it is a sense of place and shared understanding about behaviour and action in a specific culture that shapes the way we interact and communicate (Harrison and Dourish, 1996).

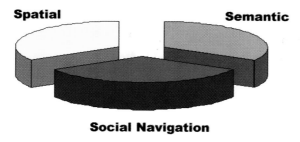

Figure 1.15   Spatial, semantic, and social navigation paradigms.

Context is a recurring concept in the design of a virtual environment that can support social interaction. Several methodologies from sociology, anthropology, and linguistics are potentially useful for exploring the structure of social interaction and how it reflects the influence of a meaningful context. Two concepts are particularly concerned with structures of social contexts: the concept of *contextualisation cues* from linguistics (Gumperz, 1982), and the concept of *frames* from sociology (Goffman, 1974). The following review is partially based on Drew and Heritage (1992).

Sociolinguistics had initially treated context in terms of the social attributes speakers bring to talk – for example, age, class, ethnicity, gender, geographical region, and other relationships. Studies of data from natural settings have showed that the relevance of these attributes depended upon the particular setting in which the talk occurred, and also upon the particular speech activities or tasks speakers were engaged in within those settings.

The dynamic nature of social contexts and the importance of linguistic details in evoking them have been studied in Gumperz (1982). It is shown that any aspect of linguistic behaviour may function as a contextualisation cue, including lexical, phonological, and syntactic choices, together with the use of particular codes, dialects, or styles. These contextualisation cues indicate which aspects of the social context are relevant in interpreting what a speaker means. By indicating significant aspects of the social context, contextualisation cues enable people to make inferences about one another's communicative intentions and goals.

The notion of contextualisation cues offered an important analytical way to grasp the relationship between language use and speakers' orientations to context and inference making. There is a significant similarity between the linguistic concept of contextualisation cues as outlined by Gumperz (1982), and the sociological concept of *frames* developed by Goffman (1974). The notion of *frames* focuses on the definition which participants give to their current social activity, to what is going on, what the situation is, and the roles adopted by the participants within it. These two concepts both relate specific linguistic options to the social activity in which language is being engaged.

Activity theory is rooted in the work of the Russian psychologist L. Vygotsky. Traditionally, this theory has a strong influence in Scandinavian countries. Since late 1980s however, there is an increasingly growing interest in activity theory in Human–Computer Interaction (HCI) (Nardi, 1996), Computer-Supported

Cooperative Work (CSCW) (Kuutti and Arvonen, 1992), and Information Science (Hjorland, 1997).

According to activity theory, cognition is an adaptation of one's knowledge to ecological and social environments. The individual's information needs, knowledge, and subjective relevance criteria should be seen in a larger context (Hjorland, 1997).

This book aims to explore and develop virtual environments that take into account the dynamics of social structures, such as rules and resources, and to provide an environment for the social construction of knowledge. We are interested in building virtual environments in which spatial, semantic, and social navigation can be organically combined together. People will be able to chat and have light conversations, but also engage in social interaction as a part of collaborative intellectual work, in particular subject domains.

1.6 Information Visualisation Resources

There has been a steady growth of interest in information visualisation and in virtual worlds. Figure 1.16 shows the results of a recent search in ISI's Science Citation Index for publications on information visualisation. It is interesting to note that the majority of authors, particularly North American authors, use the spelling visualization – both spellings are used in the search. The number of publications in the field has steadily increased over the last decade. Information visualisation as a field seems to have become established around 1991, when 79 journal articles were published on this topic, although some pioneering works had been published earlier.

Table 1.3 lists information visualisation systems. It also suggests that much of information visualisation as a field has emerged since 1991, with the notable exception of SemNet, which is now one of the most frequently cited information visualisation classics.

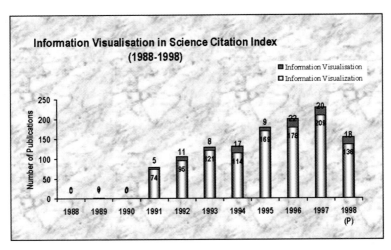

Figure 1.16   ISI Science Citation Index search results (17 August, 1998).

Table 1.3 Major information visualisation systems discussed in this book

Information visualisation	Year	Publication
SemNet	1988	(Fairchild, Poltrock, and Furnas, 1988)
Cone Trees	1991	(Robertson, Mackinlay, and Card, 1991)
Self-Organised Maps	1991	(Lin, Soergel, and Marchionini, 1991)
Tree-maps	1991	(Johnson and Shneiderman, 1991)
BEAD	1992	(Chalmers, 1992)
Envision	1993	(Fox *et al.*, 1993)
VIBE	1993	(Olsen, Korfhage, and Sochats, 1993)
LyberWorld	1994	(Hemmje *et al.*, 1994)
SCI-MAP	1994	(Small, 1994)
Starfield/FilmFinder	1994	(Ahlberg and Shneiderman, 1994)
Butterfly	1995	(Mackinlay, Rao, and Card, 1995)
Narcissus	1995	(Hendley, Drew, Wood, and Beale, 1995)
SageBook	1995	(Chuah, Roth, Kolojejchick, Mattis, and Juarez, 1995)
SPIRE	1995	(Thomas, 1995)
TileBars	1995	(Hearst, 1995)
VR-VIBE	1995	(Benford *et al.*, 1995)
Elastic windows	1996	(Kandogan and Shneiderman, 1996)
WebBook	1996	(Card, Robertson, and York, 1996)
Cat-a-Cone	1997	(Hearst and Karadi, 1997)
GSA/StarWalker	1997	(Chen, 1997)
H3 (Hyperbolic 3D)	1997	(Munzner, 1997)
NicheWorks	1998	(Wills, 1998)

The chart in Fig. 1.17 shows the search results of the ISI Science Citation Index on virtual environments. Journal articles on the topic started to appear in 1992. The number of journal publications on virtual environments in 1996 slightly offsets the increasing general trend, but there is a relatively sharp increase in 1997. It is not clear what might have caused the slow down in 1996 and the additional increase in 1997, without examining these particular publications, but factors may include the release of new browsers, cross-platform plug-in viewers, and other enabling facilities.

Apart from major conference sources such as the IEEE symposium on Information Visualisation, the World-Wide Web provides a variety of resources regarding information visualisation and virtual environments.

Paul Kahn at Dynamic Diagrams[9] presents a series of tutorials on information visualisation, especially on site maps on the Web. MAPA, Dynamic Diagrams' own visualisation tool, is introduced in Chapter 4.

The University of Maryland maintains a comprehensive resource called Online Library of Information Visualization Environments (Olive) on the Web.[10] Olive gives wide coverage of various aspects of information visualisation. Information

---

[9]http://www.dynamicdiagrams.com
[10]http://otal.umd.edu/Olive/

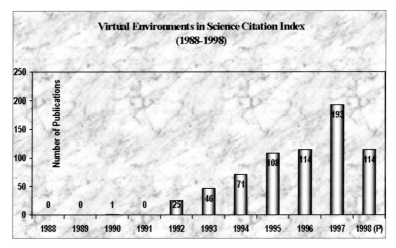

Figure 1.17   ISI Science Citation Index search results (17 August, 1998).

is organised according to the underlying data structures, e.g. tree and network structures, and includes a comprehensive bibliography of information visualisation (Shneiderman, 1996). The University of Maryland also maintains a website on virtual environments.[11]

Iowa State University maintains a clearing house website of projects, research, products, and services concerning information visualisation. The website is called the Big Picture,[12] covering issues from visual browsing on the Web to navigating in databases, notably in MARC and bibliographical databases. A general bibliography of applicable works is also included.

Finally, a wonderful collection of images and reference links on information visualisation, called the *Atlas of Cyberspaces*,[13] is maintained on the Web by Martin Dodge at University College of London. It contains screenshots of various information visualisation applications, with particular focus on geography, spatial analysis, and urban design.

1.7 Summary

In this chapter, we introduced geographical visualisations as the starting point of our journey, emphasising that the goal of information visualisation is to represent abstract information spaces intuitively and naturally. We also pointed out that the power of information visualisation will only be fully understood when information visualisation becomes an integral part of users' activity.

---

[11]http://www.cs.umd.edu/projects/hcil/vrtp.html
[12]http://www.public.iastate.edu/~CYBERSTACKS/BigPic.htm
[13]http://www.cybergeography.org/

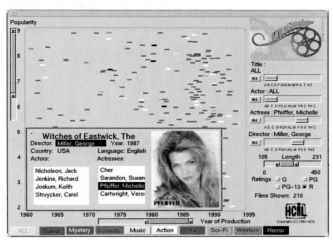

Figure 1.18 The use of Starfield displays in Film Finder (http://www.cs.umd.edu/projects/hcil/members/bshneiderman/ivwp.html). (Reprinted with permission of Ben Shneiderman).

Optimal foraging theory and cognitive maps were introduced, to provide a wider context in which to shape the requirements for information visualisation.

In Chapter 2, we focus on techniques to extract salient structures from a complex information system, for the purpose of information visualisation. In subsequent chapters, we will demonstrate the visualisation techniques available to deal with these structures.

Bibliography

Ahlberg, C, Shneiderman, B (1994). *Visual information-seeking – tight coupling of dynamic query filters with starfield displays.* Proceedings of CHI 94 (Boston, USA), ACM Press, pp. 313–17.

Barrett, E (ed.) (1989). *The Society of Text: Hypertext, Hypermedia, and the Social Construction of Information.* MIT Press (Cambridge, USA).

Benford, S, Snowdon, D, Greenhalgh, C, Ingram, R, Knox, I, and Brown, C (1995). VR-VIBE: A virtual environment for co-operative information retrieval. *Computer Graphics Forum,* 14(3): C.349–C.360.

CAIDA. (1998, 11/22/98 17:37:23). *Skitter.* CAIDA. Available: http://www.caida.org/Tools/Skitter/ [1998, 22 November 1998].

Card, SK, Robertson, GG, and York, W (1996). *The WebBook and the WebForager: An Information Workspace for the World-Wide Web.* Proceedings of the ACM Conference on Human Factors in Computing Systems (CHI 96, Vancouver, Canada, April 1996), ACM Press. Available: http://www.acm.org/sigchi/chi96/proceedings/papers/Card/skc1txt.html.

Chalmers, M (1992). *BEAD: Explorations in information visualisation.* Proceedings of SIGIR 92(Copenhagen, Denmark, June 1992), ACM Press, pp. 330–37.

Chen, C (1997). *Structuring and visualising the WWW with Generalised Similarity Analysis.* Proceedings of the Eighth ACM Conference on Hypertext (Hypertext 97, Southampton, UK), ACM Press, pp. 177–86. Available: http://www.acm.org:82/pubs/citations/proceedings/hypertext/267437/p277-chen/.

Chuah, MC, Roth, SF, Kolojejchick, J, Mattis, J, and Juarez, O (1995). *SageBook: Searching data-graphics by content.* Proceedings of CHI 95 (Denver, USA, May 1995), ACM Press, pp. 338–45. Available: http://www.cs.cmu.edu/Web/Groups/sage/SageBook/SageBook.html.

Darken, RP, and Sibert, JL (1996). *Wayfinding strategies and behaviors in large virtual worlds.* Proceedings of CHI 96, ACM Press. Available: http://www.acm.org/sigchi/chi96/proceedings/ papers/Darken/ Rpd_txt.htm.

Dillon, A, McKnight, C, and Richardson, J (1990). Navigating in hypertext: A critical review of the concept. In: EAD Diaper (ed.), *Human-Computer Interaction – INTERACT 90*, Elsevier (Oxford, UK), pp. 587–92.

Dourish, P, and Chalmers, M (1994). *Running out of space: Models of information navigation.* Proceedings of HCI 94, Available: ftp://parcftp.xerox.com/pub/europarc/jpd/hci94-navigation.ps.

Drew, P, and Heritage, J (eds.) (1992). *Talk at Work: Interaction in Institutional Settings.* CUP (Cambridge, UK).

Eckstrom, RB, French, JW, Harman, HH, and Derman, D (1976). *Kit of Factor-Referenced Cognitive Tests.* Educational Testing Service (Princeton, USA).

Fairchild, K, Poltrock, S, and Furnas, G (1988). SemNet: Three-dimensional graphic representations of large knowledge bases. In: R Guidon (ed.), *Cognitive Science and its Applications for Human-Computer Interaction.* Lawrence Erlbaum (UK), pp. 201–33.

Fox, E, Hix, D, Nowell, L, Brueni, D, Wake, W, Heath, L, and Rao, D (1993). Users, user interfaces, and objects: Envision, a digital library. *Journal of the American Society for Information Science,* 44(5):480–91.

Goffman, E (1974). *Frame Analysis.* Harper and Row (New York, USA).

Gumperz, J (1982). *Discourse Strategies.* CUP (Cambridge, UK).

Hafner, K, and Lyon, M (1996). *Where Wizards Stay Up Late: The Origins of the Internet*: Simon & Schuster.

Harrison, S, and Dourish, P (1996). *Re-place-ing space: The roles of place and space in collaborative systems.* Proceedings of CSCW 96, ACM Press, pp. 67–76.

Hearst, MA (1995). *TileBars: Visualization of term distribution information in full text information access papers.* Proceedings of ACM CHI 95 Conference on Human Factors in Computing Systems, ACM Press, pp. 59–66.

Hearst, M, and Karadi, C (1997). *Cat-a-Cone: An interactive interface for specifying searches and viewing retrieval results using a large category hierarchy.* Proceedings of the Twentieth Annual International ACM/SIGIR Conference (Philadelphia, USA, July 1997), ACM Press. Available: http://www.sims.berkeley.edu/~hearst/papers/cac-sigir97/sigir97.html.

Hemmje, M, Kunkel, C, and Willett, A (1994). *LyberWorld – A visualization user interface supporting full text retrieval.* Proceedings of the 17th Annual International ACM SIGIR Conference on Research and Development in Information Retrieval (Dublin, Ireland), Springer-Verlag (London, UK), pp. 249–59.

Hendley, RJ, Drew, NS, Wood, AM, and Beale, R (1995). *Narcissus: Visualising information.* Proceedings of Information Visualization 95 Symposium (Atlanta, USA, October 1995), IEEE, pp. 90–6.

Hjorland, B (1997). *Information Seeking and Subject Representation: An Activity-Theoretical Approach to Information Science.* Greenwood Press (Westport, USA).

Huffaker, B, Nemeth, E, and Claffy, K (1998). Otter: A general-purpose network visualization tool. Available from http://www.caida.org/Tools/Otter/Paper/.

Johnson, B, and Shneiderman, B (1991). *Tree-maps: A space filling approach to the visualization of hierarchical information structures.* Proceedings of IEEE Visualization 91 (October 1991), IEEE, pp. 284–91).

Kandogan, E, and Shneiderman, B (1996). *Elastic windows: Improved spatial layout and rapid multiple window operations.* Proceedings of Advanced Visual Interfaces Conference 96 (May 1996), ACM Press.

Kuutti, K, and Arvonen, T (1992). *Identifying potential CSCW applications by means of Activity Theory concepts: A case example.* Proceedings of CSCW 92, ACM Press, pp. 233–40.

Lamm, SE, Reed, DA, and Scullin, WH (1995). *Real-time geographic visualization of World-Wide Web traffic.* Proceedings of Fifth International World-Wide Web Conference (Paris, France, May 1996). Available: http://www5conf.inria.fr/fich_html/papers/P49/Overview.html.

Lin, X, Soergel, D, and Marchionini, G (1991). *A self-organizing semantic map for information retrieval.* Proceedings of SIGIR 91 (Chicago, USA, October 1991), ACM Press, pp. 262–69.

Lokuge, I, Gilbert, SA, and Richards, W (1996). *Structuring information with mental models: A tour of Boston.* Proceedings of CHI 96, ACM Press. Available: http://www.acm.org/sigchi/chi96/ proceedings/papers/Lokuge/sag_txt.html.

Mackinlay, JD, Rao, R, and Card, SK (1995). *An organic user interface for searching citation links.* Proceedings of ACM CHI 95 Conference on Human Factors in Computing Systems, ACM Press, pp. 67–73.

Munzner, T (1997). *H3: Laying out large directed graphs in 3D hyperbolic space.* Proceedings of the 1997 IEEE Symposium on Information Visualization (Phoenix, USA), IEEE, pp. 2–10.

Munzner, T (1998). Exploring large graphs in 3D hyperbolic space. *IEEE Computer Graphics and Applications,* 18(4):18–23.

Munzner, T, Hoffman, E, Claffy, K, and Fenner, B (1996). *Visualizing the global topology of the MBone.* Proceedings of the 1996 IEEE Symposium on Information Visualization (San Francisco, USA, October 1996), IEEE, pp. 85–92. Available: http://WWW.ERC.MsState.Edu/conferences/vis96/infoviz/infoviz.html.

Nardi, BA (1996). *Context and Consciousness: Activity Theory and Human-Computer Interaction.* MIT Press (Cambridge, USA).

Olsen, KA, Korfhage, RR, and Sochats, KM (1993). Visualization of a document collection: The VIBE System. *Information Processing and Management,* 29(1):69–81.

Pirolli, P (1998). *Exploring browser design trade-offs using a dynamical model of optimal information foraging.* Proceedings of CHI 98 (Los Angeles, USA), ACM Press, pp 33–40.

Pirolli, P, and Card, SK (1995). *Information foraging in information access environments.* Proceedings of the Conference on Human Factors in Computing (CHI 95, Denver, USA), ACM Press, pp. 51–8. Available: http://www.acm.org/sigchi/chi95/proceedings/papers/ppp_bdy.htm.

Pirolli, P, Schank, P, Hearst, M, and Diehl, C (1996). *Scatter/Gather browsing communicates the topic structure of a very large text collection.* Proceedings of the Conference on Human Factors in Computing Systems (CHI 96, Vancouver, Canada), ACM Press. Available: http://www.acm.org/sigchi/chi96/proceedings/papers/Pirolli/pp_txt.htm.

Robertson, GG, Mackinlay, JD, and Card, SK (1991). *Cone trees: Animated 3D visualizations of hierarchical information.* Proceedings of CHI 97 (New Orleans, USA, April/May 1991), ACM Press (Boston, MA), pp. 189–94.

Roth, SF, Chuah, MC, Kerpedjiev, S, Kolgejehick, J, Lucas, P (1997). Towards an information visualization workspace: combining multiple means of expression. *Human-Computer Interaction,* 12 (1&2):131–85.

Shneiderman, B (1996) *The eyes have it: a task by data type taxonomy of information visualizations.* Proceedings of IEEE Symposium on Visual Languages '96 (Los Alamos, USA, September 1996), IEEE, pp. 336–343.

Small, H (1994). A SCI-MAP case study: Building a map of AIDS research. *Scientometrics,* 30(1):229–41.

Thomas, JJ (1995). *Information visualization: Beyond traditional engineering.* Proceedings of the Workshop on Human-Computer Interaction and Virtual Environments (Hampton, Virginia, April 1995), NASA (USA). Available: http://multimedia.pnl.gov:2080/showcase/?it_content/spire.node.

Thorndyke, P, and Hayes-Roth, B (1982). Differences in spatial knowledge acquired from maps and navigation. *Cognitive Psychology,* 14:560–89.

Tolman, EC (1948). Cognitive maps in rats and men. *Psychological Review,* 55:189–208.

Tversky, B (1993). *Cognitive maps, cognitive colages, and spatial mental models.* Proceedings of COSIT 93 (Elba, USA), Springer-Verlag (London, UK), pp. 14–24.

Wills, GJ (1998). *NicheWorks: Interactive Visualization of Very Large Graphs.* Bell Laboratories (USA). Available: http://www.bell-labs.com/user/gwills/NICHEguide/nichepaper.html [1998, 4 August].

Chapter 2
Finding Salient Structures

Information overload becomes a common problem in the exponential growth of widely accessible information in modern society and efficient information filtering and sharing facilities are needed to resolve it. Information visualisation has the potential to help people find the information they need more effectively and intuitively.

Information visualisation has two fundamentally related aspects: (1) structural modelling, and (2) graphical representation. The purpose of structural modelling is to detect, extract, and simplify underlying relationships. These relationships form a structure that characterises a collection of documents or other data sets. The following questions are typically answered by structural modelling: What is the basic structure of a complex network or a collection of documents? What are the mental models of a city or a zoo in different people's minds? What is the structure of the literature of a subject domain?

In contrast, the aim of the graphical representation is to transform an initial representation of a structure into a graphical one, so that the structure can be visually examined and interacted with. For example, a hierarchical structure can be displayed as a cone tree, or a hyperbolic graph.

Although the second aspect normally concentrates on the representation of a given structure, the boundary between the two aspects is blurred, as many information visualisation systems are capable of displaying the same structure in a number of ways. In fact, the phrase *information visualisation* sometimes refers to the second aspect specifically.

In this chapter, we focus on the first aspect of information visualisation – structural modelling. Generalised similarity analysis (GSA), is introduced as a unifying framework, and as a starting point for us to interpret and evaluate visualisation systems, and to understand the strengths of a particular technical solution. GSA provides a generic and extensible framework capable of accommodating the development of new approaches to visualisation. This and subsequent chapters include some examples of how we incrementally introduce Latent Semantic Indexing and Author Co-Citation Analysis into the framework.

This chapter first examines the automatic construction of hypertext, a rich source of inspiration for information visualisation, then looks at the growing interest in the WordNet® database and its role in visualisation applications, and finally, at GSA, introduced to provide a synthesized view of the literature, and to highlight some potentially fruitful areas for research.

2.1 Virtual Structures

The outcome of structural modelling is a virtual structure. It is this virtual structure that information visualisation aims to reveal to users in a graphical and visually understandable form. Virtual structures include structures derived from a wide range of data, using computational, statistical, or other modelling mechanisms. The term 'virtual' is used here to emphasise that the structure does not exist in the original data in a readily accessible form.

A topical map of a collection of scientific papers published in a conference series is a good example to explain the difference between a virtual structure and an existing structure. The papers are independently written about related topical subjects, but they may or may not relate to each other in more specific aspects. The original data set does not usually have readily accessible information to specify whether or not two papers are related, and if so in what sense. Thus the topical map provides a means of describing the underlying connections within the collection, which is not readily available in any other form.

In order to demonstrate the process of structural modelling, we include some theoretical and practical examples, in areas such as automatic construction of hypertext, manually constructed thesaurus, and the GSA framework.

2.1.1 Automatic Construction of Hypertext

Many systems have been designed on the basis of classic information retrieval models. The most common requirement for generating hypertext automatically is to identify passages in the text that are good candidates for a hypertext link. Automatic construction of hypertext is closely related to the creation of an automatic overview map, an information visualisation area in its own right.

Automated link generation presents some of the most challenging tasks for extracting and visualising abstract information spaces. A variety of techniques have been developed; among them the classic vector space model has a profound impact on the development of visualisation systems for information retrieval. In fact, a wide range of information visualisation systems use the basic idea of a vector space model in one way or another.

The process of constructing a hypertext consists of two broad phases. In the first, known as information chunking, a document is segmented into nodes to be interconnected in the final hypertext. The second phase is linking: nodes are connected by hypertext links according to a story line, some underlying logic, or other heuristics, into a hypertext. Research in information retrieval has used clustering methods to link documents by their containing cluster.

Most approaches inspired by information retrieval models have paid little attention to the nature of the relationship underlying automatically generated links. Allan (1997), however, particularly focused on how link types can be found automatically, and how these links can be appropriately described. He classified links into three categories – manual, pattern matching, and automatic – based on whether or not their identification can be achieved automatically. For example, pattern-matching links typically rely on existing mark-ups in the text, whereas automatic link types can be derived with or without existing mark-ups. Automatic links are further divided into sub-cateogries, such as revision, summary and expansion, equivalence, comparison and contrast, tangent, and aggregate links. Equivalence links represent strongly related discussions of the same topic.

2.1.2 The Vector Space Model

Much of the work on automatic hypertext generation in large document collections has been formulated as a special case of the more general information retrieval (IR) problem. The basic premise underlying most current IR systems is that documents that are related in some way will use the same words. If two documents have enough terms in common, then we can assume that they are related, and should therefore have a link placed between them.

The vector space model (VSM) has a great impact, not only on information retrieval, but also on the design of many information visualisation systems. The SMART information retrieval system introduces the vector space model, in which both queries and documents are represented as vectors in a high-dimensional space. The dimensionality is determined by the number of unique terms in the given document collection. The magnitude of a vector in a particular dimension represents the importance of the specific term in the corresponding document (Salton *et al.*, 1994).

Since the vector space model maps both queries and documents into vectors, one can compute document–document relevance, as well as query–document relevance. The well-known *tf* × *idf* weighting scheme is typically used to compute the vector coefficients. The weight of term T_k in document D_i is defined by w_{ik} as follows:

$$w_{ik} = \frac{v_{ik}}{\sqrt{\sum_{j=1}^{t} v_{ij}^2}}$$

$$v_{ik} = tf_{ik} \cdot \log\left(\frac{N}{n_k}\right)$$

where N is the number of documents in the collection, tf_{ik} is the number of times term T_k occurs in document D_i, and n_k is the number of documents in which term T_k occurs at least once. The denominator plays a role known as *length normalisation*, which reduces the bias in favor of long documents, because they tend to have larger *tf* values.

The vector space model has several appealing features for information retrieval and information visualisation. Both queries and documents are represented as vectors. The focus of traditional information retrieval is on query–document relevance ranking, in order to find the document which best matches a given query. In contrast, information visualisation has special interests in inter-document similarities, as measured by the distance between corresponding document vectors.

Many visualisation systems are designed to visualise a sub-set of a particular collection of documents, in response to a search query. The original collection is therefore narrowed down by the search query. For example, Allan (1997) describes automated construction of hypertext with such a scenario. A hypertext, based on the results of an initial search query, is automatically generated. Users can find documents related to a chosen document in the vector space by selecting documents immediately surrounding the vector of the document.

Allan presents an example in which the user's goal was to find documents related to an encyclopedia article on 'March music'. Many of the documents retrieved according to the vector proximity turned out to be relevant to the topic. However, a number of documents retrieved in this way were not relevant, because the meaning of the word 'March' is ambiguous: it could refer to a type of music, a month of the year, or other meanings. This is a well-known problem, known in the information retrieval community as the vocabulary mismatch problem, and has drawn much attention from researchers.

In order to distinguish the meanings of words like 'March' or 'Bank' is to examine the contexts in which they occur. Latent semantic indexing (LSI), demonstrates how this problem can be tackled (Deerwester et al., 1990) (see 2.1.3). Lexical chaining (see 2.2.2) represents an alternative approach, in which the accurate information about connections between different words is derived from a thesaurus, and the information used to reduce the ambiguity of words as their contexts are taken into account (Green, 1998).

Allan (1997) describes yet another approach, where the vector space model is applied to finer-grained analysis within documents. In addition to document vectors, paragraphs and sentences in each document are also represented in the vector space model. First, two documents are deconstructed into smaller pieces so that they can be compared at a finer-grained inspection, for example, sentence by sentence, or paragraph by paragraph. Second, sentences are transformed into vectors. These sentence vectors are compared, to determine whether or not the documents share a similar context. In Allan's example, the following criteria are used to select relevant documents:

- there must be at least one pair of sentences in the two documents with a similarity of 70%;
- there must be at least one pair of sentences with at least two terms in common; and
- the most heavily weighted term must contribute more than 95% of the similarity.

There exist other alternatives to take the role of a context into account. Latent semantic indexing (LSI), also known as singular value-decomposition (SVD), is such a candidate.

2.1.3 Latent Semantic Indexing

Latent semantic indexing (LSI) is designed to overcome the so-called vocabulary mismatch problem faced by information retrieval systems (Deerwester et al., 1990; Dumais, 1995). Individual words in natural language provide unreliable evidence about the conceptual topic or meaning of a document. LSI assumes the existence of some underlying semantic structure in the data, that is partially obscured by the randomness of word choice in a retrieval process, and that the latent semantic structure can be more accurately estimated with statistical techniques.

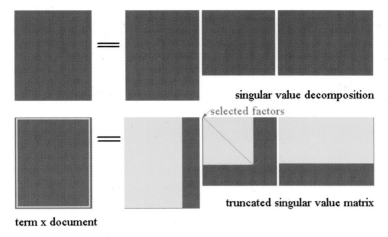

Figure 2.1   Singular Value Decomposition (SVD) and a truncated SVD matrix.

In LSI, a semantic space, based on a large term × document matrix, is constructed. Each element of the matrix is the number of occurrences of a term in a document. The document plays a contextual role, specifying the meaning of the term. LSI uses a mathematical technique called singular value decomposition (SVD). The original term × document matrix can be approximated with a truncated SVD matrix. A proper truncation can remove noise data from the original data, as well as improve the recall and precision of information retrieval. The diagram in Fig. 2.1 illustrates how a large matrix is truncated into a smaller one.

Perhaps the most compelling claim from the LSI is that it allows an information retrieval system to retrieve documents that share no words with the query (Deerwester et al., 1990; Dumais, 1995). Another potentially appealing feature is that the underlying semantic space can be subject to geometric representations. For example, one can project the semantic space into an Euclidean space for a 2D- or 3D-visualisation. On the other hand, in practice, large complex semantic spaces may not always fit into low-dimension spaces comfortably.

LSI reduces the dimensionality of a data set in a similar way to standard factor analysis. Each data point can be represented by a smaller number of underlying factors identified by LSI. In Fig. 2.2, (a) is a 2D-scatter plot of the ACM SIGCHI conference data set, containing 169 documents published between 1995 and 1997. This data set appears to be relatively well captured by the first two dimensions. In contrast, Fig. 2.2 (b) shows a scatter plot of the CACM collection, containing more than 3,200 documents. A large number of documents are plotted close to the original, suggesting that their positions in the semantic space cannot be adequately represented within its sub-spaces.

The two diagrams in Fig. 2.3 represent the singular values of the CHI and CACM data sets based on the output of LSI. They were plotted in a similar way to eigenvalue curves in standard factor analysis. The value of each point indicates the uniqueness or significance of a given factor. A higher singular value indicates

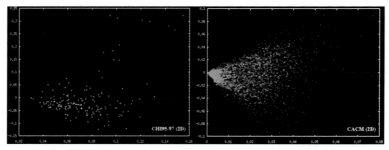

Figure 2.2 Scatter plots of CHI 95-97 (left) and the CACM collection (right)

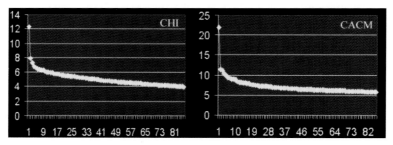

Figure 2.3 The singular value curves of the CHI and CACM data sets.

that the underlying factor explains more variance than a factor with a lower singular value. The first few dimensions typically explain a large amount of variance. Both data sets have a long, flat tail, suggesting that they are high-dimensional spaces in nature.

2.2 The Use of WordNet®

WordNet® is an on-line lexical database developed by the Cognitive Science Laboratory at Princeton University[1], on the basis of contemporary psycholinguistic theories of human lexical memory. It was first created in 1985 as a dictionary based on psycholinguistic theories, and now contains over 50,000 words and 40,000 phrases, collected into more than 70,000 sense meanings.

The basic concepts and construction of WordNet® are explained in the so-called 'Five Papers on WordNet', available on the Web.[2] A comprehensive bibliography, maintained by Joseph Rosenzweig at the University of Pennsylvania, is also available on the Web.[3]

WordNet® divides words up into synonym sets, also known as synsets. Each synonym set includes words that are synonyms of one another. These synsets are

---

[1]http://www.cogsci.princeton.edu/~wn/
[2]ftp://ftp.cogsci.princeton.edu/pub/wordnet/5papers.pdf
[3]http://www.cis.upenn.edu/~josephr/wn-biblio.html

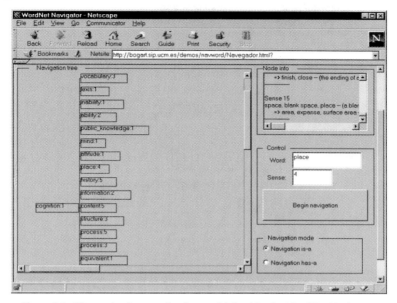

Figure 2.4   The navigation tree for the word 'place' in the WordNet Navigator.

then connected by a number of different relations such as 'is-a', 'has-a', or 'includes'. A particular word may appear in several synonym sets, depending on how many senses it has. Each sense of a word is identifiable by the word and a sense number.

A number of browsers have been designed to facilitate the access to the WordNet®. WordNet Navigator[4] is a graphical user interface, developed at the Universidad Complutense de Madrid, Spain. It can be used to display how words are related in the WordNet®. While its user interface was mainly written in Java, the communication with the WordNet® is handled in C. These two components are integrated on the Web using Common Gateway Interface (CGI).

The information is displayed on the screen in four categories: (1) Navigation Tree, a diagram of relations between words; (2) Node Info, information about a particular word; (3) Control and (4) Navigation Mode, for inputting control parameters and link types for navigation (Fig. 2.4).

The local structure surrounding a given word is displayed in the navigation tree, in which nodes represent words, and edges indicate relations such as 'is-a', 'has-a', or 'include'. Each node contains a word and a *sense number*, which identifies its synonym set. The node info displays information about synonyms and definitions. The control specifies the word with which to start. The navigation mode specifies whether the current navigation is based on the structure determined by 'is-a' or by 'has-a' links.

---

[4]http://bogart.sip.ucm.es/demos/navword/

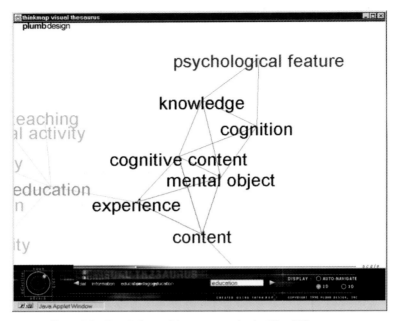

Figure 2.5   Knowledge and its synonyms in the Visual Thesaurus.

For example, suppose we are interested in the word 'place' and its synonyms. To start the navigation, type the word 'place' into the control section. The sense number is optional. If a sense number is given, only one node will appear on the screen; otherwise, the navigation tree will include all the meanings of the word 'place'. If nothing matches the query word 'place', then we may try a different word or sense number. Once the navigation tree returns, it is time to specify the navigation mode: whether the navigation should rely on 'is-a 'or 'has-a' relationships. If the user selects a node in the navigation tree, the selected node, its parent, siblings, and children will be displayed, according to the chosen navigation mode. This graphical browser provides simple but useful access to the internal structure of the WordNet®.

2.2.1 WordNet® and ThinkMap™

Visual Thesaurus[5] is developed by Plumb Design as a browser for exploring the WordNet-based thesaurus, using a Java-enabled spatial map. Visual Thesaurus is built on a graphic display tool called Thinkmap™,[6] where a network of concepts retrieved from the WordNet are visualised and animated. The topology of the map is driven by the data from the WordNet® database. The connections in

---

[5]http://www.plumbdesign.com/thesaurus/
[6]http://www.thinkmap.com/

complex data sets are displayed by dynamic Java Maplets^{TM}, which are a part of Thinkmap^{TM}.

In Thinkmap^{TM}, whenever the user clicks on a word, the clicked word moves to the centre of the display. The user can also click on any word displayed in the diagram, which may introduce more words into the local structure. Once a word moves to the centre of the display or more words emerge in the display, the map layout is adjusted instantly, so that the user can see how these words are connected with their neighbouring words. The sequence of the words selected is accessible from the user interface, so that the user can always backtrack to a word they have seen before.

The movement of words in the spatial map is determined by animated gravity and magnetic field, but more importantly, it is the WordNet® that provides the crucial knowledge and the structure of synonym words.

2.2.2 Lexical Chaining

The classic vector space model and its variants are by far the most popular options in visualising abstract information spaces for retrieval and exploration. The following example illustrates how the WordNet® can provide semantic knowledge of relationships between words, in the estimation of inter-document similarities.

An interesting alternative, lexical chaining, is described by Green (1998)[7] in an attempt to deal with two major linguistic factors that may undermine the effectiveness of traditional information retrieval models, namely, synonymy and polysemy. Synonymy refers to the use of different words to describe the same concept, for example, 'dog' and 'puppy'. Polysemy, on the other hand, refers to the use of the same word to describe different concepts, for example, 'bank'. Consequently, term occurrences may under-represent the connection between synonym words, or over-represent the connection between documents using the same word in different senses.

A lexical chain is a sequence of semantically related words occurring in a document. For example, if text contains the words 'apple' and 'fruit', then they should both appear in a chain, since an apple is a kind of fruit. It is believed that the organisation of the lexical chains in a document reflects the discourse structure, or the main theme of the document.

Lexical chains in text can be recovered using any lexical resource that relates words to their meanings. For example, Roget's Thesaurus (Chapman, 1992) and the WordNet® database (Beckwith et al., 1991) have been used to provide such semantics. Estimating the similarity between two documents is therefore equivalent to finding the similarity between a variety of lexical chains associated with these documents. Lexical chaining appears to be a promising alternative to the existing information visualisation paradigms.

---

[7]An online version of the paper is available at http://www7.conf.au/programme/fullpapers/1834/com1834.htm

2.2.3 Semantic Distance

WordNet® provides a rich source of structures to describe the relationships between words. Research has shown that the perception of such relationships in a hierarchy may be affected by some interesting factors, which are likely to have significant effects on information retrieval, especially in assessing the query–document relevance. The following example explains two major effects based on a concept of semantic distance.

There is an increasing interest in the nature of online searching. According to a constructivist analysis, during online searching, the searcher continuously constructs meaning from the perceptual phenomena appearing on the computer screen as the result of a complex interplay of the work of indexers, database designers, and everyone else who has contributed to the development of the searching environment.

Online database searching and, more recently, Web-based searching using various search engines, all resemble a black-box experience. One enters a search query and receives bibliographical records, or URLs, without a clear picture of why these results are presented, or whether they are indeed relevant. Relevance ranking algorithms cannot do the real work of information retrieval – searchers themselves must reach the ultimate judgement regarding the relevance of a listed document.

A key factor that distinguishes subject experts from non-experts is specialised vocabulary. Experts are individuals with special vocabulary and background knowledge, and they share presumptions and language.

The semantic distance model (SDM) of relevance assessment is proposed by Terry Brooks (1995). The central concept of the SDM is semantic distance. Concepts are placed in a multidimensional space, according to their values on some dimension of meaning. To create a dimension of meaning, Brooks used the generic trees of descriptors found in an existing thesaurus or a hierarchical structure, in which the semantic distance between two items is defined as the number of steps from one to another along existing links in the structure.

Brooks has shown that relevance assessments declined systematically with an increase in semantic distance. Subjects gave the highest relevance assessments to the topical subject descriptor semantically closest to the bibliographical record, and then incrementally smaller relevance assessments to descriptors more distant. This was explained as a result of the so-called semantic distance effect.

In addition, the rate of decline of the assessed relevance appeared to be different for top and bottom record in the same generic tree. This was described as the influence of the semantic direction effect. Comparing a bibliographical record from the top of a generic tree to descriptors located below it produced a rapid decline in relevance assessment. In contrast, comparing a bibliographical record at the bottom of a tree to descriptors located above it produced a slower rate of decline in relevant assessment. In other words, the perceived distance downwards to non-relevance appeared to be shorter than the distance upwards to non-relevance.

Brooks found out that topical subject expertise enhances the effects of the SDM, and the strength of the SDM is contingent on phenomenological factors of the computer-human experience. This provides empirical support for the belief that relevance is a contingent, psychological construct. The effects of the SDM may be limited on term hierarchies in which terms are spaced so far apart that they lack internal coherence and do not converge into a cohesive semantic domain.

SDM can provide important input into information visualisation, especially when dealing with a heterogeneous network of documents, topical descriptors, subject headings, and search queries.

2.3 Structural Analysis and Modelling

Botafogo *et al.* (1992) analyse the structure of a hypertext using graph decomposition methods. A graph can be decomposed into sub-graphs, so that each sub-graph is connected. Using similar methods, several different types of nodes, based on their positions in the graph, are identified. For example, two structural metrics, the relative out centrality (ROC) and relative in centrality (RIC) metrics, are introduced, to identify various structural characteristics of a node.

The ROC of a node measures whether the node is a good starting point to reach out for other nodes, whereas the RIC of a node indicates how easily the node can be found. Using a high-ROC node as a starting point, the structure of the hypertext can be transformed to one or more hierarchies, and large hierarchies can be displayed with fisheye views, which balance local details and global context (Furnas, 1986). Several examples of how hierarchical structures can be visualised are considered in Chapter 4, including fisheye and hyperbolic views in particular.

2.3.1 Discovering Landmarks in a Web Locality

A Web locality often refers to a collection of Web documents. Documents on a particular HTTP server, a collection of documents gathered from the Web using a 'spider', or perhaps even the search results returned by a Web search engine, all constitute a Web locality. Landmarks in a Web locality are simply those nodes important to the locality. However, identifying good landmarks automatically is, in general, a complex and challenging task.

Mukherjea and Hara (1997) adopt three heuristic metrics in order to identify landmark nodes within a Web locality, including connectivity, frequency of access, and depth in a hierarchy.

A landmark node should be highly connected to other nodes. If all roads lead to Rome, then Rome must be a landmark place on this planet. First of all, the 'out degree' of a node is the number of outgoing links provided by the node, whereas the 'in degree' is the number of incoming links received by the node. A node with high out and/or in degrees should be marked as a landmark.

In addition to the first order connectivity, the second-order connectivity has also been used to identify landmark nodes. This is defined as the number of nodes that can be reached from a particular node by no more than two links. Botafogo *et al.* (1992) suggest that nodes with high back second-order connectivity also make good landmarks. The back second-order connectivity is defined as the number of nodes that can reach the given node by no more than two links. For example, an index page including many anchors on the Web, tends to have high connectivity, while the home page of a large corporation is likely to have high back connectivity.

Purely connectivity-based heuristics may miss nodes that are significantly important, but are unlikely to be singled out in terms of connectivity alone. Mukherjea's formula thus takes the frequency of access into account in attempts to identify landmark nodes with reference to the perception of users. The more frequently a node is visited, the more likely that the node should be made a landmark.

The majority of Web sites put general information higher up in the hierarchy of the Web locality. Detailed information, on the other hand, is likely to be placed lower down in the hierarchy. Mukherjea suggests that the depth of a node indicates its importance. The depth of a document on the Web can be detected by decomposing its URL. For example, http://www.acm.org/ is a node with a depth of one, whereas http://www.acm.org/sigchi/chi97/ has a depth of three.

The following formula is adopted from Mukherjea and Hara (1997) for discovering landmark nodes (with simplified notations and symbols):

$$landmark(\lambda) = \frac{connectivity}{\max(connectivity)} \bullet \varpi_{connectivity} + \frac{access}{\max(access)} \bullet \varpi_{access} + \frac{1}{depth} \bullet \varpi_{depth}$$

$$connectivity = (in + out) \bullet \varpi_{first} + (in2 + out2) \bullet \varpi_{second}$$

$$\varpi_{first} + \varpi_{second} = 1$$

$$\varpi_{connectivity} + \varpi_{access} + \varpi_{depth} = 1$$

ϖ_xs are weights that can be configured by users. To be a landmark, the landmark value must exceed the threshold value λ to ensure that only real landmark nodes are selected. The default threshold value is 0.1. By default, the first-order connectivity (in and out) is weighted slightly more than the second-order connectivity (in 2 and out 2).

A landmark view generated by this formula is shown in Fig. 2.6, which visualises the Georgia Technical College of Computing Web server. The aesthetic

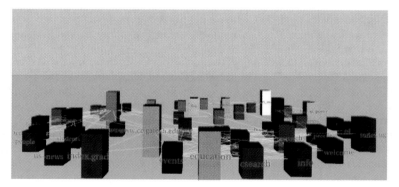

Figure 2.6 Landmark nodes in a Web locality. The taller a node, the greater its importance. Nodes with brighter colours are more popular. (Reprinted with permission of Songata Mukherjea).

layout of the landscape is generated using a force-directed graph layout algorithm (Szirmay-Kalos, 1994). These are described in detail in Chapter 3.

In this map, landmarks are displayed proportional to their importance values. The height of a node represents the importance of the node. Popular nodes are in bright colours, while less popular nodes are displayed in darker colours.

The landscape view enables the user to locate important nodes in the Web locality quickly, by navigating through the 3D space using mechanisms provided by the VRML browser.

2.3.2 Trajectory Maps

So far we have discussed structural models based on feature vectors of documents, images, or other types of objects. In addition to these vector-based models, a structure may represent the dynamics between documents and generic objects. An important family of such structures is known as procedural models, including user-centred information structures. Here, the interrelationship between two objects is determined on the basis of actions or events that directly involve the two objects.

When a user navigates the Web, a link-following event relates the source document with the destination document. Such events collectively indicate the perceived connection between the two documents. In other words, such interrelationships can be derived from behavioural models of browsing patterns. Similarly, as two publications in the literature are repeatedly cited together, the bond between them is reinforced and strengthened dynamically. Sometimes such structures are referred to as mental maps (Lokuge *et al.*, 1996). The following example is based on Lokuge *et al.* (1996) and Lokuge and Ishizaki (1995), in which mental maps of various facilities in Boston are derived as user-centred information structures.

There are many tourist attractions in Boston. How are these attractions interrelated from the point of view of an individual? Are mental models different from one individual to another? Lokuge *et al.* (1996) describe a method to structure such information using multidimensional scaling and trajectory mapping techniques.

Fifteen different tourist sites are chosen from a tourist guide to form the mental map. The interrelationships between these sites are high dimensional in nature, because they may be uniquely related in a number of ways according to different features, and they tend to vary from individual to individual.

At least two mental models of these tourist sites can be derived: one based on their geographic locations, and one based on their functions. To generate these mental models using multidimensional scaling, two subjects gave pairwise similarity judgments according to geographic locations and functions. The judgments based on geographic similarity (Fig. 2.7) are completely different from judgments based on content (Fig. 2.8).

The distance-based MDS plot is similar to the actual map of Boston. In the function-based MDS plot, similar tourist sites, such as the Aquarium and the Zoo appear near each other. This example is further discussed in Chapter 3.

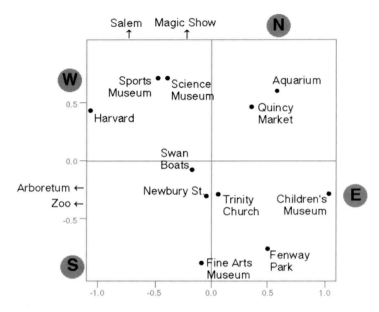

Figure 2.7   The mental model of Boston tourist sites, based on geographical locations (© 1996 ACM, Inc. reprinted with permission).

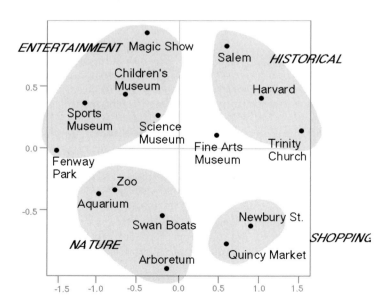

Figure 2.8   The mental model of Boston tourist sites, based on their functions (© 1996 ACM, Inc. reprinted with permission).

2.3.3 Self-organised Feature Maps

The use of self-organised feature maps forms a unique branch of information visualisation, which is primarily based on connectionism, in particular Koheon's feature maps, developed in artificial neural networks. There is an increasing interest in using self-organised maps as a means of organising complex information spaces. The term 'self-organised' refers to the fact that these feature maps are constructed by unsupervised learning algorithms.

The pioneering work in this area has been done by Xia Lin (Lin, 1997; Lin *et al.*, 1991). He classifies a set of documents and organises them into various regions in a map, which may contain multiple layers of classification. Each region contains a group of documents similar to each other in some ways. The self-organised map shown in Fig. 2.9 represents documents drawn from the Science category at the Yahoo! Web site. Words in the map, such as 'lunar', 'apollo', and 'mission', indicate the general topics of the documents grouped in these regions. Similar methods have been adopted by a research group at the University of Arizona (Chen *et al.*, 1998). They use neural network algorithms to generate a map of an information space based on more than 100,000 documents about entertainment on the Web. The resultant map is called the 'ET-Map', for entertainment (see Fig. 2.10).

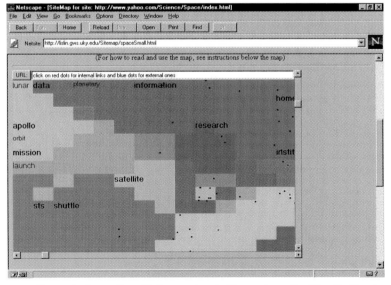

Figure 2.9   Self-organised map (http://lislin.gws.uky.edu/Sitemap/spaceSmall.html). (Reprinted with permission of Xia Lin).

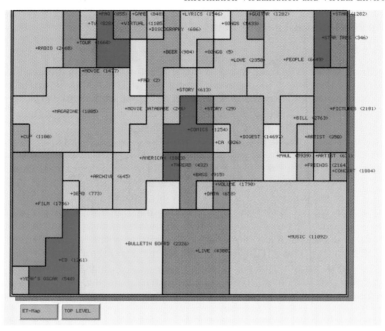

Figure 2.10 'ET-Map' – a cybermap of the information space occupied by the URLs of over 100,000 entertainment-related web pages. (Reprinted with permission of Hsinchun Chen).

2.4 Generalised Similarity Analysis: Introduction

Generalised similarity analysis (GSA) is a unifying framework developed through a series of studies in structuring and visualising complex information spaces (Chen, 1997a; Chen, 1997b; Chen, 1998a; Chen, 1998b; Chen and Czerwinski, 1997; Chen and Czerwinski, 1998). GSA aims to provide a consistent framework, with associated modelling and visualisation tools, to extract and transform a wide variety of structures inherited in a collection of documents into spatial models. For example, a number of inter-document similarity matrices have been derived: content-based similarity, cross reference-based similarity, and usage pattern-based similarity. A key element is the use of Pathfinder network scaling techniques (Schvaneveldt *et al.*, 1989).

Visualising a complex graph often needs to address a challenging problem, caused by an excessive number of links. In a spatial layout of a network representation with a large number of links, tends fundamental patterns may be lost in a cluttered display, and users may experience a cognitive overload.

Pathfinder network scaling simplifies the structure of a network by extracting and displaying only the most salient relationships, and eliminating redundant or counter-intuitive ones from the original network. Pathfinder has some desirable features over techniques, including multidimensional scaling (MDS).

In our earlier work (Chen, 1997a), we used the classic vector space model with *tf* × *idf* weighting (Salton *et al.*, 1994) to compute inter-document similarities.

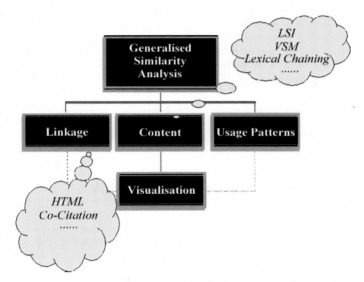

Figure 2.11   The architecture of the Generalised Similarity Analysis framework.

However, the vector space model is subject to an assumption that terms used in document vectors are independent, and it was realised that this assumption may over-simplify the interrelationships between the use of particular terms and its context, consequently leading to counter-intuitive results. Latent semantic indexing (LSI) (Deerwester *et al.*, 1990) was subsequently incorporated into the framework, in order to reveal underlying semantic structures as reflected through a collection of publications in a specific subject domain. (See related sections for more detailed descriptions of Pathfinder network scaling and LSI).

The development of GSA was initially based on three distinct interconnectivity models associated with documents on the Web: hypertext linkage, term distributions, and navigation patterns. These three examples are included in order to illustrate the extensibility of the framework.

2.4.1 Scalability of Networks

Visualising complex information structures must address two different types of scalability issue: the size of the network (in terms of the number of nodes), and the density of the network (in terms of the number of links).

SHADOCS is a document retrieval system that incorporates interactive dynamic maps into the user interface (Zizi and Beaudouin-Lafon, 1994). A large set of document descriptors is divided into smaller clusters using a dynamic clustering technique. Graphic overview maps are generated on the screen using a space-filling algorithm; each region in a map corresponds to a cluster of descriptors. The size of a region is proportional to the relative importance of those descriptors in the underlying documents.

On the one hand, a large network can be separated into a number of smaller networks by dynamic clustering algorithms, for example in SHADOCS. On the other hand, a density-related scalability issue remains a relatively challenging one. The maximum number of links in a network consisting of N nodes is N^2. When we deal with a network with a large number of nodes, we must also deal with an even larger number of links.

A commonly used strategy is to set a threshold, and consider only links whose weights are above the threshold. For instance, SHADOCS uses a straightforward threshold to control the number of links to be displayed on the screen map. However, threshold values may not adequately reflect the intrinsic structure of a network. As a result, a pruned network may look rather arbitrary, and incompatible with the layout nodes. Scalability is the ability to maintain the original integrity, consistency, and semantics associated with the network representation of an implicit structure. In the next section, this challenging problem is addressed in a more harmonious way, by a useful approach based on Pathfinder network scaling algorithms.

2.4.2 Pathfinder Network Scaling

Pathfinder network scaling is a structural modelling technique originally developed by Schvaneveldt *et al.* (1989) for the analysis of proximity data in psychology. It simplifies a complex representation of data to a much more concise and meaningful network – only the most important links are preserved, to create a Pathfinder network (PFNET).

If we consider the following three examples, the major problems with an excessive number of links in a graphical representation of a network should become clear.

Figure 2.12 shows a network structure visualised by the NavigationView-Builder (Mukherjea *et al.*, 1995), one of the most widely cited works in information visualisation. It is clear from this example that a large, connected graph would have even more edges crossing each other. One of the common criteria for general undirected graph drawing is to avoid such crossings if possible (see Chapter 3).

This illustrates the fact that underlying patterns in a complex network can be lost in a large number of links. There are several options to avoid displaying redundant links. For example, multidimensional scaling (MDS) does not usually display any links at all. The relationships between objects are purely represented by their positions in the spatial configuration. In fact, a special class of hypertext, called spatial hypertext, also known as linkless hypertext because of its reliance on spatial proximity (Marshall and Shipman, 1995), is taking a similar approach. Alternatively, redundant links from the original data may be removed in advance, including algorithms such as Pathfinder network scaling and minimal spanning trees. The spanning tree approach is used in LyberWorld (Hemmje *et al.*, 1994) and Hyperbolic 3D (Munzner, 1998).

Visualising complex information structures is much more difficult than representing regular hierarchical structures. Zizi and Beaudouin-Lafon designed SHADOCS, a document retrieval system, to incorporate interactive dynamic maps into the user interface (Zizi and Beaudouin-Lafon, 1994). SHADOCS uses a

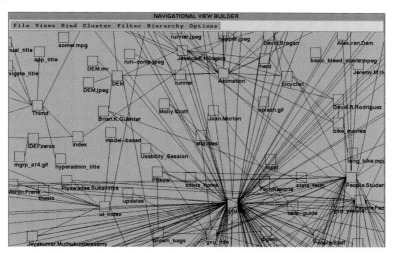

Figure 2.12 A real-world network contains many edges. (Reprinted by permission of Songata Mukherjea).

dynamic clustering technique to divide a large set of document descriptors into smaller clusters. Graphical overview maps are subsequently generated on the screen using a space-filling algorithm. Each region in a map corresponds to a cluster of descriptors, and the size of a region is proportional to the relative importance of those descriptors in the underlying documents. This is very similar to the representation of self-organised maps.

There are two types of approach towards the issue of scalability, focusing on either the size (in terms of the number of nodes), or the density of the network (in terms of the number of links). The scalability issue, in terms of the size of new networks, has been largely resolved (Zizi and Beaudouin-Lafon, 1994) by systems such as SHADOCS, which separate large networks into a number of smaller networks by dynamic clustering algorithms. However, a density-related scalability issue turns out to be more difficult.

The total number of links in a network consisting of n nodes could be as many as n^2. A commonly used strategy is to set a threshold value, and only consider links with values above the threshold. SHADOCS uses a straightforward threshold to control the number of links to be displayed on the screen map. Since the spatial relations have not been taken into account, the linkage in a pruned network may look rather arbitrary, and incompatible with the spatial layout. After all, scalability implies the ability to maintain the original integrity, consistency, and semantics associated with the network representation of an implicit structure. Pathfinder network scaling algorithms provide a useful means of dealing with this challenging problem in a more harmonious way.

Pathfinder network scaling can be seen as a link reduction mechanism that preserves the most salient semantic relations. A key assumption is the triangle inequality condition; only those links that satisfy this condition will appear in the final network. In essence, the rationale is that, if the meaning of a semantic relation can be more accurately or reliably derived from other relations, then this particular relation becomes redundant and can therefore be safely omitted. GSA extends this method to a variety of proximity data estimated by statistical and mathematical models (Chen, 1997a; Chen, 1998b). A distinct advantage is that the same spatial metaphor can be consistently used across a range of proximity data, a significant advantage for maintaining the integrity of the semantic structures generated by different theories and techniques.

Pathfinder relies on Pathfinder network scaling, the so-called triangle inequality to eliminate redundant or counter-intuitive links. The principal assumption is that if a link in the network violates this condition, then the link is likely to be redundant or counter-intuitive and should be pruned from the network.

The topology of a PFNET is determined by parameters r and q: the resultant Pathfinder network is denoted as PFNET(r, q). The weight of a path is defined, based on Minkowski metric with the r-parameter. The q-parameter specifies that the triangle inequality must be maintained against all the alternative paths with up to q links connecting nodes n_1 and n_k:

$$w_{n_1 n_k} \leq \left(\sum_{i=1}^{k-1} w_{n_i n_{i+1}}^r \right)^{\frac{1}{r}} \ \forall \ k = 2, \ 3, \ ..., \ q$$

For a network with N nodes, the maximum value of the q-parameter is N−1. PFNET($r = \infty$, $q = $ N−1) consists of the least number of links, where each path is a minimum-cost path. If there is more than one path connecting the same pair of nodes, they must have the same weight. The tightest triangle inequality ($q = $ N−1) is normally imposed, in order to achieve a concise Pathfinder network for visualisation purposes, and must be maintained throughout the entire network.

A Pathfinder network can be generated from an existing minimal spanning tree (MST) of the original network by including additional links, provided new links do not violate the triangle inequality. In fact, the minimum-cost Pathfinder network (MCN) is the set union of all the possible MSTs so that the structure of an MCN is unique for each original proximity network. The software allows us to choose an MST instead of a PFNET to represent a large network.

Figure 2.13 illustrates how the triangle inequality filter works and how its outcome should be interpreted. Suppose there are three papers: A, B, and C.

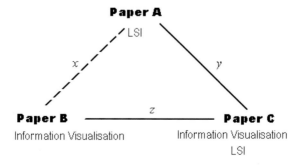

Figure 2.13   Triangle inequality: links y and z are more fundamental than x.

Paper A describes LSI. Paper B is about information visualisation. Paper C applies LSI to an information visualisation design. The relationship between papers A and B is established by the content of Paper C. Therefore the path along links y and z reflects the nature of this relationship more profoundly than link x does. Link x becomes redundant and should be removed.

Graphical representations of Pathfinder networks are generated using force-directed graph-drawing algorithms (Fruchterman and Reingold, 1991; Kamada and Kawai, 1989), which are increasingly popular in information visualisation because they tend to lay out similar nodes near to one another, and put dissimilar ones farther away. Similar algorithms are used by BEAD (Chalmers, 1992) and SPIRE (Hetzler *et al.*, 1998).

The value of Pathfinder network scaling in visualisation is its ability to reduce the number of links in a *meaningful* way, which results in a concise representation of clarified proximity patterns, a desirable feature for visualising a complex structure. Pathfinder networks provide not only a fuller representation of the salient semantic structures than minimal spanning trees, but also a more accurate representation of local structures than multidimensional scaling techniques.

Let us compare two Pathfinder networks, based on the same set of papers from the CHI 96 proceedings, but with different q parameters. The link structure in Fig. 2.14, PFNET($r = 2$, $q = 1$), keeps all the links derived from the proximity data. The meaning of $q = 1$ is that the triangle inequality is not imposed on alternative paths consisting of two or more links. In contrast, the link structure in Fig. 2.6, PFNET ($r = 2$, $q = N-1$), preserves only paths that have the minimal weights, in order to highlight salient relationships with an improved clarity. Such simplified graphs provide a natural basis for an overview map of the information space.

2.4.3 Hypertext Linkage

The structure of a network can be represented as a matrix. A network of a hypertext with N document nodes can be represented as a distance matrix, an $N \times N$ matrix. Each element d_{ij} in the matrix denotes the distance between node i and j. Botafogo *et al.* (1992) introduced two structural metrics, the relative out centrality (ROC) and relative in centrality (RIC) metrics, to identify various structural characteristics of a node.

A node with a high ROC would be a good starting point to reach out for other nodes, while a node with a high RIC should be readily accessible. Using a high-ROC node as a starting point, the structure of the hypertext can be transformed into one or more hierarchies. Botafogo *et al.* suggest that large hierarchies may be displayed with fisheye views, which balance local details and global context (Furnas, 1986). Chapter 4 includes several examples of how hierarchical structures can be visualised, using fisheye and hyperbolic views.

HyPursuit is a hierarchical network search engine based on semantic information embedded in hyperlink structures and document contents (Weiss *et al.*, 1996). HyPursuit considers not only links between two documents, but also how their ancestor and descendant documents are related. For example, if two documents have a common ancestor, they are regarded as more similar to each

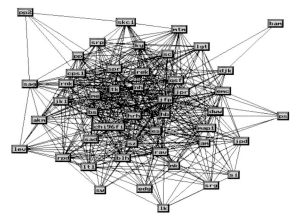

Figure 2.14   CHI 96 papers visualised, based on all the available paths (Stress < 0.005, Links = 516) (Chen, 1997a).

other. In HyPursuit, document similarity by linkage is defined as a linear combination of three components: direct linkage, ancestor, and descendant inheritance. More recently, the design of a very large Web search engine, known as Google, also relies on hypertext links to enhance the precision of search results. The Google search engine is described in Chapter 4.

Pirolli *et al.* (1996) at Xerox also use hypertext links to characterise Web documents. Documents in a Web locality, a closed subset of WWW documents, can be represented by feature vectors based on attributes such as the number of incoming and outgoing hyperlinks of a document, how frequently the document has been visited and content similarities between the document and its children. These feature vectors can be used to describe the nature of a page and predict the interests of visitors to that page.

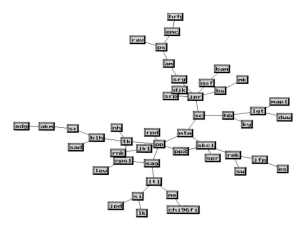

Figure 2.15   CHI 96 papers visualised, based on minimum-cost paths only (Stress < 0.005, Links = 47) (Chen, 1997a).

In generalised similarity analysis (GSA), document proximity is defined based on similarities between documents. The document similarity by hypertext linkage in GSA is defined as follows:

$$sim_{ij}^{link} = \frac{link_{ij}}{\displaystyle\sum_{k=1}^{N} link_{ik}}$$

where $link_{ij}$ is the number of hyperlinks from document D_i to D_j in a collection of N documents from the WWW, for example, from a particular server or on a specific topic. Higher-order interrelationships with ancestors and descendants are not considered, because they can be resolved by Pathfinder network scaling algorithms. This definition allows asymmetrical as well as symmetrical relationships between documents. The Pathfinder network scaling algorithms can handle both symmetric and asymmetric data. Without losing generality, we assume that these measures are symmetric unless otherwise stated. According to this definition, a similarity of 0 between two documents implies $link_{ij} = 0$, which means that one document is not linked to the other at all. On the other hand, a similarity of 1 implies $link_{ik} = 0$ for all the $k \neq j$, which means that the two documents are connected by hyperlinks to each other, but not to any other documents.

Fig. 2.16 shows the structure of a WWW site (SITE$_A$) according to hypertext linkage. Pathfinder extracted 189 salient relationships from 1,503 initial similarity measures. The spring energy in this PFNET is less than 0.005 (four isolated nodes are not shown).

Structural analysis based on hypertext links can be used to detect general interests from one Web site to others. Chen *et al.* (1988) present a connectivity analysis of the Web sites of computer science departments in 13 universities in Scotland. Fig. 2.17 shows the number of outgoing hypertext links from each of the 13 departmental Web sites in Scottish universities.

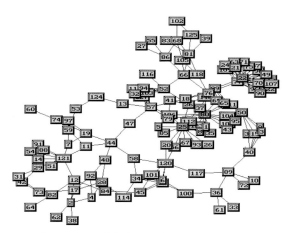

Figure 2.16   The structure of SITE$_A$ (partial) by hyperlinks, shown as a PFNET($r = \infty$, $q = N$-1 = 126) with 189 links (Chen, 1997a).

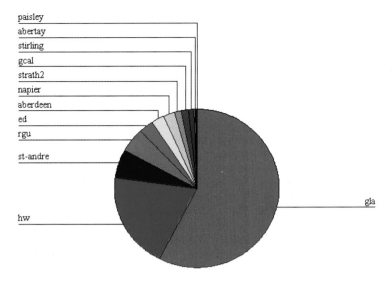

Figure 2.17 Outgoing hyperlinks from each of the 13 Scottish university sites (Chen *et al.*, 1998).

Table 2.1 shows the top 10 American and British commercial websites most frequently cited by the 13 Scottish computer science sites. A commercial site was identified by its domain name, i.e. .com for an American site, and .co.uk for a British site. They were ranked by the number of unique Scottish sites that linked to them. For example, 10 out of 13 Scottish sites had links to Java Development Toolkit at *java.sun.com*, at the time of the analysis.

An interesting pattern emerged. Links to American sites were predominated by companies providing leading Internet-related technologies and services, such as Java programming tools, Yahoo and AltaVista. On the other hand, links to British

Table 2.1 Top ten most popular American and British commercial sites cited by Scottish universities (Data: Aug/Sept, 1996)

Rank	US Site	Count	Type	UK Site	Count	Type
1	Java	188	Software	Demon	63	ISP
2	Yahoo	124	Search Engine	Telegraph	27	Media
3	AltaVista	34	Search Engine	Bookshop	35	Publisher
4	Lycos	29	Search Engine	Web13/Future	28/28	ISP/Media
5	Microsoft	30	Software	Cityscape	26	Media
6	AT&T research	51	Research	Nexor	34	ISP
7	Netscape	32	Software	OUP	16	Publisher
8	NBA	36	Sport/Music	Almac	16	ISP
9	Digital research	44	Research	Musicbase	18	Sport/Music
10	Lights	36	Others	Virgin Records	17	Sport/Music

sites were predominated by mass media and entertainment such as the Daily Telegraph and Channel 4 (at *www.cityscape.co.uk*).

The profile of top-ranked popular commercial sites is mapped into a two-dimensional configuration using multidimensional scaling (MDS). Each site is represented as a vector, based on how frequently it was referenced across the 13 Scottish sites. The frequencies are standardised over all the Scottish sites, to minimise the bias towards large sites in Scotland. Fig. 2.18 shows the MDS map generated by SPSS, a popular statistical package. It explains 85% of the variance. Annotations in the map are added by hand with lines, to highlight sites that are similar to each other.

Along Dimension 1, research laboratories in large American companies are located on the one hand, namely, **AT&T** and **Digital**, while two sites at the other end are particularly devoted to music, e.g., Virgin Music Group (**VMG**).

In contrast, Dimension 2 may reflect some aspects of particular cultures. For example, National Basketball Association (**NBA**) (American) is on the top map, whereas the **Daily Telegraph** (British) is at the bottom. The positions of **Yahoo** and **AltaVista** suggested some connections to the generic nature of their indexing and search facilities. On the other hand, popular British commercial sites clearly reflected the British culture, for example, **Daily Telegraph**, **Channel 4**, and **Oxford University Press** (OUP).

2.4.4 Content Similarity

The vector-space model was originally developed for information retrieval (Salton *et al.*, 1994; Salton *et al.*, 1996). It is an influential and powerful framework for analysing and structuring documents. Each document is

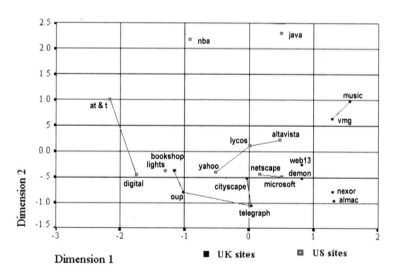

Figure 2.18 The profile of the most popular American and British commercial sites to Scottish universities (MDS Stress = 0.184, RSQ = 0.846) (Chen *et al.*, 1998).

represented by a vector of terms, and terms are weighted to indicate how important they are in representing the document. The distance between two documents can be determined according to corresponding vector coefficients.

A large collection of documents can be split into a number of smaller clusters such that documents within a cluster are more similar than documents in different clusters. By creating links between documents that are sufficiently similar, Salton *et al.* automatically generated semantically-based hypertext networks using the vector-space model (Salton *et al.*, 1994).

In GSA, we have several options to derive inter-document similarities according to term distributions. These may include, among others, the classic vector space model, the latent semantic indexing model, and dice coefficients. The following example is based on the well-known *tf* × *idf* model, term frequency × inverse document frequency, to build term vectors. Each document is represented by a vector of T terms with corresponding term weights. The weight of term T_k to document D_i, is determined by

$$w_{ik} = \frac{tf_{ik} \times log\left(\frac{N}{n_k}\right)}{\sqrt{\sum_{j=1}^{T} \left(tf_{ij}\right)^2 \times log\left(\frac{N}{n_j}\right)^2}}$$

where tf_{ik} is the occurrences of term T_k in D_i, N is the number of documents in the collection (such as the size of a WWW site), and n_k represents the number of documents containing term T_k. The document similarity is computed as follows, based on corresponding vectors: $D_i = (w_{i1}, w_{i2}, ., w_{iT})$ and $D_j = (w_{j1}, w_{j2}, ., w_{jT})$:

$$sim_{ij}^{content} = \sum_{k=1}^{T} w_{ik} \times w_{jk}$$

Figure 2.19 shows a PFNET for another departmental WWW site, SITE$_B$, with 172 HTML documents. The network has 172 nodes and 242 links. The screen display

Figure 2.19   The structure of SITE$_B$ by content similarity, shown as a PFNET ($r = \infty$, $q = N\text{-}1 = 171$), with 242 links (Chen, 1997a).

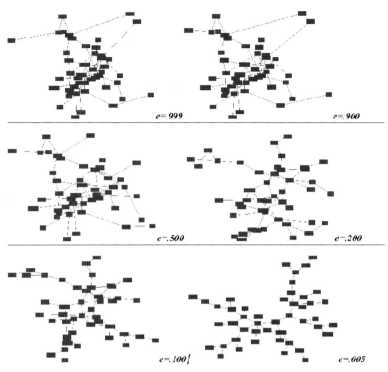

Figure 2.20 The graph layout is being optimised as the spatial configuration represents the underlying similarity model more accurately (Chen, 1998b).

becomes crowded even if numerical IDs are used in the graphical representation. This is an example of the famous 'focus *versus* context' problem: users need to access local details, while maintaining a meaningful context. In order to resolve this problem, virtual reality modelling language (VRML) comes into play. VRML provides not only new ways of interacting with graphic representations in a two- or three-dimensional space, but also a new metaphor of interaction, ranging from individual use to collaborative work.

A graph representation takes shape as the overall spring energy reduces below a threshold given in advance. Figure 2.20 shows the node placement process for CHI 96 papers at six discrete points. The value of spring energy at each point is given at the right-hand corner. For example, at an early stage, the energy of the spring system is 0.999, the energy is systematically reduced to 0.900, 0.500, 0.200, 0.100, and eventually the process is terminated at the threshold, 0.005.

2.4.5 State-transition Patterns

There is a growing interest in incorporating usage patterns into the design of large, distributed hypermedia systems, notably on the WWW. Access logs maintained by many WWW servers provide a valuable source of empirical information on how users actually access the information on a server, and which documents appear to attract the attention of users. Sequential patterns of browsing indicate, to some extent, document relatedness perceived by users. For example, Pirolli *et al.* (1996) use the number of users who followed a hyperlink connecting two documents in the past to estimate the degree of relatedness between the two documents.

The dynamics of a browsing process can be captured by state-transition probabilities. Transition probabilities can be used to indicate document similarity with respect to browsing, to some advantage. For example, the construction of the state-transition model is consistent with linkage- and content-based similarity models. In our example, one-step transition probability p_{ij} from document D_i to D_j is estimated as follows:

$$p_{ij} = \frac{f(D_i, D_j)}{\sum_{k=1}^{N} f(D_i, D_k)}$$

where $f(D_i, D_j)$ is the observed occurrences of a transition from D_i to D_j, and $\Sigma_k f(D_i, D_k)$ is the total number of transitions starting from D_i. Transition probability p_{ij} is used to derive the similarity between document D_i and D_j in the view of users:

$$sim_{ij}^{usage} = p_{ij}$$

The following example is based on state-transition patterns derived from server access logs maintained at SITE$_A$.

Figure 2.21 shows three Pathfinder networks, corresponding to three bi-monthly access log data between September 1996 and January 1997, associated with external users' access to the author's homepage. A number of predominant cycles emerged from the graph. In fact, there seemed to be some correspondence between a cycle and a set of documents of a particular type. For example, the largest cycle corresponds to top-level documents regarding general information

Figure 2.21   The structure of a subset of SITE$_A$, containing personal WWW pages, according to usage patterns (Stress < 0.005) (three bi-monthly snapshots between Sept. 1996 and Jan. 1997) (Chen, 1997a).

about the homepage (Node 7), the page counters and plans. The cycle (17-19-20-21-6-15) corresponds to some research papers. The cycle (21-22-23-33-6) corresponds to documents used in teaching. It also seemed that larger cycles corresponded to deeper browsing sequences, whereas smaller cycles tended to relate to more specific topics and shorter browsing sequences. Node 0 is an artificial node, to indicate the end of a browsing sequence.

A total of 22,209 access requests were made between 30 July and 31 September 1996, from 1,125 sources. The behaviour of the top 30 most active users is used to establish representative behavioural patterns in terms of first-order state transitions. These 30 users count for 10.7% of all the users who visited the site during this period. The number of pages visited by the top 30 users range from 13 to 115. Figure 2.22 shows a PFNET derived from similarities based on first-order state-transition probabilities. Cluster A is enlarged to Cluster A*.

The spike at the lower left half and the ring in Cluster A* essentially associate with an M.Sc. student's project on Web-based interface design. The spike at the upper right half corresponds to some research papers on hypertext.

It is possible to integrate several virtual structures derived from the same data using different structural modelling mechanisms. In the following generic formula, an existing hyperlink structure is adjusted, by incorporating the underlying semantic structure derived from content similarities:

$$sim_{ij}^{combined}(\omega_{ij}) = \frac{\omega_{ij} \cdot hyperlinks_{ij}}{\sum\limits_{k=1}^{N} \omega_{ik} \cdot hyperlinks_{ik}}$$

$$sim_{ij}^{link+content} = sim_{ij}^{combined}(\omega_{ij} = sim_{ij}^{content})$$

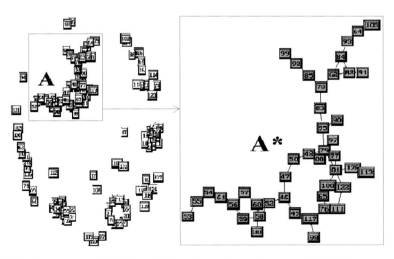

Figure 2.22 The structure of SITE$_A$ by state-transition patterns, shown as a PFNET ($r = \infty$, $q = N$-1), with 67 links (Chen, 1997a).

where the resultant similarity, $sim_{ij}^{link+content}$, represents a virtual structure, based on both hypertext linkage and term distributions.

2.4.6 Meta-similarities

A meta-similarity is an overall estimate of the strength that two similarity variables are related. To illustrate this concept, we computed Pearson's and cosine correlation coefficients among three sets of similarities associated with the website $SITE_A$, according to hyperlinks, content terms, and usage patterns. A total of 127 valid documents from the $SITE_A$ were included in our study. The linkage-content meta-similarity has the highest score on both Pearson's and cosine correlation coefficients ($r = 0.3201$ and $r_c = 0.4682$, $N = 127$) (see Table 2.2). The linkage-usage meta-similarity has the lowest score on both Pearson's and cosine correlation coefficients ($r = 0.0184$ and $r_c = 0.0644$, $N = 127$).

We analysed the changes in usage patterns associated with a collection of documents maintained by the author on the WWW over six consecutive months between August 1996 and January 1997. By comparing usage pattern-based similarity measures between adjacent months, it was found that the meta-similarity increased from 0.1967 to 0.4586 over the six months. It appears to be a trend that the meta-similarity is increasing with time (see Fig. 2.23). A possible explanation is that usage patterns become increasingly similar as the underlying structure settles down, at least for frequently visited documents. Experimental studies, and a thorough examination of specific documents and associated usage patterns, may lead to further insights into the pattern.

Table 2.2. Pearson's and cosine correlation coefficients among similarities based on linkage, content and usage patterns associated with the $SITE_A$

$SITE_A$ ($N = 127$)	Linkage	Content	Usage
Mean	0.0735	0.1671	0.0020
Std Dev	0.1413	0.3121	0.0357
$SITE_A$ ($N = 127$)	Pearson	Sig.	Cosine
Linkage-Content	0.3201	0.000	0.4682
Linkage-Usage	0.0184	0.017	0.0423
Content-Usage	0.0429	0.000	0.0644

2.4.7 Structuring Heterogeneous Information

This example briefly illustrates the design of a novel user interface for exploiting documents accumulated in an information filtering and sharing environment. In addition to visualising inter-document relationships, the visual user interface reveals the interconnectivity between user profiles and documents. The role of user profiles, based on the notion of reference points, is explored.

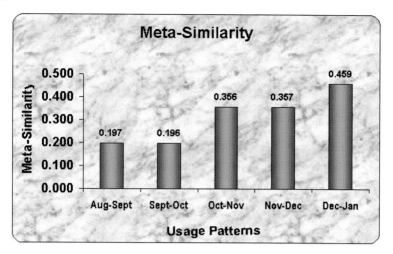

Figure 2.23 Increased meta-similarities, based on adjacent monthly usage patterns over six months.

The exponential growth of widely accessible information in modern society highlights the need for efficient information filtering and sharing. Information filtering techniques are usually based on the notion of user profiles, in order to estimate the relevance of information to a particular person.

Jasper is an information filtering and sharing system (Davies *et al.*, 1995), maintaining a growing collection of annotated reference links to documents on the World Wide Web (WWW). Currently, the interconnectivity among these accumulated documents and user profiles is not readily available in Jasper. In this chapter, we describe the design of a novel visual user interface in order to uncover the interconnectivity.

The concept of reference points was originated in psychological studies of similarity data and spatial density (Kruskal, 1977). The underlying principle is that geometric properties such as symmetry, perpendicularity, and parallelism are particularly useful in communicating graphical patterns. For example, people often focus on structural patterns such as stars, rings and spikes, in a network representation. Reference points, conceptually or visually, play the role of a reference framework in which other points can be placed.

In this example, it is hypothesized that a number of star-shaped, profile-centred document clusters would emerge if the role of reference points was activated by user profiles. Users would be able to share information more effectively, based on the additional information provided by user profiles through the visual user interface.

Based on a random sample of 127 documents and 11 user profiles from Jasper, the heterogeneous information structure is visualised within the generalised similarity analysis (GSA) framework. First, we extract and preserve only the most salient semantic relationships, in order to reduce the complexity of the visualisation network. Second, we incorporate user profile-based reference points in order to improve the clarity of the visual user interface.

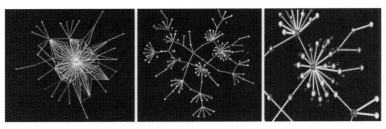

Figure 2.24   The role of reference points: disabled (left), enabled (middle), and a close-up look at a cluster (right) (cube = profile; sphere = document).

Unique behavioural heuristics are applied to distinguish user profiles and documents, in order to speed up the convergence of our self-organised clustering process. These emergent structures are derived without any prior knowledge of structural relationships. Additional structural cues are likely to result in more efficient results.

The impact of user profile-based reference points can be seen in Fig. 2.24. The left sub-figure shows the self-organised spatial layout without using the mechanism of reference points. The sub-figure in the middle shows the layout if the mechanism of reference points was utilised.

In fact, the 11 user profiles, which make up merely 8% of the 138 nodes, were associated with 69% of the links in the network, whereas the remaining 127 documents, which make up 92% of the nodes, only shared 31% of the links. Reference points have clearly improved the clarity of the overall structure. Users may now track relevant documents based on their knowledge of their colleagues' expertise.

The quality of information visualisation can be improved by incorporating user profile-based reference points, which is potentially useful for visual user interface design. The focus of empirical analyses on this type of visual user interface is usually the human factors. There are many usability evaluation methodologies available to assess whether a particular design feature, or the entire ecological system, is appropriate for users.

2.5 Summary

In this chapter, we have introduced several major aspect of information visualisation: structural modelling, in particular, the use of the vector space model and its variants, multidimensional scaling and trajectory mapping.

There was also an introduction to the generalised similarity analysis (GSA) framework, giving several examples to illustrate its extensibility and flexibility. More examples are cited in subsequent chapters.

The next chapter focuses on graphic representation, another fundamental aspect of information visualisation, introducing some of the most popular and advanced spatial layout algorithms.

Bibliography

Allan, J (1997). Building hypertext using information retrieval. *Information Processing and Management*, 33(2): pp. 145–59.

Beckwith, R, Fellbaum, C, Gross, D, and Miller, GA (1991). WordNet: A lexical database organized on psycholinguistic principles. In: U Zernik (ed.), *Lexical Acquisition: Exploiting On-Line Resources to Build a Lexicon*, Lawrence Erlbaum, pp. 211–31.

Botafogo, RA, Rivlin, E, and Shneiderman, B (1992). Structural analysis of hypertexts: Identifying hierarchies and useful metrics. *ACM Transactions on Office Information Systems,* 10(2): pp. 142–80.

Brooks, TA (1995). Topical subject expertise and the semantic distance model of relevance assessment. *Journal of Documentation*, 51(4): pp. 370–87.

Chalmers, M (1992). *BEAD: Explorations in information visualisation.* Proceedings of SIGIR 92 (Copenhagen, Denmark, June 1992), ACM Press, pp. 330–37.

Chapman, RL (ed.),(1992). *Roget's International Thesaurus* (Fifth edition), Harper Collins (London, UK).

Chen, C (1997a). *Structuring and visualising the WWW with Generalised Similarity Analysis.* Proceedings of the Eighth ACM Conference on Hypertext (Hypertext 97, Southampton, UK), ACM Press, pp. 177–86. Available: http://www.acm.org:82/pubs/citations/proceedings/hypertext/267437/p277-chen/.

Chen, C (1997b). Tracking latent domain structures: An integration of Pathfinder and Latent Semantic Analysis. *AI and Society*, 11(1–2): pp. 48–62.

Chen, C (1998a). Bridging the gap: The use of Pathfinder networks in visual navigation. *Journal of Visual Languages and Computing*, 9(3): pp. 267–86.

Chen, C (1998b). Generalised Similarity Analysis and Pathfinder Network Scaling. *Interacting with Computers*, 10(2): pp. 107–28.

Chen, C, and Czerwinski, M (1997). Spatial ability and visual navigation: An empirical study. *New Review of Hypermedia and Multimedia*, 3: pp. 67–89.

Chen, C, and Czerwinski, M (1998). *From latent semantics to spatial hypertext: An integrated approach.* Proceedings of the Ninth ACM Conference on Hypertext and Hypermedia (Hypertext 98, Pittsburg, PA, June 1998), ACM Press, pp. 77–86.

Chen, C, Newman, J, Newman, R, and Rada, R (1998). How did university departments interweave the web: A study of connectivity and underlying factors. *Interacting with Computers*, 10(4), 353–373.

Chen, H, Houston, AL, Sewell, RR, and Schatz, BR (1998). Internet browsing and searching: User evaluations of category map and concept space techniques. *Journal of the American Society for Information Science* 49(7): pp. 582–608.

Davies, NJ, Weeks, R, and Revett, MC (1995). *An information agent for WWW.* Proceedings of the Fourth International Conference on World-Wide Web (Boston, MA, December 1995). Available: http://www.w3.org/pub/Conferences/WWW4/Papers/180/).

Deerwester, S, Dumais, ST, Landauer, TK, Furnas, GW, and Harshman, RA (1990). Indexing by Latent Semantic Analysis. *Journal of the American Society for Information Science,* 41(6): pp. 391–407.

Dumais, ST (1995). *Using LSI for information filtering: TREC-3 experiments.* Proceedings of the Third Text Retrieval Conference (TREC3), National Institute of Standards and Technology Special Publication. Available: http://superbook.bellcore.com/~std/papers/TREC3.ps.

Fruchterman, TMJ, and Reingold, EM (1991). Graph drawing by force-directed placement. *Software – Practice and Experience*, **21**: pp. 1129–164.

Green, SJ (1998). *Automated link generation: Can we do better than term repetition?* Proceedings of the Seventh International World-Wide Web Conference (Brisbane, Australia, April 1998). Available: http://www7.conf.au/programme/fullpapers/1834/com1834.htm.

Hemmje, M, Kunkel, C, and Willett, A (1994). *LyberWorld – A visualization user interface supporting full text retrieval.* Proceedings of the 17th Annual International ACM-SIGIR Conference on Research and Development in Information Retrieval (Dublin, Ireland), Springer-Verlag (London, UK), pp. 249–59.

Hetzler, B, Harris, WM, Havre, S, and Whitney, P (1998). *Visualizing the full spectrum of document relationships.* Proceedings of the Fifth International ISKO Conference: Structures and Relations in the Knowledge Organization (Lille, August 1998). Available: http://multimedia.pnl.gov:2080/infoviz/isko.pdf.

Kamada, T, and Kawai, S (1989). An algorithm for drawing general undirected graphs. *Information Processing Letters*, 31(1):7–15.

Kruskal, JB (1977). Multidimensional scaling and other methods for discovering structure. In: K Enslein, A Ralston, and H Wilf (eds.), *Statistical Methods for Digital Computers*, Wiley (New York, USA).

Lin, X (1997). Map displays for information retrieval. *Journal of the American Society for Information Science*, 48(1):40–54.

Lin, X, Soergel, D, and Marchionini, G (1991). *A self-organizing semantic map for information retrieval*. Proceedings of SIGIR 91 (Chicago, IL, October 1991), ACM Press, pp. 262–69.

Lokuge, I, Gilbert, SA, and Richards, W (1996). *Structuring information with mental models: A tour of Boston*. Proceedings of CHI 96, ACM Press. Available: http://www.acm.org/sigchi/ chi96/ proceedings/papers/Lokuge/sag_txt.html.

Lokuge, I, and Ishizaki, S (1995). *GeoSpace: An interactive visualization system for exploring complex information spaces*. Proceedings of ACM CHI 95 Conference on Human Factors in Computing Systems, ACM Press, pp. 409–14. Available: http://www.acm.org/sigchi/chi95/proceedings/papers/ il_bdy.htm.

Marshall, CC, and Shipman, FM (1995). Spatial hypertext: Designing for change. *Communications of the ACM*, 38(8):88–97.

Mukherjea, S, Foley, JD, and Hudson, S (1995). *Visualizing complex hypermedia networks through multiple hierarchical views*. Proceedings of ACM CHI 95 Conference on Human Factors in Computing Systems, ACM Press, pp. 331–37. Available: http://www.acm.org/sigchi/chi95/ proceedings/papers/sm_bdy.htm.

Mukherjea, S, and Hara, Y (1997). *Focus + context views of World-Wide Web nodes*. Proceedings of Hypertext 97 (Southampton, UK), ACM Press, pp. 187–96.

Munzner, T (1998). Exploring large graphs in 3D hyperbolic space. *IEEE Computer Graphics and Applications*, 18(4):18–23.

Pirolli, P, Pitkow, J, and Rao, R (1996). *Silk from a sow's ear: Extracting usable structures from the web*. Proceedings of CHI 96, ACM Press, pp. 118–25.

Salton, G, Allan, J, and Buckley, C (1994). Automatic structuring and retrieval of large text files. *Communications of the ACM*, 37(2):97–108.

Salton, G, Singhal, A, Buckley, C, and Mitra, M (1996). *Automatic text decomposition using text segments and text themes*. Proceedings of Hypertext 96, ACM Press, pp. 53–65.

Schvaneveldt, RW, Durso, FT, and Dearholt, DW (1989). Network structures in proximity data. In: G Bower (ed.), *The Psychology of Learning and Motivation*, 24, Academic Press, pp. 249–84.

Szirmay-Kalos, L (1994). Dynamic layout algorithm to display general graphs. *Graphics Gem IV*, Academic Press.

Weiss, R, Velez, B, Sheldon, M, Nemprempre, C, Szilagyi, P, Duda, A, and Gifford, L (1996). *HyPursuit: A hierarchical network search engine that exploits content link hypertext clustering*. Proceedings of Hypertext 96 (Washington DC), ACM Press, pp. 180–93. Available: http:// www.psrg.lcs.mit.edu/ftpdir/papers/.

Zizi, M, and Beaudouin-Lafon, M (1994). *Accessing hyperdocuments through interactive dynamic maps*. Proceedings of ECHT 94 (Edinburgh, Scotland, September 1994), pp. 126–35.

Chapter 3
Spatial Layout and Graph Drawing Algorithms

This chapter focuses on the second aspect of information visualisation – graphic representation, or more generally, visual representation. Spatial layout and graph-drawing algorithms play a fundamental role in information visualisation. A good layout effectively conveys the key features of a complex structure or system to a wide range of users and audience, whereas a poor layout may obscure the nature of an underlying structure.

Graph drawing techniques have been used in information visualisation, as well as in VLSI design and software visualisation. Most graph-drawing algorithms agree on some common criteria for what makes a drawing good, and what should be avoided, and these criteria strongly shape the final appearance of visualisation.

Clustering algorithms often go hand in hand with graph-drawing algorithms, and also provide an important means of dealing with increasingly large data sets. For example, several popular graph-drawing algorithms have been developed to deal with relatively small data sets, from dozens of nodes to several hundreds. An ultimate test for such algorithms is to scale up, in order to deal with several hundreds of thousands of nodes, notably for visualisation applications on the Web.

This chapter discusses the following topics: (1) clustering algorithms, especially incremental clustering algorithms; (2) drawing hierarchical structures; (3) graph-drawing algorithms for general undirected graphs. Criteria for spatial layout are introduced, and there are in-depth discussions on force-directed graph layout algorithms. Closely related topics, such as simulated annealing, are also discussed, along with information on state-of-the-art graph drawing.

3.1 Clustering and Scaling

The goal of cluster analysis is to divide a large data set into a number of sub-sets, called clusters, according to some given similarity measures. The diagram in Fig. 3.1 illustrates this process. The original data set contains 11 balls of different colours. These balls can be grouped into three clusters of balls so that each cluster only contains balls of the same colour.

Not only has clustering analysis established many areas of application, for instance, constructing taxonomies in biology, but it can also play a significant role in information visualisation. For example, the 'Scatter/Gather' developed at Xerox helps users to deal with a large information space by repeatedly clustering

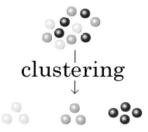

clustering
↓

Figure 3.1   The 11 balls are grouped into clusters according to their colours.

and aggregating documents at various levels in its user interface, so that the required information can be found more easily.

3.1.1 Clustering algorithms

Clustering algorithms rely on a definition of distance or similarity between two items in a data set. The Minkowski model provides a generic definition of distance:

$$d_{ij} = \left[\sum_{a=1}^{r} | x_{ia} - x_{ja} |^{p} \right]^{1/p} \quad (p \geq 1), x_i \neq x_j$$

where two data points are represented by vectors x_i and x_j. Several definitions of distances can be derived from this model; in particular, Euclidean ($p = 2$) and Dominance ($p = \infty$) can be derived from the Minkowski distance, as special cases.

A metric space is defined with the following two axioms:

1   Non-Degeneracy: $d_{ij} = 0$ if, and only if, $i = j$
2   Triangle Inequality: $d_{jk} \leq d_{ij} + d_{ik}$.

The Minkowski distance defines a metric space. Pathfinder network scaling introduced in Chapter 3 relies on an extended triangle inequality condition. If the triangle inequality can be defined in a semantic space, based on some *semantic distance*, it is then a metric space. Clustering algorithms use distance as a yardstick to either group a pair of data points into the same cluster, or separate them into different clusters.

There are three basic categories of clustering methodologies: (1) *graph-theoretical*, (2) *single-pass*, and (3) *iterative* algorithms. A graph-theoretical algorithm relies on a similarity matrix representing the similarity between individual documents. Clusters are formed by closely related documents, according to a similarity threshold. Each cluster can be represented as a connected graph. Depending on how these documents are separated, the process is known as 'single link', 'group average', or 'complete link' clustering (van Rijsbergen, 1979).

Table 3.1 Centroids of two clusters

Cluster	People	Age	Education	Salary (begin)	Salary (now)
1	401	37.55	12.77	5748.27	11290.35
2	73	35.20	17.47	12619.07	27376.99

Seed-oriented clustering is an example of single-pass clustering algorithms. In the seed-oriented clustering, clusters grow from individual data points, called *cluster seeds*. For example, document clusters can be generated by adding the documents most similar to the seeds into existing clusters. The number of clusters must be known for seed-oriented clustering to occur.

Iterative algorithms attempt to optimise a clustering structure, according to some heuristic function. An iterative algorithm can use clusters generated by other clustering algorithms, such as seed-oriented clustering, as a starting point.

Some clustering analysis routines are provided in popular statistical packages such as SPSS.[1] SPSS provides the following clustering procedures in the Professional Statistics option:

- K-means cluster
- Hierarchical cluster

K-means clustering algorithms can handle a large data set, but the number of clusters must be specified in advance. Hierarchical clustering algorithms merge smaller clusters into larger ones, without knowing the number of clusters in advance.

The example data set for the K-mean clustering method includes various personal profiles from 474 people, such as age, education, starting salary, and present salary. The goal of the example analysis is to divide these people in two groups based on their profiles. Two clusters are specified in advance, and the resulting clusters are shown in Table 3.1.

The data set is divided into two clusters by the K-mean procedure: cluster 1 contains 401 people and cluster contains 73 people. People in cluster 2 seem to be younger, better educated, and earning higher salaries.

Clustering is a useful way of dealing with very large sets of documents. However, there are few *incremental,* or *maintenance,* clustering algorithms in the literature. It is common for the clustering procedure to be repeated entirely in response to the change of the original data set. For a dynamic and evolving data set, re-clustering must be done from time to time on the updated data set, in order to keep the clusters up to date. Each time the data are updated, the whole set of clusters must be built all over again.

3.1.2 Incremental Clustering

To maintain clusters generated by graph-theoretical methods such as single-link, group-average, or complete-link clustering algorithms, similarity values are

---

[1]Statistical Package for Social Sciences (SPSS).

needed. Although the update cost of the single-link method is reasonable, the time and space requirements of the group-average and the complete-link approaches are prohibitive, because the complete knowledge of similarities among old documents is required. Therefore, an efficient maintenance algorithm would be preferable to re-clustering the whole data set.

Fazli Can (1993) has developed an incremental clustering algorithm that can continuously update existing clusters. It was tested in an experiment based on the INSPEC database of 12,684 documents and 77 queries. Empirical testing suggests that the incremental clustering algorithm is cost-effective; more importantly, the clusters generated are statistically valid and compatible with those generated by re-clustering procedures.

Can's algorithm is called *cover-coefficient-based incremental clustering methodology* (C^2ICM), and is a seed-oriented method. The cover-coefficient (CC) concept provides a measure of similarities among documents. It is first used to determine the number of clusters and cluster seeds. Non-seed documents are subsequently assigned to seeded clusters.

The CC concept is used to derive document similarities based on a multidimensional term space. An $m \times n$ (document by term) matrix D is mapped into an $m \times m$ matrix C (cover coefficient). Each c_{ij} ($l < i, j < m$) in the matrix C denotes the probability of selecting any term that appeared in document d_i from document d_j. The probability is defined as follows:

$$c_{ij} = \alpha_i x \sum_{k=1}^{n} (d_{ik} \times \beta_k \times d_{jk})$$

where α_i, and β_k are the reciprocals of the ith row sum and k^{th} column sum, respectively. Each document must contain at least one term, and each term must appear in at least one document.

This probability indicates the similarity between documents d_i and d_j, and is demonstrated as follows. First, randomly choose a term t_k from document d_i. In c_{ij}, the probability of this random selection is denoted by $\alpha_i \times d_{ik}$. The next step is to select the term t_k from document d_j (the ball of that particular colour); this probability is represented in c_{ij} by $\beta_k \times d_{jk}$. Finally, the contribution of each bag (terms of d_i) to the selection probability of a ball of that particular colour (d_j) must be taken into account, by adding these probabilities together for all.

This c_{ij} probability is a measure of similarity: it indicates the extent to which document d_i is 'covered' by document d_j. If two documents have no terms in common, then they will not cover each other at all, and the corresponding c_{ij} and

Figure 3.2   Documents (bags) contain terms (balls of different colours).

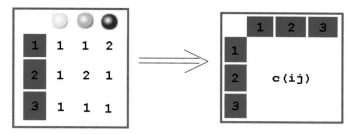

Figure 3.3 An $m \times n$ matrix is transformed to an $m \times m$ cover-coefficient matrix.

c_{ji} will be zero. In addition, Can (1993) introduces $\delta_i = c_{ii}$ as the *de-coupling coefficient,* because it is a measure of how different document d_i is from all other documents. The de-coupling coefficient is defined as $\psi_i = 1 - \delta_i.$

Based on the coupling and de-coupling coefficients, the number of clusters can be estimated as a function of the matrix D instead of a pre-defined parameter. This is the key to the incremental clustering method.

Can (1993) generated initial clusters using a method called C³M (cover-coefficient-based clustering methodology). The incremental clustering algorithm C²ICM is an extension of the C³M method; both are seed-oriented clustering algorithms.

In a seed-oriented approach, a cluster seed must be able to attract some non-seed documents around itself, and, at the same time, must be separated from other seeds as much as possible. To satisfy these constraints, Can introduced another concept, the *cluster seed power,* such that documents with the highest seed powers are selected as the cluster seeds. Once seed documents are found, the remaining non-seed documents are allocated to a cluster if its seed can provide the best cover for them, or if it has the greatest seed power.

C²ICM is a complex incremental clustering algorithm, but it is useful for updating clusters of very large and dynamic data sets. As many computational algorithms and software must be able to scale up to meet continuous challenges from increasingly large data sets, notably the Web, methods such as the incremental clustering will be an increasingly useful and generic tool.

3.1.3 Multidimensional Scaling

Scaling is an important concept in psychology, and can provide a rich source of visualisation techniques. It derives a quantitative scale to represent an internal, psychological response or reaction to stimuli, such as preference and satisfaction. A number of techniques have been developed for a variety of scaling. Multidimensional scaling (MDS) includes a family of popular scaling methods that can map high-dimensional data into a two- or three-dimensional space. It is possible to capture the nature of a data set from groupings emerging from the spatial layout in MDS.

To use MDS, the data set must provide enough information to derive and represent the distance between a pair of data points. This type of data is known as proximity data. There are several ways of obtaining it, for example, judging the

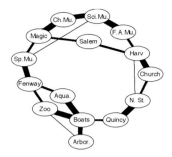

Figure 3.4   A trajectory map of Boston tourist sites (© 1996 ACM, Inc. reprinted with permission).

similarity between two documents directly, using sorting and clustering techniques. We have seen some examples in Chapter 2 using MDS, namely, the Boston tourist sites and top commercial sites cited among Scottish universities.

A special type of MDS, known as *individual differences MDS* (INDSCAL), is designed for the study of the nature of individual differences. The input is a series of matrices. For example, White and McCain (1998) used author co-citation analysis to map the field of information science. Twelve key journals in information science between 1972 and 1995 were analysed, and INDSCAL was used to identify trends in terms of top-cited authors in the field. The input was three periodical author co-citation matrices.

The results of MDS may not always be straightforward to interpret. Continuing the example of Boston tourist sites introduced in Chapter 2, according to Lokuge, Gilbert, and Richards (1996), trajectory mapping for high-dimensional feature spaces often captures the features of the data better than MDS. Instead of relying on similarity judgements as in MDS, trajectory mapping requires subjects to imagine a conceptual feature or property that links each pair of sites. The subject then extrapolates that feature in both directions, to pick two stimuli that would be appropriate from the remaining set.

A trajectory map for tourist sites in Boston is shown in Fig. 3.4. The positions of the nodes are not important; instead, the mental model is captured by the connections between the nodes. It is the choice between using spatial proximity or using explicit links that distinguishes MDS and trajectory mapping. Similarly, Pathfinder networks, a key component in GSA, also highlight the role of explicit links in structuring and visualising salient semantic structures.

3.2 Trees, Cone Trees, and Hyperbolic Views

Hierarchies, or trees, are the most basic data structures in computing systems. Visualising hierarchies is a significant aspect of information visualisation. In fact, many visualisation systems are designed for displaying hierarchical structures. For example, Fig. 3.5 shows a tree map, in which a tree is mapped onto areas of different size and colour. Tree-maps are described by Johnson and Shneiderman (1991) and Shneiderman (1992) as a space-filling approach to the visualisation of hierarchical information. Space-filling approaches have also been used in

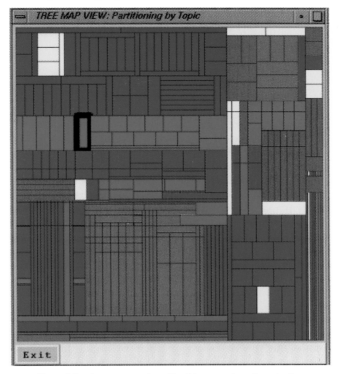

Figure 3.5 A tree map view. Partitions are based on topics.

representing self-organised maps; for example, the computer display area can be partitioned into a number of regional areas, each corresponding to an underlying topic (Lin, 1991; 1997). A related concept, also developed at the University of Maryland, is elastic windows, in which the screen is tiled by all the available windows in various sizes, so that the user can easily bring a window into focus. Further details about elastic windows can be found in Kandogan and Shneiderman (1997).

A representative approach to displaying and visualising a large hierarchical structure is to use cone trees. These were originally developed by George Robertson and his colleagues at Xerox PARC (Robertson *et al.*, 1991). The idea of cone trees has had a profound impact on information visualisation, and has been adopted in the design of a number of systems that visualise hierarchical structures. In fact, several systems derive hierarchical structures from more general network structures, and use cone trees to visualise the resultant hierarchies.

One of the well-known visualisation systems for information retrieval, LyberWorld, uses NavigationCones to visualise the context of searching. A recent example is provided by Tamara Munzner (1998b) in the design of H3 – a 3D Hyperbolic layout system. Her algorithm draws 3D cone-trees in a hyperbolic space in order to overcome common problems encountered by tree-drawing algorithms. She also uses a spanning tree as the backbone of her cone trees in a hyperbolic space, which effectively simplifies the visualisation of a general graph into the visualisation of a hierarchical structure.

3.2.1 LyberWorld

LyberWorld (Hemmje *et al.*, 1994) is a well-known example of applying metaphors of spatial navigation to abstract information spaces. The design of LyberWorld focuses on a network representation of an information space. It consists of two types of nodes: document nodes and term nodes, and three types of links: document–term links, term–term links, and document–document links.

Navigation in LyberWorld relies on the concepts of content and context spaces. The content space is the entire search space, whereas the context space is the sub-space the user has visited. Instead of using computationally expensive graph layout algorithms to map the content network into a three-dimensional space, LyberWorld derives hierarchies from the network representation of the content space and maps them onto a visualisation tool, called NavigationCones. NavigationCones visualise the navigation history of a user in the content space, along content-oriented search paths, which connect different documents in the content space.

In LyberWorld, document–term relevance is visualised by the Relevance-Sphere. Here, terms are placed on the surface of a sphere, while documents are positioned within the sphere, based on their relevance to each of the terms. Documents closer to the surface are of a greater overall relevance. This visualisation aims to improve the user's understanding of the query results, and the structure of the document space. However, no empirical studies have been found in the literature, based on the use of LyberWorld.

3.2.2 Hyperbolic in 3D

Much attention has been drawn to the 'focus versus context' issue, concerning the design of visual user interfaces. The challenge arises when users need easy access to local details related to their current focus, but at the same time they

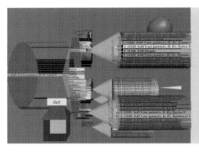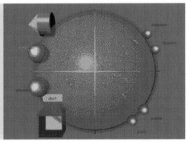

Figure 3.6 NavigationCones (left) and RelevanceSphere (right) in LyberWorld. (Reprinted with permission of Matthias Hemmje).

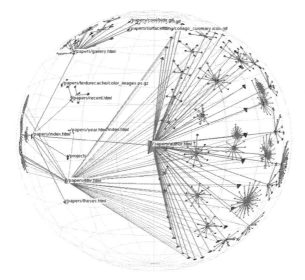

Figure 3.7 Mapping a file store into a hyperbolic space (Munzer *et al.*, 1998b) (© 1998 IEEE, reprinted with permission).

must be able to access information to help maintain a reasonable sense of context.

Cone trees can display many more nodes on the screen than traditional two-dimensional tree diagrams, and can be rotated so that users can examine a node of a tree in the display more closely. However, in an Euclidean space, there is a limit to how large a cone tree can be squeezed into a display area without losing legibility.

In order to overcome such limitations, a variety of distorted or warped spaces have been proposed and developed, including fisheye views and hyperbolic views. A recent development in this area by Tamara Munzner is the design of her H3[2] – three-dimensional hyperbolic visualisation (Munzner, 1998a; Munzner, 1998b).

The design of H3 aims to reduce visual clutter, speed up layout, and provide fluid interaction for a very large graph. The same technique has been implemented in Site Manager, a free Web publishing package from Silicon Graphics. It was used to visualise the hyperlink structure of the Stanford Graphics Group Web site, which contains 14,000 nodes and 29,000 edges. The unique features of H3 include the use of a spanning tree as the backbone visualisation model, and embedding cone trees in a hyperbolic space. The hyperbolic space is in turn projected onto a sphere in 3D Euclidean space.

One of the properties of a Pathfinder network, introduced in Chapter 2, is that the sparest Pathfinder network is the union of all the minimal spanning trees

---

[2]http://graphics.stanford.edu/~munzner/h3/

associated with the original network. Pathfinder networks represent an interesting alternative to the use of spanning trees.

3.3 Drawing General Undirected Graphs

General undirected graphs are one of the most useful data structures. We all can think of many examples of using graphs. However, the large variety of graphs and the general problems of information visualisation have caused researchers to focus on various special cases or special appearances of the layout, such as trees and directed acyclic graphs (Davidson and Harel, 1996). A comprehensive discussion and annotated bibliography of a wide range of graph-drawing algorithms can be found in the literature (Di Battista, 1998; Di Battista *et al.*, 1994).

Drawing general undirected graphs presents a challenging area to a variety of graph-drawing algorithms. They need to meet one or both of the two important requirements: (1) to draw a graph well, and (2) to draw it quickly. To meet the first requirement, algorithms may follow several commonly used heuristics. To meet the second, algorithms may need to scale up to be able to handle a large graph.

Drawing undirected graphs can be traced back to a VLSI design technique called *force-directed placement*, whose aim is to optimise the layout of a circuit with the least number of line crossings. Eades (1984) introduced the spring-embedder model, in which vertices in a graph are replaced by steel rings, and each edge is replaced by a spring. The spring system starts with a random initial state, and the vertices move accordingly under the spring forces. An optimal layout is achieved as the energy of the system is reduced to a minimal.

This intuitive idea has inspired many subsequent works in drawing undirected graphs, notably Kamada and Kawai (1989), Fruchterman and Reingold (1991), and Davidson and Harel (1996). Here their works are summarised and compared, to illustrate the influence of the spring-embedder model in graph drawing and information visualisation. The insights inspired by these works are invaluable for information visualisation in general.

3.3.1 Aesthetic Criteria for Graph Drawing

Different graph-drawing algorithms may have their own aesthetic criteria to follow. Important aesthetics for general graph drawing are given by Di Battista *et al.* (1994). Coleman (1996) also gives a list of properties towards which good graph layout algorithms should strive, covering notions of clarity, generality and ability to produce satisfying layouts for a fairly general class of graphs. Speed is also a criterion. Table 3.2 shows various criteria for drawing undirected, straight-line edge graphs. Most emphasise evenly distributed vertices and uniform edge lengths. Some algorithms make explicit efforts to minimise edge crossings, while others do not.

Some of these criteria can be mutually exclusive. For example, a symmetrical graph may require a certain number of edge crossings, even if they may be avoided. And uniform edge lengths may not always produce the most

Table 3.2 Criteria for graph-drawing algorithms

Criteria	Battista et al. (1994)	Eades (1984)	Kamada and Kawai (1989)	Fruthterman and Reingold (1991)	Davidson and Harel (1996)	NicheWorks (1997)
Symmetric	✔	✔	✔			
Evenly distributed nodes	✔		✔	✔	✔	Clustered
Uniform edge lengths	✔	✔	✔	✔	✔	Weights
Minimised edge crossings	✔		✔	✔	✔	

appropriate results. A pragmatic approach is to allow sufficient flexibility to allow algorithms to be tailored to particular applications.

NicheWorks (Wills, 1998) is a visualisation tool developed at Bell Laboratories, which aims to help an analyst to work on very large networks of telephone-calling data. A crucial requirement for NicheWorks is the ability to lay out a group of 10,000–100,000 nodes. Another important requirement is that it should be able to display both graph structure and attributes associated with node and edge, to reveal hidden patterns and information for investigating and exploring such large, complex data sets.

One strategy used by NicheWorks is to relax some of the optimisation criteria in order to speed up the process. For example, the aesthetics of evenly distributed nodes is not required for investigating traffic on a telephone network, so that this criteron was considerably relaxed by including only a final polishing algorithm to separate overlapping nodes.

NicheWorks presents a graph with straight-line edges. Instead of keeping edge lengths uniform, it is more important if the length of an edge can reflect the weight on the edge. In NicheWorks, the length of an edge is inversely proportional to the weight on the edge, so that the strongest linked nodes are closest together in the ideal layout. Fig. 3.8 shows a graph in NicheWorks.

3.3.2 Eades (1984) – the Spring-Embedder Model

The spring-embedder model was originally proposed by Eades (1984), and is now one of the most popular algorithms for drawing undirected graphs with straight-line edges, widely favored in information visualisation systems for its simplicity and intuitive appeal.

Eades' algorithm follows two aesthetic criteria: uniform edge lengths and symmetry as far as possible. In the spring-embedder model, vertices of a graph are denoted by a set of rings, and each pair of rings is connected by a spring. The spring is associated with two types of forces: *attraction* forces and *repulsive* forces, according to the distance and the properties of the connecting space.

The drawing of a graph approaches optimal as the energy of the spring system is reduced. An attraction force (f_a) is applied to nodes connected by a spring, while a repulsive force (f_r) is applied to disconnected nodes. These forces are

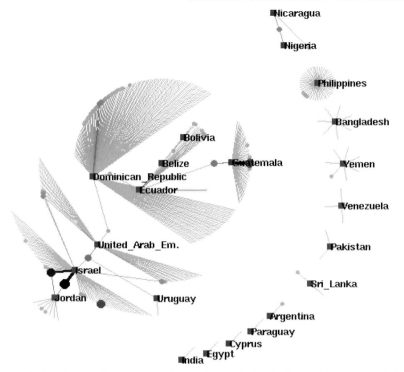

Figure 3.8 A telephone calling network visualised in NicheWorks (reprinted with permission of Graham Wills).

defined as follows:

$$f_a(d) = k_a \log(d)$$

$$f_r(d) = k_r / d^2$$

The k_a and k_r are constants and d is the current distance between nodes. For connected nodes, this distance d is the length of the spring. The initial layout of the graph is configured randomly. Within each iteration the forces are calculated for each node, and nodes are moved accordingly, in order to reduce the tension. According to Eades (1984), the spring-embedder model ran very fast on a VAX

Figure 3.9 In the spring-embedder model, the position of a vertex is dynamically determined by the attraction force (f_a) and the repulsive force (f_r).

11/780 on graphs with up to 30 nodes. However, the spring-embedder model may break down on very large graphs.

3.3.3 Kamada and Kawai (1989) – Local Minimum

The spring-embedder model has inspired a number of modified and extended algorithms for drawing undirected graphs. For example, repulsive forces are usually computed between all the pairs of vertices, but attractive forces can be calculated only between neighbouring vertices. The simplified model reduces the time complexity: calculating the attractive forces between neighbours is $\Theta(|E|)$, although the repulsive force calculation is till $\Theta(|V|^2)$, which is a great bottleneck of n-body algorithms in general.

Kamada and Kawai (1989) introduced an algorithm based on Eades' springer-embedder model, which attempts to achieve the following two criteria, or heuristics, of graph drawing:

- The number of edge crossings should be minimal.
- The vertices and edges are distributed uniformly.

The key is to find local minimum energy according to the gradient vector $\sigma = 0$, which is a necessary, but not a sufficient, condition for a global miminum. In nature's terms, this search is asking much, so additional controls are often included in the implementation to ensure that the spring system is not trapped in a local minimum valley.

Unlike Eades' algorithm, which does not explicitly incorporate Hooke's law, Kamada and Kawai's algorithm moves vertices into new positions one at a time, so that the total energy of the spring system is reduced with the new configuration. It also introduces the concept of a desirable distance between vertices in the drawing: the distance between two vertices is propotional to the length of the shortest path between them.

Following Kamada and Kawai's notation (1989), given a dynamic system of n particles mutually connected by springs, let $p_1, p_2, ..., p_n$ be the particles in the drawing area corresponding to the vertices $v_1, v_2, ..., v_n \in V$ respectively. The balanced layout of vertices can be achieved through the dynamically balanced spring system. Kamada and Kawai formulated the degree of imbalance as the total energy of springs:

$$E = \sum_{i=1}^{n-1} \sum_{j=i+1}^{n} \frac{1}{2} k_{ij}(|\, p_i - p_j \,| - l_{ij})^2$$

Their model implies that the best graph layout is the state with minimum E. The distance d_{ij} between two vertices v_i and v_j in a graph is defined as the length of the shortest paths between v_i and v_j. The algorithm aims to match the spring length l_{ij} between particles p_i and p_j, with the shortest-path distance, to achieve the optimal length between them in the drawing. The length l_{ij} is defined as follows:

$$l_{ij} = L \times d_{ij}$$

where L is the desirable length of a single edge in the drawing area. L can be determined based on the largest vertex-to-vertex distance in the graph. If L_0 is the length of a side of the square of drawing area, L can be derived as follows:

$$L = \frac{L_0}{\max_{i<j}(d_{ij})}$$

The strength of the spring connecting p_i and p_j is denoted by parameter k_{ij}:

$$k_{ij} = \frac{K}{d_{ij}^2}$$

where K is a constant. Both l_{ij} and k_{ij} are symmetrical, therefore this design yields symmetrical layouts whenever possible.

Finding a global minimum is difficult in a large search space. The strategy used in Kamada and Kawai's algorithm is to find a local minimum first. Nodes are moved into new positions if the movement leads to the fastest reduction of the total energy. The procedure is repeated until it converges – when the maximum improvement is less than a fixed small threshold ϵ. The algorithms may continuously search for a new local minimum by swapping over pairs of nodes and repeating the above procedure, provided this swapping over yields a further decrease in the energy. In genetic programming, such swapping operations are known as cross-overs.

Kamada and Kawai's algorithm has been extended from a two-dimensional space to a three-dimensional version (Kumar and Fowler, 1994).[3] The necessary condition of local minimum energy E is specified by the following equation:

$$\frac{\partial E}{\partial x_m} = \frac{\partial E}{\partial y_m} = \frac{\partial E}{\partial z_m} = 0, (1 \leq m \leq n)$$

A distinct feature of Kamada and Kawai's algorithm is that only one vertex is moved at a time, while other vertices are frozen. Typically the algorithm chooses to move the vertex v_m that is in the 'worst place', i.e., which has the largest Δ_m, as defined below:

$$\Delta_m = \sqrt{\left\{\frac{\partial E}{\partial x_m}\right\}^2 + \left\{\frac{\partial E}{\partial y_m}\right\}^2 + \left\{\frac{\partial E}{\partial z_m}\right\}^2}$$

The following pseudo-code of the algorithm is adapted from Kamada and Kawai (1989), and Kumar and Fowler (1995). Let p_1, p_2, ..., p_n denote the vertices in a graph of N nodes, and d_{ij}, l_{ij}, k_{ij}, ϵ as defined above. δx, δy, and δz denote the corresponding movement along x, y, and z dimensions.

```
compute d_ij for 1 ≤ i ≠ j ≤ N
compute l_ij for 1 ≤ i ≠ j ≤ N
compute k_ij for 1 ≤ i ≠ j ≤ N
initialise p_1, p_2, ..., p_n
while (max_i Δ_i > ε) {
    let p_m be the vertex satisfying Δ_m = max_i Δ_i
    while (Δ_m > ε) {
```

[3] http://bahia.cs.panam.edu/info_vis/spr_tr.html

```
    compute δx, δy, and δz
    xₘ = xₘ + δx
    yₘ = yₘ + δy
    zₘ = zₘ + δz
  }
}
```

The time complexity of the algorithm in Kamada and Kawai (1989) cannot be represented as a function of $|V|$ and $|E|$. Kamada and Kawai (1989) suggested a method to deal with weighted graphs. For example, *lij* can be defined as the sum of weights on the shortest path between i and j. In Pathfinder network scaling, the generic Minkowski metric can be used to compute the length of a path.

Some of the common criteria are not explicitly controlled in the spring-embedder model. For example, it does not provide an explicit mechanism to detect and minimise the number of edge crossings. Several implementations based on the spring-embedder model have introduced optimisation mechanisms. The greatest advantage of formulating such graph drawing problems as an optimisation problem is that algorithms can be made more flexible by incorporating the required criteria into the optimisation process.

3.3.4 Fruchterman and Reingold (1991) – Force Directed

A significant enhancement and adaptation of the spring-embedder model (Eades, 1984) has been made by Fruchterman and Reingold (1991). Their algorithm follows generally accepted aesthetic criteria for graph drawing, including evenly distributed vertices, minimised edge crossings, and uniform edge lengths. As in Eades (1984), attraction forces are calculated only for neighboring nodes, and repulsive forces are calculated for all pairs of nodes. According to Fruchterman and Reingold, nodes at distance d are attracted to each other by the following attraction force f_a:

$$f_a(d) = d^2/k$$

and they are pushed apart by the repulsive force f_r:

$$f_r(d) = -d^2/k$$

where k is the optimal distance between nodes in the graph, calculated from the number of nodes and the size of the drawing area. In Fruchterman and Reingold (1991), the process is carried out iteratively. Within each iteration, the forces are calculated for each node, and at its end all nodes are moved simultaneously. The process is also controlled by a temperature parameter, in a similar way to simulated annealing (see 3.3.5). The algorithm uses 50 iterations, and all the examples shown in their article were drawn in 10 seconds or less on a SparcStation. The following force-directed placement algorithm is adapted from Fruchterman and Reingold (1991):

{ a drawing frame: $W \times L$ }
$G := (V, E);$
$k := \sqrt{W * L / |V|}$
function $f_a(x) :=$ **begin return** x^2/k **end**;
function $f_r(x) :=$ **begin return** k^2/x **end**;

for i := 1 **to** *iterations* **do begin**
  {calculate repulsive forces}
  for *v* **in** *V* **do begin**
    {each vertex has two vectors: .pos and .disp}
    v.disp := 0;
    for *u* **in** *V* **do**
      if $(u \neq v)$ **then begin**
        $\Delta :=$ *v.pos* $-$ *u.pos*;
        v.disp := *v.disp* $+ (\Delta/|\Delta|)*f_r(|\Delta|)$;
      end
  end

  {calculate attractive forces}
  for *e* **in** *E* **do begin**
    $\Delta :=$ *e.v.pos* $-$ *e.u.pos*;
    e.v.disp := *e.v.disp* $- (\Delta/|\Delta|)*f_a(|\Delta|)$;
    e.v.disp := *e.v.disp* $+ (\Delta/|\Delta|)*f_a(|\Delta|)$;
  end

  {limit the maximum displacement to the temparature *t*}
  {and prevent from being displaced outside frame}
  for *v* **in** *V* **do begin**
    v.pos := *v.pos* $+ (v.disp/|v.disp|)*min(v.disp, t)$;
    v.pos.x := $min(W/2, max(-W/2, v.pos.x))$;
    v.pos.y := $min(L/2, max(-L/2, v.pos.y))$
  end
  {reduce the temperature as the layout approaches a better configuration}
  t := cool(t)
end

Figure 3.10   Force-directed placement (Fruchterman and Reingold, 1991) (© John Wiley & Sons Limited. Reproduced with permission).

3.3.5 Davidson and Harel (1996) – Simulated Annealing

Davidson and Harel (1996) describe how *simulated annealing* is applied to graph drawing. Their algorithm is also based on the spring-embedder model for drawing general undirected graphs with straight-line edges, and particularly emphasizes the aesthetic quality of graph drawing. For example, nodes and edges should be placed so that the picture is clear and pleasing. Several simple criteria are used to improve the aesthetic quality of the graph.

Simulated annealing is a flexible optimisation method originating in statistical mechanics (Kirkpartrick *et al.*, 1983; van Laarhoven and Aarts, 1987). It has been applied successfully to classical combinatorial optimisation problems, such as the 'travelling salesman' problem, and the design of VLSI. Simulated annealing differs from standard *greedy* optimisation methods by allowing 'uphill' moves, which may temporarily lead to a higher energy, but which are necessary to make a configuration out of the trap of a local minimum, and eventually reach a global minimum.

The major weakness of simulated annealing is its efficiency – simulated annealing algorithms in general are relatively slow. More fundamentally, simulated annealing may break down if the size of the graph to be drawn is very large. Davidson and Harel note that their algorithm can handle graphs of up to around 30 nodes and 50 edges, but the quality of the output deteriorates rapidly on larger graphs. In fact, their procedure is so time-consuming that they only use it to fine-tune a rough solution found using other techniques.

The major strength of simulated annealing is its ability to deal with optimisation problems in a discrete configuration space which is too large for an exhaustive search. The aim of is to minimise or maximise a cost function. Simulated annealing typically starts with a randomly chosen initial configuration and repeatedly searches for configurations that can reduce the value of the cost function.

The key function of simulated annealing is to ensure that the search does not stop at a local minimum, rather than the global minimum. It is based on an analogy to the physical *annealing* process, in which liquids are cooled to a crystalline form.

When a liquid is cooled slowly, it reaches a totally ordered *crystal* form, which represents the system with the least amount of energy. In contrast, if it is cooled rapidly, the energy of the system is higher than a crystalized state. When a liquid is cooled slowly, the atoms have time to reach a thermal equilibrium at every temperature. In this state, the system obeys the Boltzmann distribution:

$$p(E) \approx e^{-E/kT}$$

where $p(E)$ specifies the probability distribution of the energy values of the states E, as a function of the temperature T and the Boltzmann constant k. The energy is decreasing as the temperature approaches zero.

Metropolis *et al.* (1953) simulated this annealing procedure by a series of sequential moves based on a basic rule. The probability of the system changing from one state (with energy $E1$) to another state (with energy $E2$) is:

$$e^{-(E2-E1)/kT}$$

According to this rule, whenever the energy $E2$ of the new candidate state is lower than the current energy $E1$, the system will take the move. But if $E2 > E1$, the state change is probabilistic. Kirkpatrick *et al.* (1983) generalised this procedure for general optimisation problems.

A general simulated annealing algorithm is structured as follows:

```
{set initial configuration σ}
σ := σ_random
{set initial temperature}
T := T_0;
while (control condition):
```

```
{choose a new configuration σ' from the neighborhood of σ}
σ' := σ + Δ;
{let E and E' be the values of the cost function at σ and σ'}
if (E' < E) {
   {accept new configuration}
   σ := σ'
} else {
   if (r < e (E − E')/T) {
      {accept new configuration}
      σ := σ'
   }
}
{reduce temperature T}
T := cooling(T);
}
return final configuration σ.
```

Many variations on this general scheme are available in the literature; for example, van Laarhoven and Aarts (1987) describe simulated annealing in detail, and also provide an abundance of references. Simulated annealing is very good at finding minimum values that are *close* to the global minimum, but seldom does it detect the global minimum itself.

The neighbourhood of a configuration σ is defined by the set of configurations that differ from σ by the location of a single node. Each new configuration is achieved by moving a particular node to a new location. In particular, Davidson and Harel chose to limit such moves within a circle of decreasing radius around the original location of the node. The radius of the circle is relatively large at the beginning of the process so that each node has sufficient freedom to move around, but it becomes smaller and smaller as the algorithm proceeds. In fact, in their algorithm, the distance between the new location and the original location had to equal the radius of the circle, to ensure that nodes were moved around within the shrinking circle as far away as possible, throughout the process.

One further key element is the cost function, which must be optimised, and incorporate criteria to be met by the final drawing. Great care should be taken

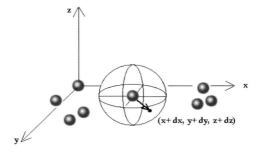

Figure 3.11   Simulated annealing accepts the new configuration if the energy is reduced; otherwise, the acceptance depends on a probability based on Boltzmann distribution.

when defining the cost function as it is the most heavy-duty computation component of the algorithm. Davidson and Harel have considered a number of criteria in their cost function.

Even node distribution in the drawing space is handled by two components in Davidson and Harel's cost function, also known as the *energy function* in this case. The first component prevents the nodes from being placed too close to each other, equivalent to the repulsive force in the spring-embedder model, while the second component deals with the placement near to the borders of the drawing space. The repulsive effect is based on the electrical potential energy. For each pair of nodes i and j, the repulsive effect is inversely proportional to the distance between them, and the energy function includes the first component as follows:

$$\sum_{i,j} \frac{\lambda_1}{d_{ij}^2}$$

where d_{ij} is the Euclidean distance between i and j. Here, λ_1 is a normalising factor defining the relative importance of this criterion compared to the others. Increasing λ_1 relative to the other normalising factors increases the cost of the repulsive effect. Therefore, more compact configurations are preferable.

In order to prevent nodes from being placed too close to the borders of the drawing space, the following term is included in the energy function:

$$m_i = \lambda_2 \left(\frac{1}{r_i^2} + \frac{1}{l_i^2} + \frac{1}{t_i^2} + \frac{1}{b_i^2} \right)$$

where r_i, l_i, t_i and b_i are the distances between node i and the right, left, top and bottom sides, respectively. Increasing λ_2 relative to λ_1 rewards configurations with more nodes towards the center, while decreasing it results in using more of the drawing space near to the borders.

Davidson and Harel included a component in their energy function to shorten the edges to the necessary minimum, without packing the entire graph too tightly. As a result, long edges are penalised in the energy function. For each edge k of length dk, the edge length component is defined as follows:

$$c_k = \lambda_3 d_k^2$$

where λ_3 is a normalising factor. As a by-product, the short-edge criterion can effectively eliminate most unnecessary edge crossings. However, some graphs may need a more specific treatment for these.

In general, minimising the number of crossings is important, but difficult to achieve. If the graph is planar, it is possible to eliminate all the edge crossings. Algorithms do exist for producing a crossing-free picture of a planar graph, but many algorithms rely on more essential criteria to eliminate them. Although the number of crossings might not be minimal (and some crossings might remain even in planar graphs), the resultant graph drawing could still be pleasant and satisfactory.

Davidson and Harel deal with edge crossings by adding a simple constant penalty, λ_4, to the cost function for every pair of crossing edges. Increasing λ_4 imposes a heavier penalty to edge crossings, and results in drawings with fewer crossings on average, probably at the expense of other aesthetics.

The cooling schedule is one of the most delicate parts of the annealing algorithm. Since the initial configuration of the system is chosen at random, the initial temperature can be set high enough to accept almost any move at the beginning. The goal is to 'shake' the graph thoroughly. The exact value of the temperature parameter needs to be determined empirically. Davidson and Harel used a geometric cooling rule. If Tp is the temperature at stage p, then the temperature at the next stage is given by

$$T_{p+1} = \gamma T_p$$

with γ falling between 0.6 and 0.95. Davidson and Harel (1996) use $\gamma = 0.75$ in most of the examples, to achieve a relatively rapid cooling. Cooling too rapidly results in sub-optimal drawing. Davidson and Harel (1996) use a linear number – 30 times the number of nodes – to determine the number of trials at each temprature. For particularly difficult examples, running the algorithm with a larger number of trials per temperature may yield only marginal improvement. Davidson and Harel's algorithm runs in time at most $O(|V|^2|E|)$.

Figure 3.12 includes nine snapshots of a simulated annealing process, using an energy function based on Kamada and Kawai's algorithm. The energy function is based on Kamada and Kawai's partial differential equation's solution, in an attempt to identify a local minimum, as part of our GSA environment.

The graph is a 25-node grid. The initial configuration of the node positions is randomly assigned. The energy function also includes a component that prevents nodes being placed too near to each other. Edge crossings are neither to be specifically detected, nor particularly penalised. A number of iterations are made at each temperature, and each not only attempts to move a node closer to a local minimum, but also randomly accepts a move such that a node may escape the

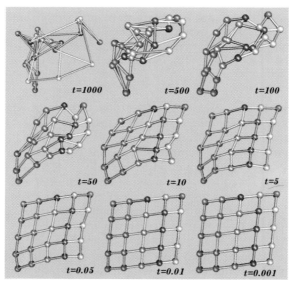

Figure 3.12   Snapshots of a modified simulated annealing process, based on Kamada and Kawai's local minimum partial differential equations.

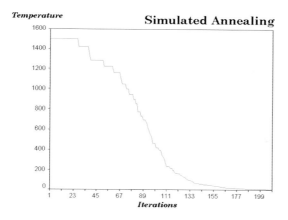

Figure 3.13   The temperature of the system decreased gradually.

valley of local minimum and lead to a global minimum. The magnitude of a move reduces as the temperature gradually decreases.

The first snapshot was made at the early stage of the simulated annealing, when the temperature was 1000. The layout revealed little about the structure of the grid. In the second and the third, the structure started to emerge, and became clearly visible by the time the temperature was decreased to 10. Finer tuning is shown in the last three snapshots, in which the basic shapes of these drawings are essentially the same, while some local adjustments took place.

Figure 3.13 shows how the temperature was gradually decreased through the simulated annealing process, although actually decreasing very quickly, although a slower decreasing rate may be appropriate for a more complex graph.

The curve of the energy function is shown in Fig. 3.14. The energy was rapidly reduced at the early stage of simulated annealing. As the temperature approached zero, the reduction of the energy was slowed down, and the process converged when the reduction of the energy was less than a small threshold.

3.4 Examples of Graph Drawing

The following examples represent applications of graph drawing techniques. Chapter 4 also includes visualisation systems that use graph-drawing techniques in a number of ways.

3.4.1 Representing Structures Using Graphs

Much attention has been given to the study of social networks as a potential application area, graph drawing techniques have been used to reveal their structures.

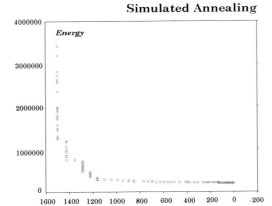

Figure 3.14   The value of the energy function is approaching to a global minimum as the temperature decreases.

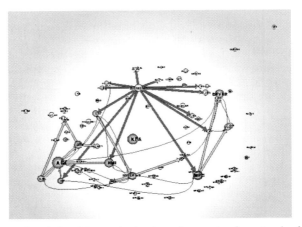

Figure 3.15   Access of an industrial organisation to various parts of a network of state sponsored research laboratories (http://www.mpi-fg-koeln.mpg.de:80/~lk/netvis/access.html). (Reprinted with permission of Lothar Krempel).

Figure 3.15 is a social network in which an industrial organisation has access to various parts of a network of research laboratories sponsored by the German government.

Many networks are homogenous, containing a single type of node, whereas heterogeneous networks contain several types of nodes. As in LyberWorld for example, a network of an information space may contain documents, terms, and queries as nodes. It is important to find out how these nodes are distributed and connected in a graphic representation. This task is equivalent to finding the two-dimensional convex hull for each of these data types. A convex hull[4] marks an

---

[4]Software for computing convex hull is available at http://www.geom.umn.edu/

area populated by all members of a given type of node. Analysing the distribution of various types of data can lead to valuable insights into profound connections between different types of data.

Figure 3.16 shows an interesting example. Several different types of research institutions in Germany are included in a heterogeneous network. For example, blue stars represent basic research institutions; yellow pentangles represent national research laboratories; green squares represent research institutions that focus on applied research; and red triangles represent industrial organisations. The visualised network provides a valuable resource for industrial partners and others who want to find out about the invisible network of research organisations.

A rapidly growing application of graph-drawing techniques is in visualising information spaces, to visualise a network of documents. Figure 3.17 displays a visualisation of the ACM SIGCHI's conference proceedings (1995–1998) as a semantic graph, rendered in VRML. The edges in the graph represent the strongest semantic relationships derived from the contents of documents within the GSA framework. The use of GSA in information visualisation and virtual environments is further discussed in subsequent chapters.

The graph in Fig. 3.18, also rendered in VRML, represents the structure of a network of Gopher servers in Europe. Connections are denoted by links between different nodes. This example is included in the Atlas of Cyberspace, maintained at the University College of London.

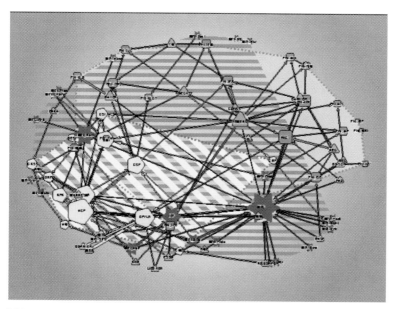

Figure 3.16 Heterogeneous research institutions: basic research (blue stars), national research laboratories (yellow pentangles), applied research (green squares), and industrial organisations (red triangles) (http://www.mpi-fg-koeln.mpg.de:80/~lk/netvis/domains.html). (Reprinted with permission of Lothar Krempel).

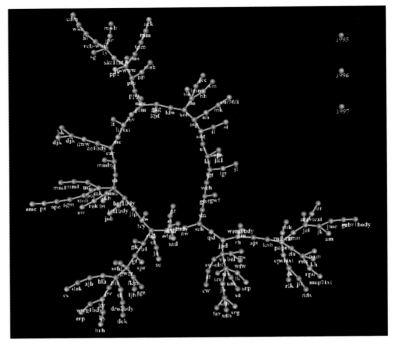

Figure 3.17   A visualisation of ACM SIGCHI's conference proceedings (1995–1997) in GSA.

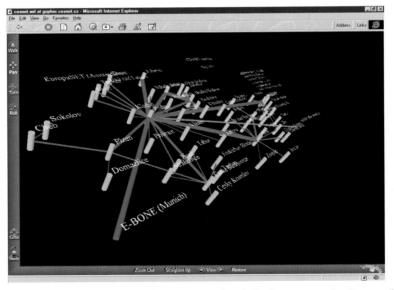

Figure 3.18 This Cesnet Map visualises a network of Gopher servers in Europe (http://
gopher.cesnet.cz/cesnet.wrl).

3.4.2 Atlas of Science

The idea of mapping the tracks of science is explained by Garfield (1994). The aim of such work is to identify research front specialties in a field of study. A specialty is characterised by its influence on the development of a given field, and can be identified by the number of citations that it receives. Our aim here is to identify some of the most predominant specialties in the field of hypertext, and to use author co-citation maps as a means of trailblazing the literature of hypertext.

In 1981, the Institute for Science Information (ISI) published the ISI Atlas of Science in Biochemistry and Molecular Biology (ISI, 1981). Articles published during a certain period of time were selected and ranked according to a citation index. A set of highly cited works were selected and labeled 'citation classics'. The distance between articles in the given period of time was then computed, based on the number of citation classics that they had in common.

102 distinct clusters of articles were identified, named 'research front specialties', to give an overview of significant research activities in biochemistry and molecular biology.

Over 100 people were involved in the project for several months, and the end product was an atlas providing a clear, distinct snapshot of the scientific network, and how it was structured. More recently, ISI developed Sci-Map software, for users to navigate the citation network (Small, 1994; Small, 1997).

Author co-citation analysis focuses on interrelationships among influential authors in the literature, rather than in individual publications. White and McCain (1998) present an extensive author co-citation analysis of information science, based on publications in 12 key journals in information science over a 23-year period (1972–1995). The top 120 authors were selected for their study according to citation counts. Maps were generated for the top 100 authors in the field using multidimensional scaling (MDS). The factor analysis reveals that information science consists of two major specialties, with little overlap in their memberships: experimental retrieval and citation analysis.

3.4.3 3D Spring-Embedder Model and Narcissus

Kamada and Kawai's influential algorithm was originally presented for graph drawing in a 2D drawing space, but the extension of a 2D to a 3D drawing space is relatively straightforward. A 3D version[5] of Kamada and Kawai's algorithm is described in Kumar and Fowler (1994).

Narcissus is an information visualisation system developed at the University of Birmingham (Hendley *et al.*, 1995). It aims to visualise highly interconnected structures in a 3D space, for software visualisation, and is based on self-organised graph drawing techniques and virtual reality, to reveal a complex structure. It is proposed to use Narcissus to display the dependencies between various components of a software system.

Figure 3.19 is a screenshot of the Narcissus system. The graph layout is generated by following the same principle as the spring-embedder model, and

---

[5]http://bahia.cs.panam.edu/info_vis/spr_tr.html

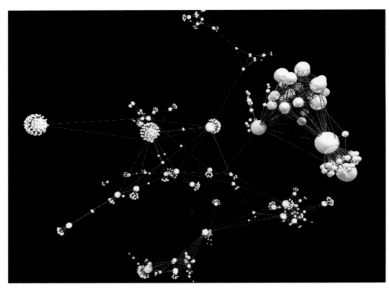

Figure 3.19 Visualisation in Narcissus rendered by ray-tracing (reprinted with permission of Bob Hendley).

was drawn in a 3D space. Ray-tracing techniques are used to render the final display. It is clear from the layout that Narcissus clusters nodes as much as possible, instead of producing an even distribution. Layout of the graph is performed using a self-organised graph-drawing technique. New nodes are introduced into the structure by being assigned a random location.

Simulated annealing algorithms in general can be degenerated quickly as the size of a graph increases. The spring-embedder model and its variants are likely to break down on very large graphs. For example, Fig. 3.20 is a visualisation of co-authorships among 555 scientists, generated with a method similar to the spring-embedder model. Its aim is to reveal patterns in a social network of co-authorships.

The spatial layout here appears to be cluttered with links crossing each other over long distance. It highlights two issues: first, a highly interconnected graph like this is unlikely to be planar. It is difficult to project such graphs onto a two-dimensional space without losing clarity. The second observation is that the size of the graph becomes too large for self-organised graph-drawing heuristics to handle.

To address the first issue, the interconnectivity of the graph can be simplified by deriving representative sub-structures from it, such as a minimal spanning tree, or a Pathfinder network. Chapter 5 includes an example in which a fundamental structure is derived from a substantial part of the literature of hypertext. This structure is then simplified into a Pathfinder network for visualisation.

To address the second issue, a hybrid strategy may work well. A very large data set may be divided into smaller, more homogenous sub-sets using various clustering algorithms. Self-organised graph-drawing algorithms are used only if

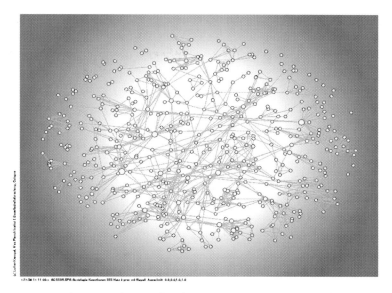

Figure 3.20 Visualisation of co-authorships among 555 scientists (http://www.mpi-fg-koeln.mpg.de:80/~lk/netvis/Huge.html). (Reprinted with permission of Lothar Krempel).

the clustering process results in clusters that can be comfortably handled. Alternatively, as with NicheWorks, one can always relax certain less important criteria to improve the overall quality of a graph drawing.

A serious problem with self-organised graph drawing techniques, including the spring-embedder model, is that the configuration in the drawing space is not a continuous function of the underlying structure of the graph; small change in the graph structure can lead to a much different configuration in its layout. Instead of placing new nodes randomly in the drawing space, a more sensible approach would be to use methods equivalent to incremental clustering techniques (see 3.1.2), so that the essential structure can be carried out into new configurations in a meaningful way. An incremental update of spatial layout would help users to reduce their cognitive load in dealing with these graphic representations.

An alternative to incremental updates is to animate the transformation from a previous drawing to the current one so that the user can see the changes in the structure as they are taking place. For example, in VRML 2.0 two consecutive frames can be interpolated to form an animation. More examples of information visualisation are included in Chapter 4, with emphasis on the connection between a visualised structure and the mental model of the user.

3.4.4 Summary

Davidson and Harel's simulated annealing approach is more similar to Kamada and Kawai (1989) than to those of Eades (1984) or Fruchterman and Reingold

Table 3.3 Drawing undirected graphs: the spring-embedder and its variants

Models	Attraction force	Repulsive force	Energy function
Eades (1984) Spring-Embedder	$f_a(d) = k_a \log(d)$	$f_r(d) = k_r/d^2$	
Kamada and Kawai (1989) Local Minimum			$E = \sum\limits_{i=1}^{n-1} \sum\limits_{j=i+1}^{n} \frac{1}{2} k_{ij}(\mid p_i - p_j \mid -l_{ij})^2$
Fruchterman and Reingold (1991) Spring-Embedder	$f_a(d) = d^2/k$	$f_r(d) = -d^2/k$	
Davidson and Harel (1996) Simulated Annealing			uneven-node-distribution-penalty + edge-crossing-penalty + long-edge-length-penalty.

(1991). In Kamada and Kawai (1989), the energy of the spring system is reduced in stages, node after node, as in simulated annealing, but in a deterministic way. An attractive feature of Kamada and Kawai's algorithm is that only one expression is needed for the energy function. In order to escape from a local minimum, the locations of two nodes can be swapped in simulated annealing.

Fruchterman and Reingold's algorithm (1991) has a unique feature: all the nodes are moved together, making it possible to reach configurations that are not necessarily in the vicinity of the current local minimum.

There is flexibility in the construction of the cost function: other criteria for aesthetics could probably be added without much trouble, and the relative weights of the criteria can be varied, thus making it possible to have some control over the final appearance of the graph.

The simulated annealing approach is competitive in terms of the quality of the resulting layouts, although, as mentioned earlier, it inherits its unattractive running time from the general framework of simulated annealing.

For large graphs (say, over 60 nodes), simulated annealing does not scale up well. An alternative is to use simulated annealing only after a rather complex series of preprocessing stages.

Simulated annealing can indeed be used in graph drawing, but is probably better employed in a tandem system whose front-end contains more specific heavy-duty tools for finding a reasonable first-cut solution.

The following chapters include a wider variety of works in both information visualisation and virtual environments. The major graph-drawing criteria and heuristics described in this chapter may provide a useful standing point for the reader to assess the design rationale of particular information visualisation. Further usability criteria will be introduced in Chapter 5, taken from the perspective of individual differences in cognition.

3.5 Graph Drawing Resources

There are a number of graph-drawing packages available in the public domain. Many of them implement the spring-embedder model or its variants. A list of these packages is included in the Appendices.

GraphViz[6] is a set of graph drawing software developed at AT&T Research Laboratories. It includes software for drawing undirected and straight line edges. GraphViz 1.3 can be downloaded from AT&T's Web site.[7]

GEM3D[8] is software for drawing undirected graphs in three dimensions, based on the spring-embedder model. Edges are drawn as straight lines, and the length of edges is as uniform as possible. It is designed for fast interactive 3D graph visualisation. Arne Fricks has been maintaining information about *GEM3D* on the Web (see Table 3.4).

Another interesting graph layout tool in the public domain is *VGJ*, written in Java. *VGJ* includes routines for drawing hierarchies, undirected graphs (using the spring-embedder model), and hierarchical directed graphs (using clan-based decomposition). The tool supports 3D and file input/output in GML, an upcoming graph specification standard.

Not surprisingly, the Web has been the major source of graph-drawing literature. An annotated bibliography of graph drawing can be found on the Web.[9] The following personal pages are from people who are active in graph drawing, and have maintained informative resource links on the Web.

Tom Sawyer Software's homepage[10] and the Geometry Center at University of Minnesota[11] are also good sources of graph-drawing related information. The next one is Graph Drawing '99.[12] Graph Drawing is an annual conference devoted to graph-drawing algorithms, theories, and applications. Links to previous Graph Drawing conferences can be found on Tamassia's Web page listed in Table 3.4.

Table 3.4 Personal pages on the Web, leading to resources of graph drawing

Name	URL on the Web
David Eppstein	http://www.ics.uci.edu/~eppstein/gina/gdraw.html
Arne Frick	http://i44s11.info.uni-karlsruhe.de:80/~frick/former.html
Lothar Krempel	http://www.mpi-fg-koeln.mpg.de:80/~lk/netvis/
Tamara Munzner	http://graphics.stanford.edu/courses/cs348c-96-fall/resources.html
Georg Sander	http://www.cs.uni-sb.de/RW/users/sander/
Roberto Tamassia	http://www.cs.brown.edu/people/rt/gd.html

---

[6]http://www.research.att.com:80/orgs/ssr/book/reuse/licence/packages/95/graphviz_1_0.html
[7]http://www.research.att.com/sw/tools/graphviz/
[8]ftp://i44ftp.info.uni-karlsruhe.de/pub/papers/frick/gem3Ddraw.tar.gz
[9]file://ftp.cs.brown.edu/pub/papers/compgeo/gdbioblio.ps.gz
[10]http://www.tomsawyer.com/
[11]http://www.geom.umn.edu/
[12]http://www.ms.mff.cuni.cz/acad/conferences/gd99.html

Bibliography

Can, F (1993). Incremental clustering for dynamic information processing. *ACM Transactions on Information Systems*, 11(2):143–64.

Coleman, MK (1996). Aesthetics-based graph layout for human consumption. *Software – Practice and Experience*, 26(12):1415–438.

Davidson, R, and Harel, D (1996). Drawing graphs nicely using simulated annealing. *ACM Transactions on Graphics*, 15(4):301–31.

Di Battista, G (1998). *Graph Drawing: Algorithms for the Visualization of Graphs*, Prentice Hall (Upper Saddle River, USA).

Di Battista, G, Eades, P, Tamassia, R, and Tollis, I (1994). Algorithms for drawing graphs: An annotated bibliography. *Computational Geometry*, 4:235–82.

Eades, P (1984). A heuristic for graph drawing. *Congressus Numerantium*, 42:149–60.

Fruchterman, TMJ, and Reingold, EM (1991). Graph drawing by force-directed placement. *Software – Practice and Experience*, 21:1129–64.

Garfield, E (1994). Scientography: Mapping the tracks of science. *Current Contents: Social & Behavioural Sciences*, 7(45):5–10.

Hemmje, M, Kunkel, C, and Willett, A (1994). *LyberWorld – A visualization user interface supporting fulltext retrieval*. Proceedings of the Seventeenth Annual International ACM-SIGIR Conference on Research and Development in Information Retrieval (Dublin, Ireland), Springer-Verlag (London, UK), pp. 249–59.

Hendley, RJ, Drew, NS, Wood, AM, and Beale, R (1995). *Narcissus: Visualising information*. Proceedings of Information Visualization 95 Symposium (Atlanta, GA, October, 1995), IEEE, pp. 90–6.

ISI (1981). *ISI Atlas of Science: Biochemistry and Molecular Biology, 1978/80*. Institute for Scientific Information (Philadelphia, USA).

Johnson, B, and Shneiderman, B (1991). *Tree-maps: A space filling approach to the visualization of hierarchical information structures*. Proceedings of IEEE Visualization 91 (October 1991), IEEE, pp. 284–91.

Kamada, T, and Kawai, S (1989). An algorithm for drawing general undirected graphs. *Information Processing Letters*, 31(1):7–15.

Kandogan, E, and Shneiderman, B (1997). *Elastic windows: Evaluation of multi-window operations*. Proceedings of CHI 97, ACM Press. Available: http://www.cs.umd.edu/users/kandogan/papers/chi97/ek.htm.

Kirkpartrick, S, Gelatt Jr, CD, and Vecchi, MP (1983). Optimization by simulated annealing. *Science*, 220(4598):671–80.

Kumar, A, and Fowler, RH (1994). *A spring modeling algorithm to position nodes of an undirected graph in three dimensions* (Technical Report). University of Texas – Pan American (Edinburg, Texas, USA).

Lokuge, I, Gilbert, SA, and Richards, W (1996). *Structuring information with mental models: A tour of Boston*. Proceedings of CHI 96, ACM Press. Available: http://www.acm.org/sigchi/ chi96/proceedings/papers/Lokuge/sag_txt.html.

Metropolis, N, Rosenbluth, A, Rosenbluth, M, Teller, A, and Teller, E (1953). Equation of state calculations by fast computing machines. *Journal of Chemical Physics*, 21:1087–91.

Munzner, T (1998a). *Drawing Large Graphs with H3 Viewer and Site Manager*. Proceedings of Graph Drawing 98 (Montreal, Canada), Springer-Verlag (London, UK). Available: http://graphics.stanford.edu/papers/h3draw/.

Munzner, T (1998b). Exploring large graphs in 3D hyperbolic space. *IEEE Computer Graphics and Applications*, 18(4):18–23.

Robertson, GG, Mackinlay, JD, and Card, SK (1991). *Cone trees: Animated 3D visualizations of hierarchical information*. Proceedings of CHI 9 (New Orleans, LA, April/May, 1991), ACM Press, pp. 189–94.

Shneiderman, B (1992). Tree visualization with tree-maps: A 2-d space filling approach. *ACM Transactions on Graphics*, ACM Press.

Small, H (1994). A SCI-MAP case study: Building a map of AIDS research. *Scientometrics*, 30(1):229–41.

Small, H (1997). Update on science mapping: Creating large document spaces. *Scientometrics*, 38(2):275–93.

van Laarhoven, PJM., and Aarts, EHL (1987). *Simulated Annealing: Theory and Applications*. Reidel (Dordrecht).

van Rijsbergen, CJ (1979). *Information Retrieval.* (2nd ed.). Butterworths (London, UK).

White, HD, and McCain, KW (1998). Visualizing a discipline: An author co-citation analysis of information science, 1972–1995. *Journal of the American Society for Information Science,* 49(4):327–56.

Wills, GJ (1998). *NicheWorks: Interactive visualization of very large graphs.* Bell Laboratories. Available: http://www.bell-labs.com/user/gwills/NICHEguide/nichepaper.html [August 1998].

Chapter 4
Information Visualisation Systems and Applications

In Chapters 2 and 3, essential methods and quality criteria for analysing and modelling implicit and explicit structures were introduced. A graph-drawing algorithm, for example, usually aims to achieve a layout with the least number of edge crossings, an even distribution of nodes, and/or uniform edge lengths. This chapter illustrates applies these methods and criteria to information visualisation in a wider range of systems and applications.

There are both theoretical and pragmatic implications of using a particular visualisation technique in relation to an overall design principle. The strengths and weaknesses of visualisation techniques can be analysed in the context of their design principle. Chapter 5 will further investigate the impact of information visualisation on navigation and information retrieval, with special focus on the role of individual differences.

4.1 Navigation in Large Information Structures

Hierarchies are one of the most commonly used data structures. The organisational structure of a file system can be represented as a hierarchy; the structure of a classification system is a hierarchy; and a taxonomy of all animals is also a hierarchy. Hierarchical structures not only play significant roles in their own right, but also provide a means of representing a complex structure in a simplified form. Since there are probably more tools for visualising hierarchical structures than for visualising general network structures, transforming a general network structure into a hierarchy is likely to widen the range of tools available to deal with the data structure.

Navigation in a hierarchical structure involves moving from one node to another, along the existing hierarchical links in the structure. When the size of a hierarchy becomes large, it is desirable to enable users to have easy access to contextual information, as well as local details. This is a challenging requirement for the design of a graphical user interface. Embedded in it is the infamous 'focus versus context' problem that many information visualisation systems have attempted to address.

Furnas (1986), a classic work in the literature, presents fisheye views as a way of displaying large hierarchies. To overcome the 'focus versus context' problem, the display is distorted so that local details are enlarged, but the context of the focal point is displayed at the same time, in smaller or less detailed forms.

4.1.1 Displaying Large Hierarchies

A relatively recent visualisation technique for displaying a large hierarchical structure is known as hyperbolic views. It was originally developed at Xerox PARC, and is now available from its spin-off company, *inxight*. Hyperbolic visualisation is also licensed to Microsoft's SiteMap. Much of the work in hyperbolic views is motivated to balance both the focus and its context in each screen display.

A hyperbolic view is specified by a mathematical model, especially suitable to display a large, unbalanced hierarchy. The greatest advantage is that nodes higher up in the hierarchy are initially displayed in the centre of the view, while nodes further down in the hierarchy are displayed with an increasingly reduced screen estate.

Unfortunately, node labels are difficult to read in *inxigth*'s user interface, with white characters printed on a yellow background (see Fig. 4.1). To illustrate what it is like to navigate within a hyperbolic view, the following screen images use corrected colours.

Figure 4.2 also shows a hyperbolic view of the 'Library of Congress', which is the root node of the entire hierarchy at the web site of the Library of Congress. It has over 20 top-level sub-trees, including 'Welcome to Library of Congress' at the lower central position, and 'Publication', the second node to the right. We can see that the publications node itself contains a substantial number of nodes. Our example is based on a navigation scenario, starting from the 'Library of

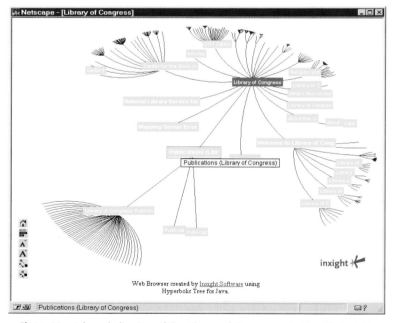

Figure 4.1   A hyperbolic view of the Library of Congress web site with *inxight*.

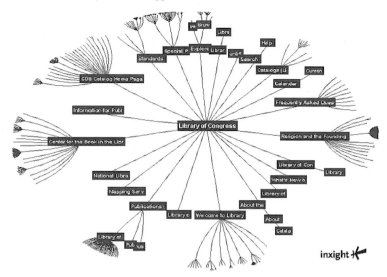

Figure 4.2   The starting node is at the centre of a hyperbolic view.

Congress' node (Fig. 4.2), selecting 'Publications' node at the lower left corner (Fig. 4.3), and targeting the final cluster of nodes (Fig. 4.4).

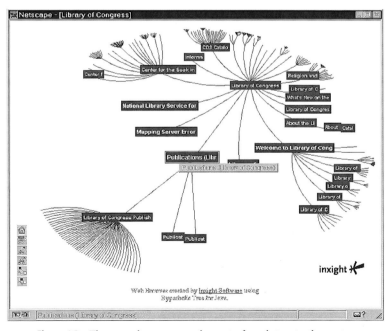

Figure 4.3   The second step moves the root of a sub-tree to the centre.

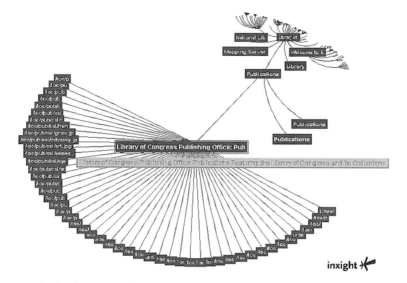

Figure 4.4   The third step moves further down along the hierarchy. The names of leaf nodes start to appear in the display.

4.1.2 Focus + Context Views

A focus + context view displays the details of a particular node, plus the neighbouring nodes that are directly linked to the focal node. Figure 4.1 shows an example of a focus + context view, generated by Sougata Mukherjea on his own homepage at Georgia Tech (Mukherjea and Hara, 1997). The focal node is represented as a sphere. Non-focal nodes are represented as cubes, the size of which is proportional to the relative importance of the node in the Web locality at Georgia Tech. Landmark nodes are coloured in red and non-landmark nodes are in green.

Blue links indicate incoming links and purple links are outgoing ones. The layout of the view is split into left and right by the focal node: the paths consisting of incoming links are placed to the left of the focal node, and the paths with outgoing links to the right of the node.

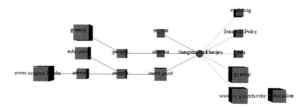

Figure 4.5   A Focus + Context view of Sougata Mukherjea's homepage. (Reprinted with permission of Sougate Mukherjea).

This focus + context view includes the immediate neighbourhood of Mukherjea's homepage, as well as shortest paths from several landmark nodes. A path from *alumni* indicates that he is an alumni of the College. The path from *gvutop* suggests that his research area was in Graphics, Visualization and Usability (GVU). In this way one can quickly understand the nature of various connections within this Web locality.

4.1.3 Zooming User Interfaces

The term *zooming user interface* (ZUI) is relatively new, although similar ideas and techniques have been used in computer systems for remote sensing image processing and geographical information systems for years. The most essential requirement for a ZUI is that the user interface must allow the user to zoom in and out freely and easily, across various levels of detail.

One representative ZUI example is Pad++, a multiple scale display tool jointly developed by a number of universities, including New York City University and the University of Maryland. A ZUI designed with PAD++ would enable users to zoom across a wide range of granularities. For example, one could design a ZUI of our universe and allow users to explore the universe at various levels. Users can infinitely zoom in and out: from an overview of our solar system, the earth, London, to a model of a human body, the human's heart, blood cells, and so on. A recent description of the design and evaluation of PAD++ in visualisation is presented in Hightower *et al.*, (1998) and Bederson and Meyer (in press) on the Web.[1] ZUI is closely related to the notion of multi-scale interfaces, as introduced by Furnas (1997). The system resembles a fractal graphical user interface, in which one can explore structures infinitely.

Figure 4.6 is the screen image of a site map of the Pad++ Web site, maintained at the University of Maryland, designed using a Java-version of Pad++. The structure is visualised as containers: a higher-level structure contains lower-level structures. Only two shapes are used: squares and circles. These two shapes are alternately used with a combination of colours. Users can not only click on colour objects to zoom in on one or more levels down the hierarchy, but also click on the background to zoom one level up out of the hierarchy.

Figure 4.7 includes three consecutive screen shots, moving from the paper directory down to directories containing papers by the year of publication, and finally to the papers published in 1998. The rim colour of each image is the colour of its parent level.

The Papers node is yellow in the left image, and the yellow colour is inherited by the border colour of the image in the middle. This is very convenient if we want to backtrack our own trail: we simply click in the yellow border area.

The ability to move freely in a spatial user interface is a desirable feature of a modern information system. A large class of information visualisation systems incorporate virtual reality techniques to enable users to explore an information space in more intuitive ways. Many system designers and analysts choose to use open standard virtual reality techniques, namely virtual reality modelling

---

[1] http://www.cs.umd.edu/hcil/pad++/

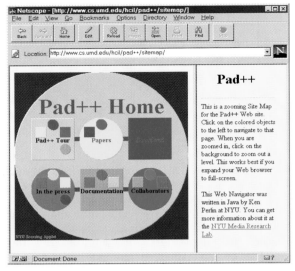

Figure 4.6   A zooming site map for the Pad++ web site.

Figure 4.7   Zooming in on the Pad++ site map across three layers.

language (VRML). Approaches based on open standards have the obvious advantages of easy exchange, and a wider community.

4.2 Visualising Search Results

Many information visualisation systems are designed to make information retrieval tasks easier, especially in terms of assessing the document–query relevance. The examples included in this section demonstrate how individual components can be usefully incorporated into a larger system.

4.2.1 Visualising Digital Libraries with Envision

Envision is one of the pioneering multimedia digital libraries of computer science literature (Fox *et al.*, 1993; Heath *et al.*, 1995). It includes publications of the ACM, and other literature to meet the needs of computer science researchers, teachers, and students at all levels of expertise. Envision was designed with full text searching and content retrieval capabilities. Search results from the Envision database can be visualised as a matrix of icons (Nowell *et al.*, 1996), which enable users to assess the results of a search graphically, based on a variety of document attributes. For example, a year-by-relevance layout can reveal peaks and valleys of document–query relevance at a glance. The design of the Envision user interface uses colours and shapes to convey important characteristics of documents. The colour of an icon indicates the degree of relevance: the most relevant documents in orange, documents marked by users as useful in red; and documents marked by users as not useful in white. A star icon indicates that the document is in the top 35% of relevance range; a diamond indicates its position in the next 35% of the range; and a triangle denotes a document in the bottom 30% of the range. The notion of peaks and valleys of relevance has also been used in more recent visualisation systems, especially ones with various spatial metaphors.

4.2.2 Visual Metaphors for Exploring Databases

VIRGILIO is a research project developed at GMD-IPSI in Germany, in cooperation with the University of Rome 'La Sapienza'. The name VIRGILIO stands for visual metaphors for database exploration. It is designed to provide novel, intuitively usable visual user interfaces, in order to reduce the cognitive load of the user significantly when working with multimedia database. Virgilio enables users to explore deeply structured information by using virtual reality techniques with metaphorical representations. It aims to build a visual representation of information, according to the structure of the result of the query from users.

Virgilio renders 3D scenes in VRML to represent the results of a search query. Users can explore the virtual world, interact with the objects embedded in the

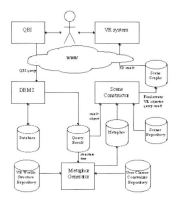

Figure 4.8   The architecture of VIRGILIO (http://www-cui.darmstadt.gmd.de:80/~hemmje/Activities/ Virgilio/vmdescr.html). (Reprinted with permission of Matthias Hemmje).

Figure 4.9 The first scene in response to a query. The structure of the building implies a classification of information (http://www-cui.darmstadt.gmd.de:80/~hemmje/Activities/Virgilio/example.html). (Reprinted with permission of Matthias Hemmje).

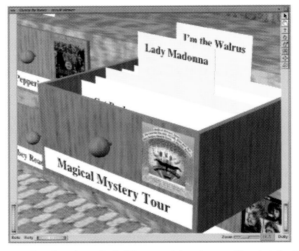

Figure 4.10 The user has found musical CDs, sorted by singers. (Reprinted with permission of Matthias Hemmje).

virtual space, and navigate across different levels of data in different scenes, from buildings, to rooms, and individual drawers.

Each drawer corresponds to a musical CD and its related information. The title of the CD and its cover image are displayed on each drawer. The smallest objects in this virtual world are songs, stored in different folders in each drawer.

Virgilio attempts to provide users with a familiar environment to access to a musical database. The greatest advantage of using a physical world metaphor is that users can easily understand how the virtual world is structured.

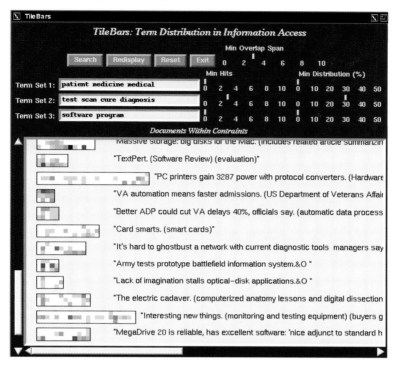

Figure 4.11   Visualisation of term distribution in documents in TileBars (© 1997 ACM, Inc. reprinted with permission).

4.2.3 Assessing Relevance with TileBars

TileBars offers an intuitive and easily understandable display of query–document relevance in information retrieval (Hearst and Karadi, 1997; Hearst, 1997). The distribution of each term in a query is marked in corresponding positions in a document. Based on where a term occurs, the user can quickly decide the nature of specific query–document relevance. For example, if a term is evenly distributed throughout a document, then the document has some profound relations with the query. On the other hand, if the term only appears at the beginning of a document, then the document is probably only marginally related to the query. TileBars also enables the user to detect the context of term occurrences. For example, the tilebars of three sets of terms can be easily compared to determine the nature of their contexts.

Figure 4.12 shows the results of a search on 'landmark' and 'California', in an attempt to search for landmarks in California. The summary shows that there is one strong co-occurrence of the two terms. For example, they may occur within the same sentence.

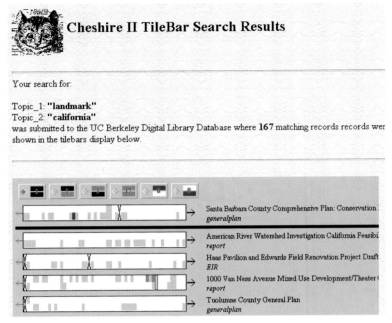

Figure 4.12   Search results displayed as a TileBar on the Web (http://elib.cs.berkeley.edu/cgi-bin/tilebars.ch.tcl).

4.2.4 Categorising Documents with Cat-a-Cone

Many information visualisation systems map each document to a single point of a semantic space, in which documents are clustered according to overall inter-document similarities. A cluster-based visualisation can be useful for many purposes, such as getting an overview of a collection's contents. On the other hand, an alternative way to visualise document similarities is to display documents according to orthogonal semantic attributes or category labels, such as the Dewy Decimal Classification Scheme. The design of Cat-a-Cone reflects some interesting insights into this issue (Hearst and Karadi, 1997).

Marti Hearst explains that when documents are clustered or grouped according to their overall similarities, it becomes harder for users to find out the unique distinctions between documents. Cat-a-Cone is designed to match the results of a search, in the context of a cone tree. It uses animation and a 3D graphical information workspace to accommodate the category hierarchy, and to store intermediate search results in a book.

The prototype of Cat-a-Cone was built on the basis of 3D cone-tree visualisation and animation from the Xerox PARC Information Visualizer (Robertson *et al.*, 1993). Cone trees are used in order to fit the entire display of a very large category hierarchy into one window. Category labels displayed in the cone tree can be easily rotated from the background to the foreground with a simple click on the label of their parent category. The user may control the

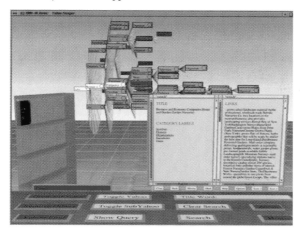

Figure 4.13   Yahoo Forager showing hierarchies in Yahoo in Cat-a-Cone (http://www.sims.berkeley.edu/~hearst/cac-overview.html). (© 1997 ACM, Inc. reprinted with permission).

details displayed in the hierarchy by pruning or growing a particular part of the hierarchy.

Another important component used in Cat-a-Cone is based on the WebBook, also developed at Xerox PARC (Card *et al.*, 1996). The WebBook and the Web Forager are designed to provide a more intuitive way for users to access interconnected information.

Figure 4.13 is a screenshot of the Cat-a-Cone user interface, with the cone tree in the background. Category labels are only displayed if they match the current document displayed in the focal book in the foreground. This information workspace also includes a bookcase. The user can search the collection of documents and save the results of a search as a book. If a book is not currently in use, it can be put into the bookcase. The example shown in the figure is a sub-structure of the Yahoo hierarchy.

A unique and significant design feature of Cat-a-Cone is the separation of the categorical hierarchy and the content of a document. It is also an example of how local details and a global context can be balanced using information visualisation techniques. The cone tree provides a global context, while the WebBook provides details of the focal point. The focal point is mirrored in the cone tree, because only category labels relevant to the current document are displayed.

4.2.5 Searching for Images with AMORE[2]

NEC Laboratories have developed an image search engine on the Web, known as Advanced Multimedia Oriented Retrieval Engine (AMORE) (Mukherjea and Hara, 1997). AMORE retrieves images based on user specified keywords. The keywords associated with an image are determined from the Web page containing the image, using various heuristics. The user can also find images

---

[2]http://www.ccrl.com/amore

Figure 4.14 Standard search results from AMORE. Retrieved images are ranked by visual similarity to the query image (Mukherjea, in press). (Reprinted with permission of Sougata Mukherjea).

visually similar in shape and colour to a specified image, and can retrieve images that are semantically similar to a specified image. The semantic similarity is determined by the keywords associated with an image.

AMORE often retrieves a large number of images in response to a query image. The relevance of a particular image to the query may be based on criteria such as shape, colour and semantic similarity values, as well as the relevance of the retrieved images to the user-specified keywords. The 3D scatterplot in Fig. 4.15 illustrates the results of a search along three dimensions: shape (X), semantics (Y), and colour (Z).

Retrieved images are represented as cubes, wrapped by corresponding images as texture maps. The query image specified by the user appears at the top right corner, because the image is 100% similar to itself in shape, semantics, and colour.

The 3D scatterplot can help the user to understand how retrieved images match to the query image. An interesting observation is that most images are either visually similar (high values for shape and colour similarity, and thus large x and z values), or semantically similar (large y value). Very few images are both visually and semantically similar.

Different viewpoints allow the user to zoom in to the image that is most semantically similar, visually similar, and so on. The user can also plot other search criteria, such as how relevant the images were to user-specified keywords in the visualisation.

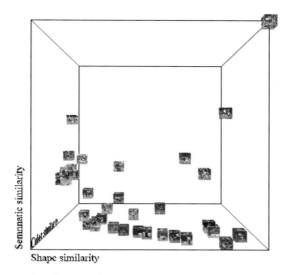

Semnnatic similarity

Colour similarity

Shape similarity

Figure 4.15   3D scatterplot of retrieved images using the AMORE search engine. (Reprinted with permission of Sougata Mukherjea).

4.3 Spatial Metaphors for Information Exploration

Spatial metaphors are among the most popular design options in information visualisation. Many influential information visualisation systems are based on them, including SemNet (Fairchild *et al.*, 1988), BEAD (Chalmers, 1992), LyberWorld (Hemmje *et al.*, 1994), Starfield (Ahlberg and Shneiderman, 1994), VR-VIBE (Benford *et al.*, 1995), and SPIRE (Hetzler *et al.*, 1998a).

Earlier geographical information systems (GIS) have been a major source of inspiration for the design of more recent information visualisation systems, using the universe, the solar system, galaxies, or other spatial metaphors. In a GIS system, tourist attractions, electricity consumption, water supply, crime, spending power, and many other types of information can be intuitively superimposed over the natural layout framework provided by geography. Figure 4.16 shows the appealing features of a geographical information system of the Boston area, and Chapter 2 discussed how multidimensional scaling and trajectory mapping techniques were used to derive structural connections among various tourist sites in Boston.

4.3.1 SemNet (1989)

SemNet (Fairchild *et al.*, 1988) is a classic study of 3D visualisation. It is designed to help people understand the complex relationships within large knowledge bases. SemNet visualises relationships that already exist within a knowledge base.

Fairchild *et al.* discuss a number of design issues in association with mapping a high dimensional data set into a 3D space. They analyse the complexity issue for displaying the semantic network derived from very large knowledge bases,

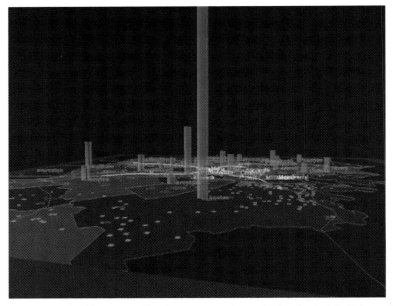

Figure 4.16   Geographical layout provides the most natural organisational principle (Lokuge, Gilbert, and Richards, 1996). (© 1996 ACM, Inc. reprinted with permission).

and rightly point out that simply using a graphical representation does not solve the problems inherent in exploring, manipulating, understanding and modifying large knowledge bases. This highlights an important need to reduce the visual complexity of graphical representations.

The layout of SemNet is designed to reflect the relatedness between nodes, measured by the number of interconnections. Highly interconnected nodes are placed much closer together than unconnected nodes. SemNet has had a profound influence on subsequent works in information visualisation.

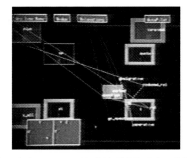

Figure 4.17   SemNet (http://panda.iss.nus.sg:8000/kids/fair/webdocs/viz/viz-1.html). (Reprinted with permission of Kim Fairchild).

4.3.2 Bead (1992)

Bead (Chalmers, 1992) is well known for its design rationale, which is based on the metaphor of information landscape, and generated using multidimensional scaling. The interrelationships among a set of documents are mapped to a geographical-like model within the DIVE virtual reality environment. Bead makes use of a variant of simulated annealing to lay out documents within a 3D space. The layout algorithm aims to map a semantic space into a 3D space, so that semantic proximity is preserved in the 3D representation.

The similarity between two documents is based on co-occurrences of terms, and measures the number of words occurring in both documents. This is very similar to the Dice coefficients, normalised word co-occurrences between two documents.

Experiences with Bead highlight some challenging issues concerning the visual complexity of 3D models and navigating within them. As a result, Bead restricts the layout of documents to a flatter landscape model – a small range of fluctuation is allowed in the third dimension. This is why a space is sometimes called a 2.1D or 2.5D space. The document nodes are meshed together by polygonal shapes, and distribution of the nodes in the landscape model tends to resemble the population on the land and on the coast to the sea. The colours in Fig. 4.18 clearly reinforce this land-and-sea metaphor, the central area being the land, and the surrounding area the sea. Bead is in fact a multi-user virtual environment; the information landscape can be populated by multiple users.

It also supports search facilities. The results of a search are highlighted in the visualised document landscape. If a document is relevant in a search, then its neighbours are likely to be worth pursuing as well, even if they are not shown as relevant to the initial search. The layout algorithm tends to place documents that are marginally related to the main theme towards the coastlines. This geographical metaphor, the coastline and the mainland, is powerful and

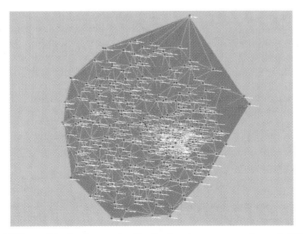

Figure 4.18 A bibliographic landscape in Bead, showing an overview of 500 bibliographical references (http://www.ubs.com/research/ubilab/Projects/hci/viz.html). (Reprinted with permission of Matthew Chalmer).

intuitive. Users can build their own mental model of how the data are organised, and their implications in terms of their locations in the visualisation.

4.3.3 VR-VIBE (1995)

VR-VIBE is a virtual reality-based information system developed at the University of Nottingham. It is an extension of the *Visual Information Browsing Environment* (VIBE) originally developed at the University of Pittsburgh (Olsen *et al.*, 1993).

VR-VIBE represents the interrelationships among documents in response to queries based on user-specified keywords, in a 3-dimensional space rendered in virtual reality (Fig. 4.19).

VR-VIBE is designed to visualise the results of a search query in such a space. A virtual reality scene in VR-VIBE is based on a number of keywords initially specified by users, and the documents that are relevant to these keywords. Both keywords and resultant documents are placed in the 3-dimensional space. The document-keyword relevance is based on the number of matches of the keyword in the given document and the position of a document is constrained according to the significance of each keyword given by the user. A document placed an equal distance from two keywords would be equally relevant to both keywords, while a document next to a particular keyword should be strongly relevant to that keyword. Only documents that are closely relevant to query keywords are displayed according to a threshold. Less relevant documents are omitted from the scene. VR-VIBE also enables multiple users to browse the same scene.

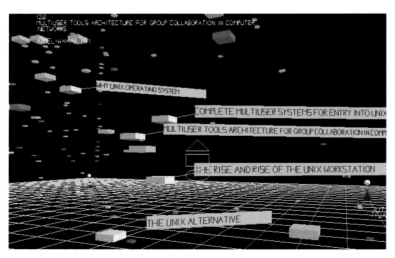

Figure 4.19   A screen shot of VR-VIBE. (Reprinted with permission of Steve Benford).

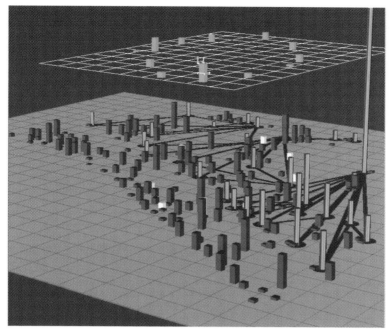

Figure 4.20 A spatial shift operation allows the user to manipulate selected components in a spatial model (vertical movement) (http://www.cs.cmu.edu/Groups/sage/project/samples/sdm/figure2.gif). (Reprinted with permission of Mark Derthick).

4.3.4 Sage Visualisation Environment

SAGE[3] is an integrated visualisation environment developed by a group of researchers at Carnegie Mellon University, incorporating a variety of graphic design tools, interactive exploration techniques, and information visualisation facilities. SageBook is an application from the SAGE environment (Chuah *et al.*, 1995).

SAGE provides some powerful operations. For instance, users can select objects and lift them to the original model of the scene. This operation is particularly useful when users want to concentrate on a sub-set of data whilst maintaining a certain amount of context. Users can also shift selected objects vertically or horizontally (see Fig. 4.20 and Fig. 4.21). SAGE calls these operations spatial shift operations.

In Fig. 4.20, the spatial shift operation moves a group of objects upwards from the original visualisation model, so that the structure of this group is clear and easy to understand. In Fig. 4.21, the spatial shift operation moves the selected sub-structure horizontally.

---

[3] http://www.cs.cmu.edu/Groups/sage/sage.html

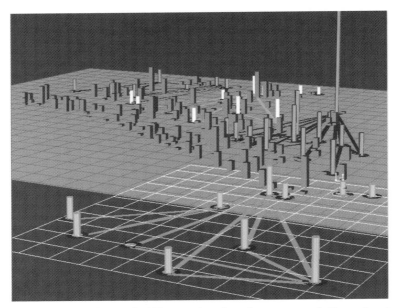

Figure 4.21 A horizontal spatial shift operation (http://www.cs.cmu.edu/Groups/sage/project/ samples/sdm/figure3.gif). (Reprinted with permission of Mark Derthick).

4.3.5 SPIRE (1998)

SPIRE[4] – Spatial Paradigm for Information Retrieval and Exploration – is a suite of information visualisation tools developed at Pacific Northwest National Laboratory (PNL) in the USA. It aims to help users explore a large number of textual documents with an intuitive spatial metaphor (Wise *et al.*, 1995; Hetzler *et al.*, 1998a; Hetzler *et al.*, 1998b). One of the design requirements of SPIRE is that users without special domain knowledge should be able to use these visualisation tools to explore and discover topical themes and other underlying relationships among documents. The design of SPIRE is based on word similarities and themes within text. SPIRE supports two types of visualisation: 'galaxies' and 'themescapes'.

   Visualisation in galaxies is based on the popular document-clustering concept. It provides an overview of the entire set of documents; documents are represented as a galaxy of star clusters in the night sky (see Fig. 4.22). These stars are called *docustars* in the galaxy visualisation. Like many other visualisation systems using spatial metaphors, similar documents are represented by stars near to each other in the galaxy, whereas documents about different topics are separated by greater distance. This metaphor intuitively suggests that

[4]http://multimedia.pnl.gov:2080/infoviz/technologies.html

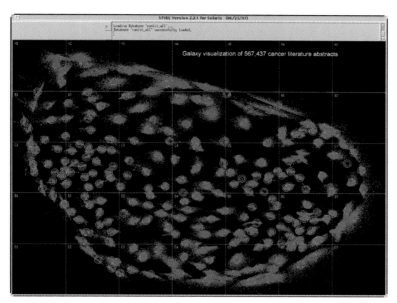

Figure 4.22   Galaxy visualisation of 567,437 abstracts from the cancer literature (SPIRE version 2.2.1). (Reprinted with permission of Beth Hetzler).

documents within each cluster are closely related, and documents between different clusters are less closely related. Analytical tools provided by SPIRE may be used to investigate the document groupings, query the document contents, and investigate time-based trends.

The themescape visualises the presence of specific themes across different documents as mountains in a relief map of natural terrain. The height of a peak indicates the relative strength of a given topic in the document set. Similar themes are grouped into a neighbourhood, whereas unrelated themes are separated by greater distance. These visualisation tools can be used to identify unanticipated relationships and examine changes in topics over time. One may also examine these thematic spaces over time, in order to understand vast interrelated dynamic changes simply not possible to detect using traditional approaches. Structuring abstract digital documents in general presents a challenging issue.

In the themescape[5] visualisation, the mountains in the visualisation indicate dominant themes. The height of the peaks indicate the relative strengths of the topics in the document set. Again, similar themes are grouped into neighbourhood, while themes separated by larger distances are unlikely to be related. Analysts can use this tool to identify unanticipated relationships, and examine changes in topics over time.

PNL is currently developing a Web-enabled version of SPIRE, called WebTheme[TM]. It visualises data gathered from the WWW, either as the result of performing a search query, or by traversing specific areas of a web site.

---

[5]PNL has recently renamed the landscape image as a ThemeView[TM].

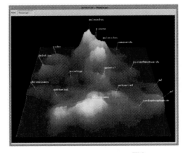

Figure 4.23 Peaks and valleys of themes in ThemeView™. (Reprinted with permission of Beth Hetzler).

As with Themescape, users can identify themes and concepts found among thousands of pages of text, and then further explore areas of interest.

SPIRE was originally developed for the US intelligence community, and has a wide variety of potential applications. Corporations researching competitive products, health care providers searching patient records, or attorneys reading through previous cases could all benefit from the SPIRE technology. For example, a researcher could use SPIRE to find out the direction in which the United States was heading in breast cancer research (see Fig. 4.22). Drawing from a large, unstructured document base of information, the researcher uses SPIRE's visualisation tools to automatically organise the documents into clusters according to their content similarities, and into thematic terrain according to the themes in the text. Observation of these thematic spaces over time will help

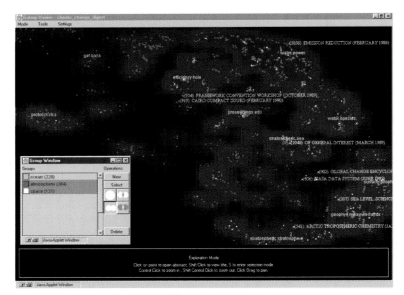

Figure 4.24 A screenshot of WebTheme™ (http://multimedia.pnl.gov:2080/infoviz/webtheme800.-gif). (Reprinted with permission of Beth Hetzler).

the user to understand vast interrelated dynamic changes simply not possible to detect using traditional approaches.

This technology has been used on many topical and current issues of national security, and results have yielded insight into complex issues, with enormous time savings. Discovering trends, finding inter-relationships among topics, and rapidly identifying key issues are all benefits of using SPIRE.

4.4 Visualising the Literature

So far, the focus of our discussion has been individual documents in an existing collection, a Web locality, or a set of search results. In this section, we include some examples in which the unit of analysis and visualisation is more than an individual document. In some cases it can be a person, making the resultant network a social one. In other cases, the unit could be a country; the visualisation would then reveal international relationships in trading and other aspects.

The thematic spaces in Themescape are based on terms occurring in documents, for example, 'oil', 'OPEC', and 'crisis'. An alternative way of identifying topical trends and predominant research areas in a field is by citation analysis. In this section, we demonstrate how author co-citation analysis can lead to insightful visualisations of the structure of a dynamic research field, in terms of topical trends and focal points of research. Furthermore author co-citation analysis can be naturally incorporated into our generalised similarity analysis (GSA) framework, so that techniques such as Pathfinder network scaling and virtual reality modelling can be directly applied to the new class of data. By analysing a Pathfinder network of author co-citation patterns, we may gain further insights into the Pathfinder network scaling itself, as well as into hypertext as a field of study.

4.4.1 Citation Networks

In a citation network, the interrelationships among nodes are based on citation-related information. The type of nodes can be researchers who have published in a given subject domain, as well as individual articles published in the literature.

The structure of a citation network provides a snapshot of the literature, based on interrelationships perceived by a specialised scientific community as a whole. It is therefore important to make the structure and associated insights easily accessible and understandable.

One example of visually navigating a citation network is provided in the design of Butterfly (Mackinlay et al., 1995). Butterfly was developed at Xerox PARC as a graphical user interface to access bibliographical records stored in DIALOG, and designed to work particularly with bibliographic resources such as Science Citation Index, Social Science Citation Index, and INSPEC. The user interface of Butterfly is shown in Fig. 4.25.

The head of the butterfly is the article of the focus. The two wings are associated with two types of citations: the left wing contains the original references cited by the focal article, while the ring wing lists articles that cite the current article. The following examples will show that citation and co-citation

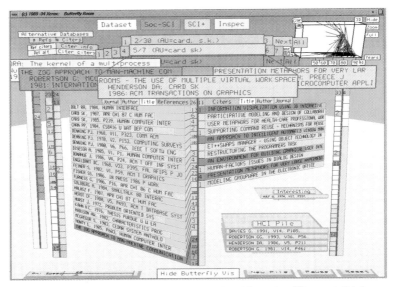

Figure 4.25   The user interface of Butterfly for citation-based browsing (© 1995 ACM, Inc. reprinted with permission).

indices provide a valuable source for information visualisation. The unit of analysis can range from individual documents to people who have contributed to the literature of a subject domain and emergent patterns may be identified through visualised citation structures.

The aim of mapping a scientific discipline is to identify sub-fields or specialties of research, and their interrelationships within the scientific discipline (Garfield, 1994). The following examples focus on research areas predominant in the field of hypertext and the use of author co-citation maps to visualise the literature of hypertext. We now need to find out whether author co-citation maps can be used to structure the literature in a similar way to SPIRE's themescape: the visualisation is concerned not only with individual documents, but also thematic topics and predominant research areas that may emerge across individual documents (see 4.3.5).

In 1981, the Institute for Science Information (ISI) published the ISI Atlas of Science in Biochemistry and Molecular Biology (ISI, 1981). The Atlas was based on a co-citation index, based on the publications in the field over a one-year period, and over 100 people were involved in the project for several months. 102 distinct clusters of articles, known as research front specialties, were identified, to depict a snapshot of significant research activities in biochemistry and molecular biology. More recently, ISI developed Sci-Map software for users to navigate the citation network (Small, 1994; Small, 1997), but unfortunately, the work at ISI largely remains unknown to the hypertext and digital library communities, for whom a major concern is to make the literature of a subject domain widely accessible.

4.4.2 Author Co-citation Analysis

Author co-citation analysis focuses on interrelationships among influential authors in the literature, instead of on individual publications. White and McCain (1998) present an extensive author co-citation analysis of information science, based on publications in 12 key journals in information science over a 23-year period (1972–1995). The top 120 authors were selected for the study according to citation counts. Several maps were generated for the top 100 authors in the field, using multidimensional scaling (MDS), and a factor analysis was conducted to identify major specialties in information science, which revealed that information science consists of two major specialties with little overlap in their memberships: experimental retrieval and citation analysis.

Author co-citation is a more rigorous grouping principle than that of typical subject indexing, because the connectivity is based on repeated and collective views of subjects experts expressed in their publications (White and McCain, 1998). Authors cite for a variety of reasons in various contexts. An important hallmark for research is whether or not it can make an impact on researchers in the same field. In addition, author co-citation analysis should help us to interpret and understand computationally constructed visualisation structures.

A number of author co-citation analyses have used multidimensional scaling techniques to depict the co-citation patterns. However, this option is often limited by the capacity of multidimensional scaling routines implemented in statistical packages such as SPSS. For example, White and McCain (1998) noted that they had to limit the visualisation to the top 100 authors in their study, because 100 is the maximum number of authors that can be handled by multidimensional scaling in the current version of SPSS. In this analysis, we were able to include 367 authors in our map without compromise.

Two sets of data were used in the analysis to delineate both the structure of the hypertext literature and the structure of the hypertext field. First, the structure of the hypertext literature were derived from all the full papers published in the entire ACM Hypertext conference series (1987–1998). Most electronic copies of these papers were available from the ACM Digital Library, and the rest were retrieved from the ACM Hypertext Compendium, which covers the 1987, 1989, and 1991 conference proceedings. The title, the names of authors, and the abstract of each paper were included in the final collection for content-similarity analysis. This collection were automatically analysed and modelled with generalised similarity analysis tools, particularly LSI and Pathfinder network scaling techniques (Chen, 1998a; Chen, 1998b; Chen and Czerwinski, 1998), and the resultant model rendered in VRML 2.0.

The second data set includes author co-citation counts based on all the papers in the conference series (1989–1998), with the exception of the first conference in 1987. In addition to full papers, the second data set also included data derived from short papers. Author co-citation counts were computed for all the authors cited five times or more during the whole period. This selection criterion resulted in a pool of 367 authors for the entire period. In order to discover significant advances and trends in the history of the field, the series of nine conferences were grouped into three sub-periods, each consisting of three consecutive conferences (Table 4.1). Author co-citation matrices were generated for the three sub-periods

Table 4.1. Three sub-periods of the series

Sub-periods	I (1989–1991)	II (1992–1994)	III (1996–1998)
Number of authors	196	195	195
Conferences	Hypertext '89	ECHT '92	Hypertext '96
	ECHT '90	Hypertext '93	Hypertext '97
	Hypertext '91	ECHT '94	Hypertext '98

using the same criterion. 196 authors were short-listed for Period I, 195 authors for Periods II and III.

Factor analysis was conducted on SPSS for Unix Release 6.1, because of the size of the overall author co-citation matrix, and the computation-intensive nature of the analysis. Following White and McCain, (1998), the raw co-citation counts were transformed into Pearson's correlation coefficients using the factor analysis, which were used to measure the proximity between authors' co-citation profiles. Self-citation counts were replaced with the mean co-citation counts for the same author. In the factor analysis, principal component analysis with varimax rotation was used to extract factors. The default criterion, eigenvalues greater than one, was specified, to determine the number of factors extracted. Missing data were replaced by mean co-citation counts for corresponding authors.

Pearson's r was used as a measure of similarity between author pairs, because, according to White and McCain, (1998), it registers the likeness in shape of their co-citation count profiles over all other authors in the set. Pearson correlation matrices were submitted to the GSA environment for processing, including Pathfinder network scaling and VRML-scene modelling. An author co-citation map was then generated automatically, with hypertext reference links provided within these maps: the name of an author in the co-citation map at Brunel University is linked to the corresponding bibliographical details maintained at Southampton University. In fact, much of the verification of author co-citation maps was based on the provision of these links. Three sub-period data sets were analysed with the same methodology.

4.4.3 Author Co-citation Maps

The overall author co-citation map included 367 authors who have made an impact in the field of hypertext over the last decade (1989–1998). This map is annotated by hand in Fig. 4.26, based on automatically displayed node labels. The map is essentially a connected graph, based on various computational algorithms used and our experiences in similar visualisation models. For example, a node on the main spine of the map is likely to belong to a much larger number of shortest paths connecting two nodes in the graph than to a leaf node. Thus, a spinal node often plays a more significant part in mediating different nodes than a leaf node. One may expect to find a highly cited article near to the centre of the map.

Indeed, names such as Engelbart, Nelson, Halasz, Trigg, and Streitz appear near to the centre of the map. Many major groups of authors are connected only because of these centrally positioned authors. For example, if we remove Streitz from the map, many of the insights into the interrelationships among several clusters of authors would be lost. This example also illustrates the role of the triangular inequality condition used in Pathfinder network scaling.

We know that nodes near to the centre of the map are more essential to the field of hypertext in terms of co-citation patterns. Branching nodes are also significant in identifying the sub-fields of hypertext. We particularly verified branching nodes, and used our knowledge about them to suggest the nature of a specialty, which typically includes all the authors in the branch. Eight major specialties can be identified from the map:

- Classics
- Design Models
- Hypertext Writing
- Information Retrieval
- Open Hypermedia
- Information Visualisation
- Structural Analysis
- User Interface

In Fig. 4.28, Salton is at a branching position, via which three branches are connected to the central spine of hypertext. Salton's work in information retrieval and automated hypertext generation is well known in both information science and hypertext. We also checked leaf nodes of these branches, as they represent some unique characteristics. We found that the leaf node of the far right branch is van Rijsbergen, whose name is prominent in information

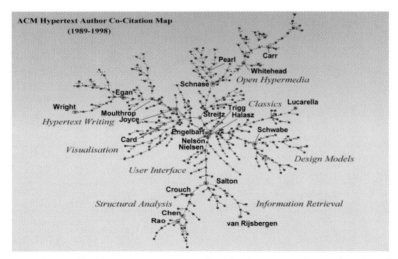

Figure 4.26 The overall author co-citation map and predominant research areas based on the ACM Hypertext conference proceedings (1989–1998).

retrieval; it then became apparent that this branch represents a specialty with strong connections with information retrieval, and therefore called the information retrieval specialty.

This map is incorporated into an interactive user interface on the WWW. Users can click on the name of an author in the map and follow links to the corresponding bibliographical entry of the same author. It was actually used in the exploration of the map and verification of various citation details. More thematic groups can be identified and discussed using this method.

The following analysis focuses on the evolution of the hypertext field over three 3-year sub-periods since 1989. The predominant authors in each period are identified, based on author co-citation maps, and patterns are compared across periods.

Figure 4.27 includes three author co-citation maps: Map (A) for (1989–1991), Map (B) for (1992–1994), and Map (C) for (1996–1998). Map A includes 196 authors with five or more citations during the first period. We followed the links from the map to detailed citation information and found that authors were clearly grouped with reference to papers describing hypertext systems, which are all well-known today, including NoteCards, Intermedia, KMS, and Microcosm. A specialty of information retrieval was already in place in the first period.

The second period, 1992–1994, is predominated by SEPIA, a collaborative hypermedia system developed at GMD in Germany. The central area of Map B is occupied by six members of GMD. In this map, Pearl became the branching node for the microcosm group. Leggett and *Pearl*'s branches appear on the same major branch. We have identified an open hypermedia specialty in the overall author co-citation map, indicating the emergent open hypermedia specialty. Remarkably, Salton and Croft are not in the same major branch in this map.

The latest period ranges from 1996 to 1998. During this period the WWW has dominated many areas of research and development, including hypertext. We expected author co-citation analysis in this period to reveal an emergent specialty of the World-Wide Web, given the apparent influence of the rapid

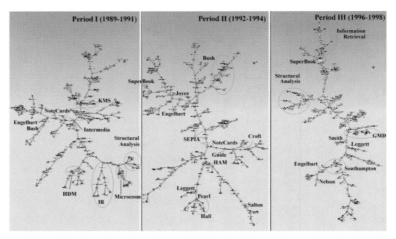

Figure 4.27   Three snapshots of the evolution of the hypertext field: Map A (1989–1991), Map B (1992–1994), and Map C (1996–1998).

advances of the Web and the growth of the WWW as a research field. However, this is not clear from Map C. There may be a number of reasons to explain the absence of a WWW specialty in the citation data, for instance, the existence of the WWW conferences, and preferences for journal publications. The influence of the WWW is so profound that it may be difficult to single out a specialty in the field of hypertext, and we thus need to examine the citation details more thoroughly. For instance, mapping the literature of related disciplines collectively, such as the WWW and digital libraries, is likely to lead to more insights. The information retrieval specialty is located towards the north of the map, and the structural analysis specialty is located to the west of the map.

4.4.4 A Semantic Space of the Hypertext Literature

Figure 4.28 shows a screenshot of the semantic space derived from 269 full papers published in the ACM Hypertext conference proceedings throughout the last decade (1987–1998). The latent semantic space was rendered in VRML 2.0. In this VRML model, each sphere represents a paper published in one of the ACM Hypertext conference proceedings. The colours of the spheres indicate the 'age' of corresponding papers: those in the earlier years are darker, and those in recent years are lighter. A light-coloured cluster of publications may reveal emergent research areas, whereas darker clusters near to the centre of the semantic structure may indicate classic research areas in the field of hypertext.

In addition to the overall semantic space, the example in Fig. 4.28 incorporates the results of a search returned by LSI. The search query included three terms: 'visualisation', 'spatial', and 'map'. The results are represented by red spikes vertical to the global structure. The higher the spike, the larger the query–document similarity. The locations of spikes reveal two major clusters of papers

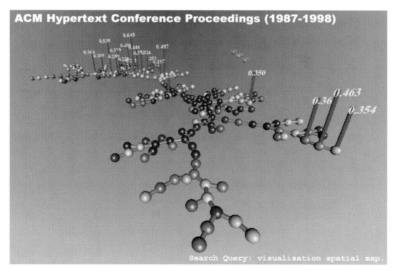

Figure 4.28 A content-similarity map of the ACM Hypertext conference proceedings (1987–1998).

Table 4.2 Eigenvalues of the top four factors

Factor	Eigenvalue	Pct of Var	Cum Pct
1	110.72	30.2	30.2
2	39.53	10.8	40.9
3	23.39	6.4	47.3
4	17.63	4.8	52.1

relevant to the search. The cluster at the far end is relatively new because it has many recently published documents (lighter coloured ones), whereas the cluster at the near end includes papers published some years ago.

The centre of the semantic structure is occupied by a large number of dark spheres, which indicate papers published in the early years of the ACM Hypertext conference series. Many of them are classic citations in the hypertext literature. This pattern suggests that papers near to the centre of the structure may play an important role in connecting papers across different areas. In the subsequent author co-citation analysis and associated co-citation maps, this pattern becomes even stronger and more intuitive.

Factor analysis extracted 39 factors from the co-citation matrix of 367 authors. These factors explain 87.8% of the variance. The top four factors alone explain 52.1% of the variance (Table 4.2). In terms of specialties, these four factors imply some substantial sub-fields of study in hypertext. These specialties will be discussed further with reference to author co-citation maps.

In order to understand the nature of each specialty associated with an identified factor, we rank the authors according to their loadings on each factor, and categorise the corresponding specialty according to the profiles of the top 20 authors. Of course, we could describe a specialty more accurately, if we have more detailed information about the nature of a particular co-citation pattern, for example, which particular piece of an author's work was referred to by citing authors.

Table 4.3 lists the top 20 authors on each factor. Note that these authors may also have significant loading on other factors. The names in the Factor 1 column are well known to the hypertext community, and represent the impact of classic hypertext systems. Therefore, we named Factor 1 as 'Classics'. The nature of Factor 2 is also apparent – we can easily recognise the names of authors whose work was focused on information retrieval, for example, Salton, Crouch, and Sematon. The third factor includes names such as Rao, Pitkow, and Jones. We suggest that this factor is about graphical user interfaces, and probably an information visualisation-related specialty. The membership of the fourth factor is clearly about links and linking mechanisms, especially the Southampton group. In the following discussion on author co-citation structures, we will identify further specialties, based on topological patterns suggested by the co-citation maps.

Table 4.3 The top 20 authors with the highest loadings on each of the first four factors*

Authors	F1	Authors	F2	Authors	F3	Authors	F4
Trigg, R	0.921	Laurel, B	0.592	Duda, A	.701	O'Hara, K	0.523
Smith, J	0.906	Chignell, M	0.588	Sheldon, M	0.686	Schilit, B	0.523
Moran, T	0.901	Gloor, P	0.575	Weiss, R	0.686	Levy, D	0.519
Halasz, F	0.885	Cousins, S	0.570	Szilagyi, P	0.681	Sellen, A	0.505
Schwartz, M	0.883	Schneiderman, B	0.564	Velez, B	0.681	Sawhney, N	0.498
Conklin, J	0.883	Crouch, C	0.564	Gifford, D	0.654	Golovchinsky, G	0.456
Streitz, N	0.875	Salton, G	0.559	Jones, S	0.620	DeRoure, D	0.445
Coombs, J	0.870	Crouch, D	0.559	Danzig, P	0.611	Maurer, H	0.429
Rogers, R	0.870	Andreas, G	0.554	Rao, R	0.587	Fountain, A	0.426
Marshall, C	0.868	Hearst, M	0.547	Lucarella, D	0.562	Carr, L	0.414
Thuring, M	0.848	McGill, M	0.543	Pitkow, J	0.544	Jones, R	0.406
Engelbart, D	0.848	Mylonas, E	0.537	Goble, C	0.541	Hill, G	0.395
McCracken, D	0.848	Egan, D	0.523	Scholl, M	0.531	Andrews, K	0.392
Akscyn, R	0.844	Allan, J	0.521	Chen, C	0.522	Bouvin, N	0.381
Begeman, M	0.843	Buckley, C	0.521	Zanzi, A	0.518	Davis, H	0.378
Brown, P	0.840	Smeaton, A	0.519	Agosti, M	0.482	Heath, I	0.377
Meyrowitz, N	0.836	Glushko, R	0.513	Rada, R	0.472	McKnight, C	0.375
Yankelovich, N	0.836	Landauer, T	0.512	Mendelzon, A	0.469	Hall, W	0.375
Hannemann, J	0.834	Guinan, C	0.510	DeRoure, D	0.455	Haas, C	0.370
Parunak, H	0.834	Waterworth, J	0.508	Bruza, P	0.454	Dillon, A	0.367

*The complete table is available from the author on request.

4.5 The Web and Online Communities

The World-Wide Web (WWW) has sparked many challenging problems concerning information visualisation, especially site maps or visualisation of navigation trails. One of the earliest attempts to visualise the Web was done by Tim Bray (1996). Here, Web sites are represented as ziggurats with globes on top: the diameter of the base indicates the number of pages, the height represents the visibility, the luminosity is denoted by the size of the globe on the top, and the domain of a site is colour-coded (see Table 4.4).

Web sites are placed in space, based on the strength of the linkages between them. Figure 4.29 shows the group of Web sites most closely linked to NASA (the

Table 4.4 Visualising web sites

Site features	Definition	Visualisation
Visibility	The number of citing sites	Height
Size	The number of pages the site contains	Diameter
Luminosity	The number of outgoing links	Size of the globe
Domain	Domain names org, gov, edu, com, etc.	Colour

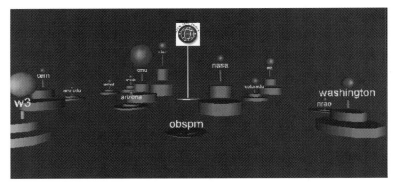

Figure 4.29   NASA's neighbourhood (reprinted with permission of Tim Bray).

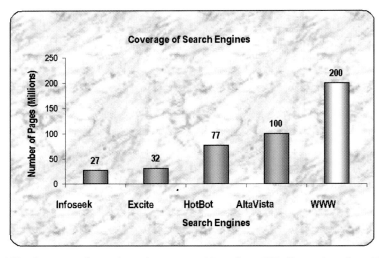

Figure 4.30   Coverage of search engines, as at November 1997 (Source:http://www7.conf.au/programme/fullpapers/1937/com1937.htm).

red site in the middle). Government sites are coloured in red, academic sites in green and nonprofit organisations in gold. CMU, where the Web Consortium site resides, provides a large number of outgoing links. NASA itself provides relatively few links to other sites.

Bharat and Broder (1998) estimated that by November 1997 the total size of the static web was 200 million pages, and search engines indexed only 160 million pages. It was estimated that Alta Vista indexed 100 million pages, Hot Bot 77 million, Excite 32 million and Infoseek 27 million (Fig. 4.30).

The Web is not only growing fast, but also changing rapidly. According to a survey[6] published in the seventh WWW conference, the average life span of documents on the Web is around 50 days, broken links occur with 5–7% of

---

[6]http://www7.conf.au/programme/fullpapers/1877/com1877.htm

Table 4.5 A maintainability survey of documents on the web

Attributes	Results
File size (HTML)	Average 4–6Kb (median 2Kb)
File size (images)	Average 14Kb
Life span of documents	50 days
Broken links	5–7% of access requests
Redirected links	13–19% of access requests
Documents requested per site	Average three, but distribution is heavily tailed
Site popularity (by traffic)	25% Web servers attract more than 85% of the traffic
Time spent per page	Heavily tailed distribution (standard deviation of 100 seconds): average 30 seconds, median 7.

access requests, and redirected links are between 13 and 19% of access requests (Table 4.5).

4.5.1 Information Farming and Spatial Hypertext

This section introduces concepts and metaphors concerning information organisation with a spatial metaphor. These concepts and systems not only provide a special means of information visualisation, but also suggest new ways of interacting with computers beyond the desktop metaphor.

Storyspace is a commercial product from the Eastgate Systems[7], a publisher of hypertext works. It was designed as a tool for hypertext writers, and provides a variety of maps and views to help writers create, organise, and revise. Items appearing in each view can be directly manipulated.

The most powerful and distinctive Storyspace view is the Storyspace map (Figure 4.31). Each box in the map represents a separate page or writing space, and each arrow represents a link between writing spaces. Each space may contain text, graphics, and sounds. In addition, writing spaces can contain other spaces.

A new links is created by drawing a line between two writing spaces – even if the two spaces appear in different maps. Links can connect entire writing spaces, or specific sections within a space. Storyspace can open many different maps onto a single document, allowing writers (and readers) to view various sections simultaneously. Links always stay connected as the document changes; if a new structure is unsatisfactory, it can be taken apart and improved. A similar but more intuitive example of a working space is 'information farms', which were also developed by the Eastgate Systems.

The term 'information farming' may remind us the concept of information foraging. But information farming puts more emphasis on the active role of users in terms what, how, and where they can arrange information in their own land.

---

[7]http://www.eastgate.com/squirrel/

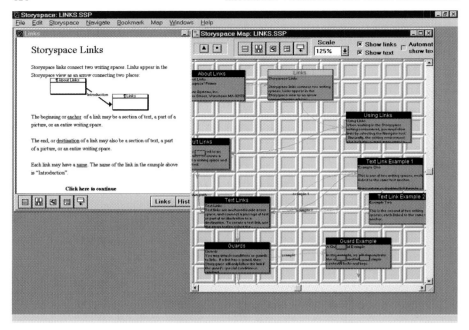

Figure 4.31   A Storyspace map, showing connections among several writing spaces.

Information farms refer to a metaphor for information organisation and knowledge management. As with a farm in the physical world, one can store, cultivate, organise, and harvest information. The Eastgate Systems Web Squirrel^{TM} is software that can build information farms. A key to information farms is that the information organised in a farm is persistent and evolving in nature, a similar concept to a personalised digital library, in where digital information can be arranged to suit personal interests and frequently accessed. Information farms can be represented graphically. Because these graphical representations reveal intrinsic structures of information, they are a special type of information visualisation metaphor. There are indeed several concepts similarly motivated, including answer gardens, information gardens, knowledge trees, and knowledge gardens.

Figure 4.32 shows an example of an information farm – the Hypertext Farm, generated by the Eastgate Systems Web Squirrel^{TM}. It provides an introduction to the hypertext research literature, and indeed the hypertext research community, and includes spirals for conferences, Eastgate (as a hypertext publisher), resources, and people.

Spatial hypertext is a special form of hypertext, in which the role of explicit links is largely replaced by the spatial proximity displayed on the computer screen. A major motivation of spatial hypertext is rooted in a common problem with hypertext authoring, known as 'pre-mature linking'. This refers to the cognitive overload when making connections between information before the user can fully understand the overall context and possible implications of adding a particular link.

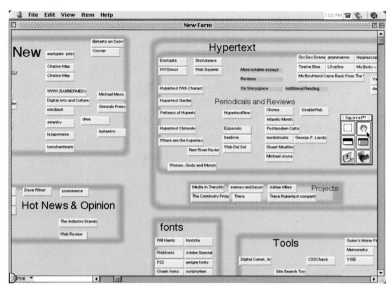

Figure 4.32 The Hypertext farm information structure, created by the Eastgate Systems Web Squirrel™ (reprinted with permission of Mark Bernstein).

Spatial hypertext, such as VIKI (Marshall *et al.*, 1994), has evolved into a unique design paradigm. A spatial hypertext allows authors to convey volatile, implicit, and more importantly, emergent patterns in a document space.

4.5.2 Searching and Exploring the Web

Millions of users on the Internet are by now familiar with the fact that they have a variety of search engines at their disposal, but exactly how these search engines work behind the scenes still remains a mystery to them. Search engines tend to give little information to the user about why documents in the search results are indeed *relevant* to a search query; users must judge this for themselves.

Exploring the Web, or information foraging on the Web, for particular topical subjects across a number of Web servers, is one area in which information visualisation has been actively pursued. The following examples include search engines that use hypertext linkage to improve the precision of search results, as well as information visualisation designed to help users to access information on the Web in a more intuitive way.

One of the most in-depth public descriptions of a large-scale search engine to date, is provided by Brin and Page (1998). They describe a search engine developed at Stanford University, and known as Google.[8] Google's prototype[9] currently contains more than 24 million pages. It aims to improve the precision

---

[8]Google is a common spelling of googol 10^{100}, i.e. very large.
[9]http://google.stanford.edu/

Figure 4.33   Searching for 'spatial +hypertext' with Google (3 July, 1998) (http://google.stanford.edu/).

of retrieval. A unique feature of the Google search engine is that information conveyed via hypertext links is heavily used to provide a better assessment of document–query relevance.

Google takes into account information reflected by hyperlinks on web resources, in order to improve the quality of search results. Such techniques can be used for searching resources that cannot be directly indexed, for example, Postscript files, images, computer software, and multimedia files.

An alternative to standard search engines' ranked lists of search results is to use information visualisation techniques to represent a set of documents as a whole, so that users can explore an information space at their own pace. Such examples include IBM's WebCutter,[10] presented at the sixth WWW conference, Silicon Graphics' Site Manager (see also Hyperbolic 3D, discussed in Chapter 3), and WebQuery.[11]

The WebBook[TM] is a 3D interactive book of HTML pages. It allows rapid interaction with objects at a higher level of aggregation than pages. The Web Forager[TM] is an application that embeds the WebBook[TM] and other objects in a hierarchical 3D workspace. Both designs are developed at Xerox PARC, intended as exercises to play off against analytical studies of information workspaces. Both WebBook[TM] and Web Forager[TM] are explained in (Card et al., 1996).

Figure 4.34 is a screenshot of WebBook[TM], which uses a book metaphor to organise Web pages. A collection of Web pages can be displayed as a collection using an augmented simulation of a physical book. 3D graphics and interactive animation are used to give the user a clear indication of the relationship between the pages of the book. Each page of the WebBook[TM] is a page from the Web. The

---

[10]http://www6.nttlabs.com/HyperNews/get/PAPER40.html
[11]http://www6.nttlabs.com/HyperNews/get/PAPER96.html

Figure 4.34 The WebBook™ (http://www.acm.org/sigchi/chi96/proceedings/papers/Card/skc1txt.html) (© 1996 ACM, Inc. reprinted with permission).

colour of a link helps the user to distinguish a reference within the same book (red links) from a reference outside the book (blue links). Choosing a red link will animate the turning of pages to the desired page; choosing a blue link will close the current WebBook and look for the page elsewhere. If the page is in another WebBook stored on a bookshelf, then that WebBook is opened and turned to the desired page. If the page is in none of the WebBooks, then the Web Forager is used to display the individual page in the user's information workspace.

Figure 4.35 shows the Webforager workspace. This is arranged hierarchically (in terms of interaction rates) into three main levels:

1. a full-sized book or page is called a focus place, for direct interaction between the user and the content;
2. the desk and the surrounding space implies an immediate memory space, where pages or books can be placed when they are in use, but not the immediate focus, and

Figure 4.35 The user interface of the Webforager™ (© 1996 ACM, Inc. reprinted with permission).

3. the bookcase represents a tertiary place where many pages and books can be stored.

4.5.3 Site Maps

Site maps are one of the most predominant applications of information visualisation on the Web. There is a wide variety, ranging from hand-made site maps, to automatically generated ones.

MAPA is a site map construction tool developed by Dynamic Diagrams. Figure 4.36 is a site map of their own homepage, generated by MAPA. The three-dimensional layout is based on existing hypertext links. MAPA relies on a Web walker, or Web spider to gather documents for pre-processing. Its design is a good example of a site map that is simple, clear, and easy to follow.

Figure 4.37 shows a screenshot of a site map created by MAPA for the *java.sun.com* Web site. To some extent the site map looks like several different types of cards placed on a table. Some cards represent pages containing higher-level information, while some represent the pages themselves.

Figure 4.38 illustrates the process of navigating through a website with MAPA. Four consecutive screenshots highlight the contextual information available to the user at each stage. Different webpages are grouped on carpet-like areas. Parent pages are displayed in front of the current page to give the user a sense of context.

In Chapter 3, we saw an example of how self-organised maps can be used to categorise and visualise a document collection (Lin *et al.*, 1991). ET-Map[12] is another example of site maps on the Web. It is a prototype Internet homepage categorization system developed at the University of Arizona (Chen *et al.*, 1998),

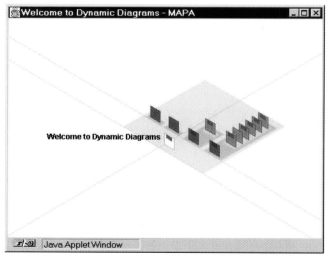

Figure 4.36 MAPA by Dynamic Diagrams (http://www.dynamicdiagrams.com/). (Reprinted with permission of Paul Kahn).

---

[12]http://ai2.BPA.Arizona.EDU/ent/

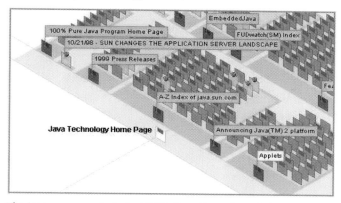

Figure 4.37   The java.sun.com website in MAPA (http://www.dynamicdiagrams.com/mapa/cgi-bin/linklist.cgi?db=javasoft&dest_id=1).

and aims to demonstrate a scalable, automatic, and concept-based approach to Internet homepage categorisation and search.

Figure 4.39 shows the top layer of a multi-layered map, based on the contents of more than 110,000 entertainment-related homepages. These maps are generated automatically using artificial neuro-network techniques, and each layer has different subject regions. Larger subject regions occupy a larger space on the map, and conceptually related subjects are often grouped in close proximity. Regions which contain 100 URLs or more produce another map; regions which contain fewer than 100 URLs produce a ranked list of URL summaries.

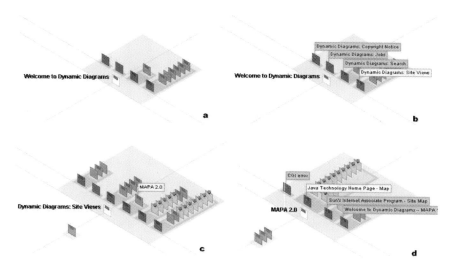

Figure 4.38   Navigating through a website with MAPA.

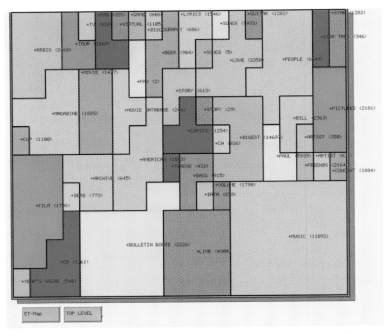

Figure 4.39 ET-Map (http://ai2.BPA.Arizona.EDU/ent/entertain1/entertain.gif). (Reprinted with permission of Hsinchun Chen).

WEBSOM[13] is yet another example of how self-organised maps may be used to organise textual documents for exploration and search. WEBSOM has been used to map discussion groups (Kohonen, 1998). Figure 4.40 shows the top level of a WEBSOM map of a newsgroup on neural networks.

Clicking in any area on the map will lead to a zoomed view. Colour denotes the density or the clustering tendency of the documents: lighter areas are clusters, and darker areas are empty space between the clusters.

The most specific discussions are mostly found in the clearest 'clusters', i.e. light regions surrounded by darker colour. Near the edges of the map are typically the most 'unusual' documents represented on the map. In the central areas, the discussions are more 'typical', or may concern many different topics found on the map.

4.5.4 Footprints

Social navigation, in the context of exploring abstract information spaces, refers to a strategy of searching information by following 'like-minded' users within the information spaces. The Footprints system was developed at MIT Media Lab. It visualises the paths of users moving from one document to another on a Web

---

[13]http://websom.hut.fi/websom/

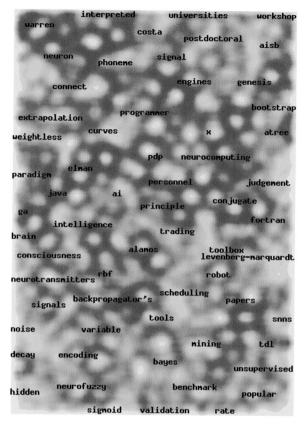

Figure 4.40   The top level of a WEBSOM map of *comp.ai.neural-nets* (http://websom.hut.fi/websom/comp.ai.neural-nets-new/html/root.html). (Reprinted with permission of Samual Kaski).

server. Figure 4.42 shows its screen layout. Footprints includes only documents that have been visited at least once. The visualisation is useful for system administrators to help spot broken links or other problems which could otherwise be hard to detect.

The system falls into a new paradigm of information organisation and social interaction. Support for it is rather limited on today's Web, because much more information is needed to make social navigation practically pursuable.

4.5.5 Collaborative Browsing

Collaborative Browsing (CoBrow)[14] is a joint European project between the University of Ulm, the University of Lancaster, and the Swiss Federal Institut of

---

[14]http://www.cobrow.com/

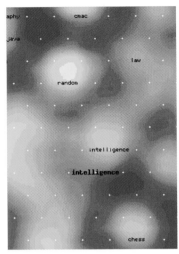

Figure 4.41 Migrating to the second level of the WEBSOM map on 'intelligence'. (Reprinted with permission of Samual Kaski).

Technology in Zurich (ETH). Its aim is to encourage and enhance communication and collaboration using the Web, by establishing a new form of collaborative work on the Internet and transforming the Web into an environment where people meet, share information, collaborate, and perform other social activities. Figure 4.43 is the screenshot of a CoBrow prototype created by Klaus Wolf and Holger Boenisch, which presents a graphical representation of a number of Web pages linked by hypertext links. Each sphere represents a document, and the sphere is wrapped by a miniature image of the document as a texture map.

Figure 4.44 shows another example from CoBrow. Edges in the 3D graph represent hypertext reference links provided by each Web page. One of CoBrow's unique features is to use miniature images as document icons, to allow users to determine whether or not to pursue a particular page.

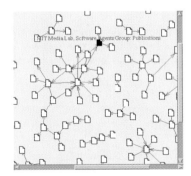

Figure 4.42 Visualised browsing paths in an earlier version of Footprints. (Reprinted with permission of Alan Wexelblat). The latest version is available at http://footprints/media.mit.edu (Wexelblat, 1999).

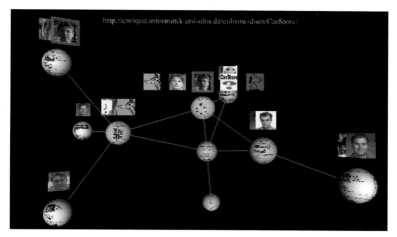

Figure 4.43 CoBrow (http://enrique.informatik.uni-ulm.de/cobrow/docs/CarStore/). (Reprinted with permission of Klaus Wolf and Holger Boenisch).

However, it is not clear how CoBrow would pursue its goal for people to meet and interact with each other, although one obvious option is to use multiuser virtual environments as a vehicle for social interaction.

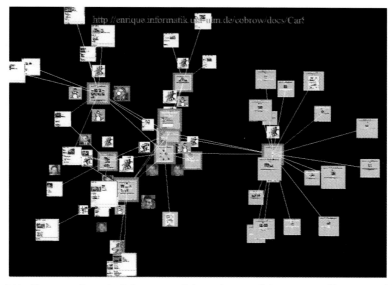

Figure 4.44 Document icons in CoBrow are miniature images of the corresponding pages. Links are hypertext reference links (http://enrique.informatik.uni-ulm.de/cobrow/docs/CarStore/). (Reprinted with permission of Klaus Wolf and Holger Boenisch).

4.5.6 Sociable Web

Currently, surfing on the Web is largely an individual experience. Users cannot tell from their browsers whether other people are also visiting the same Web page at the same time. The invisible nature of browsing is a feature that distinguishes a multiple user system from a collaborative one.

To solve this problem, Donath and Robertson at MIT Media Lab have developed a Sociable Web, consisting of a modified Web server and browser. On the Sociable Web, users have access to a list of people concurrently browsing on the same Web page. Concurrent visitors communicate with each other using a tool called WebTalk, sharing, for example, URLs, sounds, and graphics. In fact, the user does not even have to hang around the same page to 'stay tuned' to a group of people.

Social Web explores several interesting concepts: visibility among Web users on the same page, synchronous collaboration among Web users, and the sharing of URLs for a group of people to browse together. However, the system relies on a modified server and browser, which may prevent Social Web from being widely accessed and integrated into the current Web infrastructure.

4.5.7 Online Communities

An increasingly popular approach to the development of a virtual place for people to meet and chat is to use open standards such as VRML, and to incorporate the capabilities of Java-enabled applications or simply Java applets, tiny programming components that can be easily sent through computer networks.

Several front-runners in virtual reality-based multiuser environments include Online Community from blaxxun interactive, Community Place from Sony, and ActiveWorlds from The Circle of Fire Studio. The first two are VRML-based. ActiveWorlds is built on a format called Renderware, which only recently started to enable some basic VRML features.

The basic concepts and design principles behind a virtual environment are given in Chapter 6. The discussion here is to highlight the broad implications of social-navigation trends regarding the role of the Web in the future, and how such trends and the field of virtual environments might converge in future generations of Web-based applications and information services.

Several platforms for multiuser virtual environments have been developed over the past few years. *blaxxun*'s Online Community server-client architecture, as suggested by the name, aims to foster virtual communities on the Internet. It focuses activities entirely on three-dimensional virtual reality worlds, and the VRML standard. Users are able to explore and interact with virtual reality worlds via the WWW.

In these virtual worlds, users are represented as some form of 3D graphical icon known as an avatar. People use various avatars, from human figures, to birds, sharks, and dinosaurs. A potentially useful feature of avatar-based user interfaces is that one can see the movement of an avatar and follow the trail of it, which fosters an intuitive metaphor of social navigation. In addition to the visual effects in virtual reality applications, people visiting the same virtual environment can communicate with other people via chat facilities.

An important insight from the social navigation trends is that like-minded people may form a group or even a crowd as they are attracted by the content of a Web page. In social navigation, people gather together because they are all interested in a particular topic. This distinguishes the concept from traditional chat rooms, where a considerable number of people come, just for the sake of talking to someone.

This contrast leads to a far-reaching question: if the virtual reality-based virtual environment can bring like-minded people together on topical subjects in a given domain, will that enable people to experience more engaging and more focused social interaction? If so, such virtual environments might bridge the gap between chat- and collaboration-oriented virtual environments. Collaborative virtual environments have a wide range of applications, such as distance learning, digital libraries, and online communities.

4.6 Online Resources

The major sources of information visualisation literature include the IEEE symposium and conferences on information visualization. The publications of the ACM, especially SIGGRAPH, SIGIR, and SIGCHI, include the most influential works in this field.

There are a number of excellent Web sites focusing particularly on information visualisation. For example, the Atlas of Cyberspaces[15] is a web site maintained at the Centre for Advanced Spatial Analysis (CASA), University College of London (UCL). It was launched as a dissemination project in spatial analysis, and provides a wide range of reference information and image galleries on information visualisation.

The On-line Library of Information Visualization Environments[16] (Olive), created by a class of students at the University of Maryland, includes comprehensive bibliographical information, as well as brief summaries of various techniques.

A comprehensive literature review of 3D information visualisation was given by Peter Young (1996) on the Web. This review is a technical report of the Department of Computer Science at the University of Durham.

Homepages of individuals are another source of information visualisation resouces, e.g. Tamara Munzner's homepage[17] on Information Visualization Resources on the Web, and Marti Hearst's homepage.

---

[15]http://www.geog.ucl.ac.uk/casa/martin/atlas/atlas.html
[16]http://www.otal.umd.edu/Olive/
[17]http://www-graphics.stanford.edu/courses/cs348c-96-fall/resources.html

4.7 Summary

This chapter has introduced a number of information visualisation systems with applications in several categories. It has drawn attention to how a particular information visualisation mechanism can be adapted to meet various requirements from users. For example, cone trees have been used in several systems with different design rationales, such as LyberWorld, Cat-a-Cone, and Hyperbolic 3D.

One section has been devoted to the design of systems based on a spatial metaphor. This metaphor that will form the basis for further discussions in subsequent chapters on virtual environments. An extended example of visualising the literature of hypertext was used to demonstrate the flexibility and extensibility of the methodology of GSA.

One key feature distinguishes works such as Social Web and Collaborative Browsing from general-purpose chat rooms, or even virtual-reality-based environments is the motivation of gathering together. In Social Web, visitors are interested in the co-presence of others, because it is the topical content that attracts these people to visit a Web page in the first place. In these cases, the motivation is social navigation – to follow like-minded people. In contrast, the lack of depth in many chat rooms and 3D virtual environments probably results in differences in the dynamics and structures of social interaction.

Before we continue to explore how social navigation and virtual environments may converge in Chapter 6, Chapter 5 will focus on the role of human factors in the use of information visualisation techniques. Three empirical studies will investigate the impact of individual differences on information retrieval and foraging with spatial metaphors. Cognitive factors such as spatial ability and associative memory are explored.

Bibliography

Ahlberg, C, and Shneiderman, B. (1994). *Visual information-seeking – Tight coupling of dynamic query filters with starfield displays.* Proceedings of CHI 94 (Boston, MA., April 1994), ACM Press, pp. 313–17.

Bederson, B, and Meyer, J (in press). Implementing a zooming user interface: Experience building Pad++. *Software: Practice and Experience.*

Benford, S, Snowdon, D, Greenhalgh, C, Ingram, R, Knox, I, and Brown, C (1995). VR-VIBE: A virtual environment for co-operative information retrieval. *Computer Graphics Forum,* 14(3):C.349-C.360.

Bharat, K, and Broder. (1998). *A technique for measuring the relative size and overlap of public Web search engines.* Proceedings of the Seventh International World Wide Web Conference (Brisbane, Australia, April 1998). Available: http://www7.conf.au/programme/fullpapers/1937/com1937.htm.

Bray, T (1996). *Measuring the Web.* Proceedings of the Fifth International World Wide Web Conference (Paris, France, May 1996).

Brin, S, and Page, L (1998). *The anatomy of a large-scale hypertextual web search engine.* Proceedings of the Seventh International World Wide Web Conference. (Brisbane, Australia, April 1998). Available: http://www7.conf.au/programme/fullpapers/1921/com1921.htm.

Card, SK, Robertson, GG, and York, W (1996). *The WebBook and the Web Forager: An Information Workspace for the World-Wide Web.* Proceedings of the ACM Conference on Human Factors in Computing Systems (CHI 96) (Vancouver, Canada, April 1996), ACM Press. Available: http://www.acm.org/sigchi/chi96/proceedings/papers/Card/skc1txt.html.

Chalmers, M (1992). *BEAD: Explorations in information visualisation.* Proceedings of SIGIR 92 (Copenhagen, Denmark, June 1992), ACM Press, pp. 330–37.

Chen, C (1998a). Bridging the gap: The use of Pathfinder networks in visual navigation. *Journal of Visual Languages and Computing,* 9(3):267–86.

Chen, C (1998b). Generalised Similarity Analysis and Pathfinder Network Scaling. *Interacting with Computers,* 10(2):107–28.

Chen, C, and Czerwinski, M (1998). *From latent semantics to spatial hypertext: An integrated approach.* Proceedings of the Ninth ACM Conference on Hypertext and Hypermedia (Hypertext 98) (Pittsburgh, PA., June 1998), ACM Press, pp. 77–86.

Chen, H, Houston, AL, Sewell, RR, and Schatz, BR (1998). Internet browsing and searching: User evaluations of category map and concept space techniques. *Journal of the American Society for Information Science,* 49(7):582–608.

Chuah, MC, Roth, SF, Kolojejchick, J, Mattis, J, and Juarez, O (1995). *SageBook: Searching data-graphics by content.* Proceedings of CHI 95 (Denver, CO, May 1995), ACM Press, pp. 338–45. Available: http://www.cs.cmu.edu/Web/Groups/sage/SageBook/SageBook.html.

Fairchild, K, Poltrock, S, and Furnas, G (1988). SemNet: Three-dimensional graphic representations of large knowledge bases. In: R Guidon (ed.), *Cognitive Science and its Applications for Human-Computer Interaction,* Lawrence Erlbaum, pp. 201–33.

Fox, E, Hix, D, Nowell, L, Brueni, D, Wake, W, Heath, L, and Rao, D (1993). Users, user interfaces, and objects: Envision, a digital library. *Journal of the American Society for Information Science,* 44(5):480–91.

Garfield, E (1994). Scientography: Mapping the tracks of science. *Current Contents: Social & Behavioural Sciences,* 7(45):5–10.

Hearst, MA (1997). Interfaces for searching the Web. *Scientific American,* (3).

Hearst, M, and Karadi, C (1997). *Cat-a-Cone: An interactive interface for specifying searches and viewing retrieval results using a large category hierarchy.* Proceedings of the Twentieth Annual International ACM/SIGIR Conference (Philadelphia, PA, July 1997), ACM Press. Available: http://www.sims.berkeley.edu/~hearst/papers/cac-sigir97/sigir97.html.

Heath, L, Hix, D, Nowell, L, Wake, W, Averboch, G, Labow, E, *et al.* (1995). Envision: A user-centered database of computer science literature. *Communications of the ACM,* 38(4):52–3.

Hemmje, M, Kunkel, C, and Willett, A (1994). *LyberWorld – A visualization user interface supporting fulltext retrieval.* Proceedings of the Seventeenth Annual International ACM SIGIR Conference on Research and Development in Information Retrieval (Dublin, Ireland), Springer-Verlag (London, UK), pp. 249–59.

Hetzler, B, Harris, WM, Havre, S, and Whitney, P (1998a). *Visualizing the full spectrum of document relationships.* Proceedings of the Fifth International ISKO Conference: Structures and Relations in the Knowledge Organization (Lille, France, August 1998). Available: http://multimedia.pnl.-gov:2080/infoviz/isko.pdf.

Hetzler, B, Whitney, P, Martucci, L, and Thomas, J (1998b). *Multi-faceted insight through interoperable visual information analysis paradigms.* Proceedings of IEEE Information Visualiza-tion 98 (1998), IEEE. Available: http://multimedia.pnl.gov:2080/infoviz/ieee98.pdf.

Hightower, RR, Ring, LT, Helfman, JI, Bederson, BB, and Hollan, JD (1998). *Graphical multiscale Web histories: A study of PadPrints.* Proceedings of the Ninth ACM Conference on Hypertext and Hypermedia (Hypertext 98) (Pittsburgh, PA), ACM Press. Available: http://www.cs.umd.edu/hcil/pad++/papers/hypertext-98-padprints/hypertext-98-padprints.pdf.

ISI (1981). *ISI Atlas of Science: Biochemistry and Molecular Biology, 1978/80.* Institute for Scientific Information (Philadelphia, PA).

Kohonen, T (1998). Self-organization of very large document collections: state of the art. *Proceedings of the 8th International Conference on Artificial Neural Networks,* Springer-Verlag (London, UK), pp. 65–74.

Lin, X, Soergel, D, and Marchionini, G (1991). *A self-organizing semantic map for information retrieval.* Proceedings of SIGIR 91 (Chicago, IL, October 1991), ACM Press, pp. 262–69.

Lokuge, I, Gilbert, SA, and Richards, W (1996). *Structuring information with mental models: A tour of Boston.* Proceedings of CHI 96, ACM Press. Available: http://www.acm.org/sigchi/ chi96/proceedings/papers/Lokuge/sag_txt.html.

Mackinlay, JD, Rao, R, and Card, SK (1995). *An organic user interface for searching citation links.* Proceedings of ACM CHI 95 Conference on Human Factors in Computing Systems, ACM Press, pp. 67–73.

Marshall, CC, Shipman, FM, and Coombs, JH (1994). *VIKI: Spatial hypertext supporting emergent structure.* Proceedings of ECHT 94 (Edinburgh, Scotland, September 1994), ACM Press, pp. 13–23.

Mukherjea, S (in press). Using VRML-based visualizations to facilitate information retrieval in the World-Wide Web. *Virtual Reality: Research, Development, and Applications.*

Mukherjea, S, and Hara, Y (1997). *Focus + context views of World-Wide Web nodes.* Proceedings of Hypertext 97 (Southampton, UK), ACM Press, pp. 187–96.

Nowell, LT, France, RK, Hix, D, Heath, LS, and Fox, EA (1996). *Visualzing search results: Some alternatives to query-document similarity.* Proceedings of the Nineteenth Annual ACM SIGIR Conference (Zurich, Switzerland, August 1996), ACM Press, pp. 67–75.

Olsen, KA, Korfhage, RR, and Sochats, KM (1993). Visualization of a document collection: The VIBE System. *Information Processing & Management,* 29(1):69–81.

Robertson, G, Card, S, and Mackinlay, J. (1993). Information visualization using 3D interactive animation. *Communications of the ACM,* 36(4):57–71.

Small, H (1994). A SCI-MAP case study: Building a map of AIDS research. *Scientometrics,* 30(1):229–41.

Small, H (1997). Update on science mapping: Creating large document spaces. *Scientometrics,* 38(2):275–93.

Wexelblat, A (1999). History-based tools for navigation. Proceedings of the Thirty-Second Annual Hawaii International Conference on System Sciences (HICSS-32) (Maui, Hawaii, January 1999). Available: http://wex.www.media.mit.edu/people/wex/HICSS-32.html.

White, HD, and McCain, KW (1998). Visualizing a discipline: An author co-citation analysis of information science, 1972–1995. *Journal of the American Society for Information Science,* 49(4):327–56.

Young, P (1996). Three dimensional information visualisation. Durham University.

Chapter 5
Individual Differences in Visual Navigation

Users bring to the computer a wide variety of categories and factors individual to them, such as relevant experience, domain knowledge, and a number of cognitive abilities and styles. Empirical evidence and theoretical studies in the literature suggest that there may be some profound connections between visual user interfaces and a number of cognitive factors that have been extensively studied in related disciplines.

In previous chapters, we have focused on techniques to help detect and extract useful structures of information, with examples to show how they can be effectively displayed and manipulated in spatial form.

Information visualisation is a rapidly advanced discipline, an integral part of which is evaluation of its interest to users, and how well users understand the information as part of their cognitive tasks and intellectual activities.Established disciplines, such as human-computer interaction (HCI), experimental information retrieval, and navigation theories in hypertext, may provide valuable insights into how the value of information visualisation can be assessed.

Information visualisation has its unique goals and characteristics, to which existing evaluation methodologies need to be tailored. This chapter examines how individual differences in information visualisation can be assessed in empirical studies. Cognitive factors, such as spatial ability and associative memory, are particularly examined, as an integral component of our development, and an evaluation framework for information visualisation systems and virtual environments.

5.1 Introduction

Information visualisation is still a relatively young field of research and development, and evaluating the usefulness of its techniques effectively and efficiently is an integral part of the field. Many evaluation methods in the literature must be re-examined and adjusted, to meet the special characteristics of information visualisation.

Despite the rapid growth of information visualisation as a research field, there are still relatively few empirical studies in the literature. There have been little data and few criteria for assessing the effectiveness and usability of 3D interfaces, and of visualisation techniques in general (Sutcliffe and Patel, 1996). The lack of empirical studies underlines the urgent need for generic evaluation methodologies relevant to the field.

CHI 94 included a workshop called 'The challenges of 3D interaction (Herndon *et al.*, 1994)', which addressed a set of goals towards which the virtual environment community could work. Boyd and Darken organised a workshop at CHI 96 with more focused themes on psychological issues (Boyd and Darken, 1996), and have identified some major human aspects of virtual environment (VE) interaction, in particular the psychological difficulties encountered when using them. Here are some examples:

- spatial orientation and wayfinding in virtual worlds
- designing the virtual world to relate to human perceptual abilities, not just striving for photo-realism
- means of travelling from one virtual location to another, directed or browsing, and for acting in the environment
- designing the controlling inputs to take advantage of human physical abilities, and adapting to disabilities
- evaluating VE interfaces, experiences with usability testing of whole systems
- appreciating the interdependence between task features and interface design
- understanding the dimensions of usefulness and complexity for VE interfaces.

It was clear that the foci of these two workshops were mainly on psychological issues associated with the use of a virtual environment, some of which have been addressed in the previous chapter. A workshop even more directly related to social interaction was held in Stockholm in March 1998,[1] organised by IFIP working group WG13.2 and the Navigation SIG of Esprit's I[3]-net (Information Intelligence Interfaces). The abstracts of papers presented at the workshop are available on the WWW.[2] The focus of the Stockholm workshop was personalized and social navigation in information space.

Individual differences have been a unique area of study in related disciplines, such as psychology and human computer interaction, and extensive works have produced useful frameworks and valuable empirical findings.

The use of information visualisation techniques may widen the gap between individuals as they interact with, and within, an information-intensive environment. Some may like the idea of a spatial metaphor, and some may prefer a textual user interface. Some may enjoy walking or flying through a virtual landscape or a virtual galaxy; others may choose a hierarchically organised filing system or a relation database. Some may enjoy navigating and chatting with others in a group; others may prefer not to be disturbed. Individual differences are just one aspect of the dynamics of using information visualisation and virtual environments. Social and ecological dimensions are equally important in understanding how people perceive and behave in a virtual environment. These dynamics in virtual environments will be discussed in Chapter 6.

This chapter focuses on how individual differences influence a user's information-foraging performance and their satisfaction. Individual differences could be related to age, experience, domain knowledge, cognitive styles, or

---

[1]http://www.sics.se/humle/projects/persona/web/workshop/index.shtml
[2]http://www.sics.se/humle/projects/persona/web/littsurvey/abstracts.htm

learning styles. We introduce a set of established cognitive factors, and demonstrate how they can be used to evaluate and interpret information visualisation design. A series of empirical studies are included, in an attempt to stimulate further studies on the interplay between human cognition and information visualisation.

From a methodological point of view, the introduction to representative factor-referenced cognitive tests in Eckstrom *et al.* (1976) is the first step for an inter-disciplinary and long-term research programme. Is it sensible to test an information visualisation design with the whole range of cognitive factors? Is it a practical starting point to establish a baseline of representative information visualisation design? Can factor-referenced cognitive tests provide researchers and designers with common ground for analysing and comparing the effects of different information visualisation options in comparable cognitive tests?

The following sections focus on three well-studied cognitive factors, and how they may interact with tasks performed on a spatial user interface: spatial ability, associative memory, and visual memory. All three are found to be influential in situations similar to the use of information visualisation systems (Benyon, 1993; Carroll, 1993; Dahlbäck *et al.*, 1996; Dillon and Watson, 1996; Höök *et al.*, 1996; Vicente and Williges, 1988).

The first example is an empirical study focusing on spatial ability and visual information retrieval. The second example is on associative memory and visual memory, and the third is the most extensive experimental study of the three, focusing on the role of both spatial ability and associative memory in visual information retrieval.

5.1.1 Cognitive Factors

The first comprehensive introduction of individual differences into human-computer interaction (HCI) is Egan's seminal work (1988), which has inspired many studies in the field over the last decade. According to Egan (1988), differences between users can be in the order of 20:1 for common computing tasks, such as programming and text editing. Such differences can be understood and predicted, as well as modified through design. In fact, there are two general views on individual differences. One believes that the differences can be reduced through education and training, while the other believes that these differences are difficult to change, but may be accommodated through the use of specially designed tools. The special issue on *Individual Differences in Virtual Environments* (Chen *et al.*, forthcoming) presents the latest developments in this area.

The most influential and updated work on the study of individual differences in psychology is presented by Carroll (1993). Cognitive factors are grouped into a three-level hierarchy: the top level is general intelligence (*g*), the second level consists of eight ability categories, and the third level includes first order factors derived from these general ability types.

At the second level, the eight general ability categories are:

- crystallised intelligence
- fluid intelligence

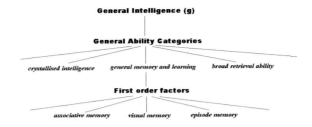

Figure 5.1   Cognitive factors are grouped into a three-level hierarchy.

- general memory and learning
- broad visual perception
- broad auditory perception
- broad retrieval ability
- broad cognitive speed
- processing speed.

The third level further divides each of these general ability types into first order factors (for example, memory is divided into associative memory, visual memory, episodic memory, and memory span); this hierarchical organisation has been highly praised as the likely standard conceptualisation for the foreseeable future (Dillon and Watson, 1996; Kline, 1994).

Recently, Dillon and Watson (1996) presented a thought-provoking review of the study of individual differences, and its position in the field of HCI. According to Dillon and Watson, a core number of basic cognitive abilities have been reliably and validly identified, as influencing the performance of specific tasks in predictable ways. Several areas are potentially fruitful for HCI. They recommend that psychological measures of individual differences should be used as a basis for establishing context, and achieving a greater degree of generalisability of HCI findings.

The empirical studies investigate the relationship between individual differences and information foraging within a semantically organised virtual world. This virtual world is constructed automatically, based on the results of information visualisation. Three cognitive factors are specifically examined in the use of the semantically organised virtual world: spatial ability, associative memory, and visual memory. Studies of these not only illustrate a generic methodology for evaluating the usefulness of information visualisation design, but also highlight cognitive factors that may lead to insights into information visualisation design itself.

5.1.1.1 Spatial Ability

An individual's visualisation ability is defined as the ability to manipulate or transform the image of spatial patterns into other arrangements (Eckstrom *et al.*, 1976). The role of spatial ability in navigating through information structures has received much attention over the last decade, ranging from large file structures and database systems, to hypermedia, and virtual reality-based spatial models. For example, Vicente and Williges (1988) found that spatial ability affected the user's ability to navigate a large file structure. Campagnoni and Ehrlich (1989) reported that users with good visualisation ability used the top-level table of contents less frequently than users with lower visualisation ability, suggesting that a good spatial ability may help in memorising how the information is organised.

Benyon and Murray (1993) found a clear influence of spatial ability on navigation in a database with a command interface. They showed that many limitations on subjects' performance on the command interface, which related to their spatial ability, could be overcome with experience. The meta-analysis in Chen and Rada (1996) synthesised findings in experimental studies concerning individual differences of cognitive styles, learning styles, and spatial ability in using hypertext systems, but the synthesised data only revealed a small effect size across the empirical findings by that time. On the other hand, it was clear that not all the limitations of low spatial ability were compensated for by high experience. Eisenberg et al. (1997) explored the role of spatial cognition in user modelling with 3D user interfaces.

More recently a similar result is found in Dahlbäck et al., (1996), with navigating through a hypermedia system. The strongest correlation was found between users' abilities on tests of the mental rotation of images and their task completion time. The fastest subject solved the tasks 19 times faster than the slowest subject. More importantly, their study concluded that there is a difference between spatial ability for solving problems in the world, and the spatial ability needed for solving problems in the abstract world of information space.

The relationship between spatial ability and visual navigation in a virtual reality-based spatial user interface was studied by Chen and Czerwinski (1997). Spatial ability, as measured by paper-folding tests (VZ-2) included in Eckstrom et al. (1976), was strongly correlated with the accuracy of sketches made by subjects after they searched within a semantically organised spatial model. The spatial ability was positively correlated with the differences between the main structure in the spatial layout and the sketches made by individuals (Spearman's $r = 0.774$, $p = 0.004$, one-tailed). Similarly, a strong correlation was found between spatial ability and the secondary structures in the spatial layout, and structures memorised by individuals (Spearman's $r = 0.591$, $p = 0.036$, one-tailed).

5.1.1.2 Associative Memory

According to Carroll (1974), associative memory refers to the ability to recall one part of a previously learned, but otherwise unrelated, pair of items, when the other part of the pair is presented. This factor involves the storage and retrieval of information from intermediate-term memory. Individual differences observed in such conditions may be largely due to the successful use of strategies such as rehearsal, and using mnemonic mediators.

In the following examples, the spatial user interface is designed to represent latent semantic structures derived from a set of documents in a virtual world. In the spatial virtual world, each document is displayed as a coloured sphere. The initials of authors of the document are displayed next to the sphere. We are interested in the role of associative memory in visual navigation for several reasons. It should help a user to build up a mental map of the virtual environment relatively more quickly, based on both the graphical and textual cues available in the spatial layout. It is further hypothesised that if users can develop their own mental maps effectively, they could probably benefit from these mental maps in their navigation. The role of a virtual world is not to replace individuals' mental maps; but rather to stimulate and help users to develop their mental maps more easily and intuitively.

5.1.1.3 Visual Memory

Visual memory is the ability to remember the configuration, location, and orientation of figural material, another potentially useful cognitive factor for the use and evaluation of a virtual environment, based on a spatial metaphor. According to Eckstrom *et al.* (1976), visual memory involves different cognitive processes from those used in other memory factors. A good visual memory should enable users to memorise and locate local structures more efficiently; thus more effective information search and information foraging is possible.

The three empirical studies described in this chapter closely follow the factor-referenced cognitive tests specified in Eckstrom *et al.* (1976). Spatial ability is measured in VZ-2 scores, while associative memory is measured in MA-1 scores, as described in Eckstrom *et al.* (1976), and visual memory in MV-1 scores. A challenging issue in measuring the performance of information foraging is how the relevance of a document to a given task is assessed. The problems with using recall and precision as a measure for evaluating interactive information retrieval are now well-known, especially the relevance according to judgements from experts, rather than the searchers themselves (Veerasamy and Belkin, 1996). Some topics may be relatively easy to retrieve with visual user interfaces, while others may be more appropriate for analytical user interfaces. In order to account for inter-topic differences, one may need to find enough subjects to explain inter-subject differences.

5.1.2 Visual Navigation

Information foraging is a broad term, covering activities associated with assessing, seeking, and handling information sources. The term 'foraging' refers both to the metaphor of organisms browsing for sustenance, and to indicate a connection to the more technical optimal foraging theory found in biology and anthropology. Information foraging theory is essentially an ecological approach to the study of information seeking behaviour (Pirolli and Card, 1995), and adopts the optimal foraging theory of biology and anthropology, which analyses the value of food-foraging strategies, and whether they should be adapted, given a particular situation. Information foraging theory applies similar trade-off analytical techniques in modelling the value of information gains against the costs for the user.

The design of an information space should optimise information foraging within that abstract space. Dourish and Chalmers (1994) discussed three types of metaphors for the design and use of an information space: spatial navigation, semantic navigation, and social navigation. A spatial metaphor provides users with various cues in association with an underlying spatial model, such as a room, a city, or landscape. Semantic navigation focuses on how users can effectively search in an information space based on semantic relationships. Instead of focusing on geometrical or semantic cues, the idea of social navigation follows the clustering of like-minded individuals in an information environment.

If users have a better understanding of the way a virtual environment is organised, they may be able to optimise their information foraging strategies. A key to the construction of the underlying virtual environment in the following examples is a semantically organised spatial metaphor. In this virtual environment, semantic structures are transformed and characterised by geometrical and topological properties. Similar documents are clustered together within the virtual environment in order to reduce the costs for the user.

The tension between a visual structure and the latent semantics has attracted attention from a number of research communities. The increasing interest also highlights the importance of understanding the role of individual differences in adapting effective navigation strategies in an information space, especially ones that rely on the abilities of individuals, notably spatial ability and memory abilities.

5.1.3 Wayfinding in Virtual Environments

Benyon and Höök (1997) presented an interesting overview of individual differences and navigation through an abstract information space, identifying three categories that could support information navigation: using appropriate metaphors, using virtual reality and 3D interfaces, and using adaptive interfaces that accommodate individual differences in users' navigation ability. The essence of navigational behaviour, either in an information space or in a physical world, is clearly described in their article:

'How do people work out how to reach their destination?. The answers to this question are many, and often unsurprising: people use maps and guides. They exploit landmarks in order to have something to aim for, and to recognise when they arrive, or use "dead reckoning" at sea when there are no landmarks.'

In reality, capabilities, preferences and skills vary from one individual to another. For example, Streeter et al. (1985) clearly showed that some individuals like using maps and some don't; some prefer graphical representations and others like verbal instructions.

Several studies investigated wayfinding behaviour in virtual environments. For example, Lokuge et al. (1996) introduced a geographical information system called GeoSpace, to help people to find various resources in the Boston urban area. The user interface of GeoSpace was implemented in a 3D graphical language, OpenGL. They found that users developed different mental maps of an area, based on the nature of the interrelationships concerned.

Darken and Sibert (1996) studied whether or not people use physical world wayfinding strategies in large virtual worlds. They examined a complex searching task in a number of virtual worlds, with different environmental cues, and their study showed that subjects were often disoriented in virtual worlds without any landmarks or cues. Simply adding cues, such as borders, boundaries and gridlines, significantly improved navigation performance. Since wayfinding strategies and behaviours were strongly influenced by the environmental cues in the Darken and Sibert study, the results reflected underlying principles for design. In other words, an organisational metaphor, with landmarks and navigational cues, was of utmost importance in successfully navigating these virtual worlds.

Darken and Sibert (1996) also investigated their subjects' spatial memory in connection with using a virtual environment, by asking them to sketch an overall organisation of the virtual environment, in which they searched for ships on the sea. They found that different organisational cues resulted in significant differences in terms of the recall accuracy of the spatial layout of the sketch, and for individual targets in the environment.

5.2 A Semantically Organised Virtual Environment

The virtual environment used in subsequent studies is uniquely designed. It is built on the basis of a visualised semantic structure of a subject domain – human-computer interaction (HCI), a semantic space automatically derived from a collection of 169 papers from three consecutive ACM CHI conference proceedings (CHI 95, CHI 96, and CHI 97, 1995–1997). The detailed structuring and modelling techniques are described in Chen (1998a, b) and Chen and Czerwinski (1998).

The content similarity between a pair of papers in the proceedings was computed according to latent semantic indexing (LSI) (Deerwester *et al.*, 1990), a sophisticated indexing technique developed for information retrieval (see Chapter 2).

The strongest inter-document relationships were extracted as a similarity matrix, using Pathfinder network scaling (Schvaneveldt *et al.*, 1989), which can provide more accurate details on local structures than the widely used multidimensional scaling techniques (MDS) (see also Chapter 2).

The resultant semantic space was then rendered in virtual reality modelling language (VRML) 2.0, and made accessible on the World-Wide Web (WWW). Users can walk and fly through the semantic space: it is, in effect, a zoomable user interface. The design rationale aims to reduce the tension between maintaining a focused view and a global view of the context. Given that the document collection is presented in semantically-related clusters in the virtual environment, we are particularly interested in whether users are influenced by the organisational cues in their information foraging activities.

In the subsequent empirical studies, the user interface is accessible via the Netscape Communicator 4.05, and Cosmo Player 2.0 VRML viewer plug-in. Figure 5.2 is a screenshot of the spatial user interface. The screen is split into two frames:the semantic space is displayed as a virtual world in the left-hand side frame. Coloured spheres in the virtual world represent papers published in different years: red (1995), green (1996), and blue (1997). Each sphere is labelled with the initials of authors of the paper. Clicking on the sphere will bring up the abstract in the right-hand side frame.

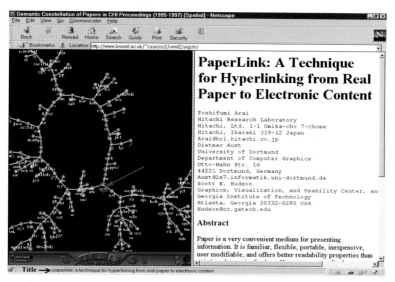

Figure 5.2   The spatial user interface used for exploring interrelationships between cognitive factors and information visualisation.

The overall landscape is designed according to the theory of cognitive maps (Chen, 1998a), the main concepts of which are introduced below.

5.2.1 Cognitive Maps

A cognitive map is an internalised analogy of the physical layout of the environment in the human mind (Tolman, 1948). The concept of cognitive maps plays an influential role in the study of navigation strategies, such as browsing in hyperspace (Edwards and Hardman, 1989), and wayfinding in virtual environments (Darken and Sibert, 1996). The acquisition of navigational knowledge proceeds through developmental stages, from the initial identification of landmarks in the environment, to a fully formed mental map (Dillon *et al.*, 1990). In this section, we use the concept of the cognitive map as the basis of our user interface design, in which a virtual world is structured to encourage the cognitive mapping between the abstract information space and users' mental maps.

5.2.1.1 Levels of Knowledge

Landmark knowledge is the basis of a cognitive map. According to Anderson (1980), as summarised in (Dillon *et al.*, 1990), the development of visual navigation knowledge starts with highly salient visual landmarks in the environment, such as unique or magnificent buildings, or natural landscape. One associates location in the environment with reference to these landmarks.

The acquisition of route knowledge is the next stage of developing a cognitive map. Route knowledge is characterised by the ability to navigate from point A to point B, using landmark knowledge acquired to make decisions about when to take turns, without association with surrounding areas. Once off the route, it would be very difficult for someone without route knowledge to backtrack to the route on their own. They may easily get lost, even though they can start their navigation all over again based on their landmark knowledge. Route knowledge does not, however, provide enough information about the contextual structure to enable the person to optimise his route for navigation.

The cognitive map is not fully developed until survey knowledge is acquired. According to Tolman (1948), the physical layout of the environment must be internalised in the human mind to form a cognitive map.

Dillon *et al.* (1990) have noted that when users navigate through an abstract structure such as a deep menu tree, if they select wrong options at a deep level they tend to return to the top of the tree altogether, rather than just take one step back. This strategy suggests the absence of survey knowledge about the structure of the environment, and a strong reliance on landmarks to guide navigation. It is not clear whether each individual develops through all stages in such a logical sequence. Nevertheless, studies suggested that intensive use of maps tends to increase survey knowledge in a relatively short period of time.

It is clear that visual navigation will rely on the cognitive map, and the extent to which users can easily connect the structure of their cognitive maps with the visual representations of the underlying information space. The concept of the cognitive map suggests that users need information about the structure of a complex, richly interconnected information space. On the other hand, if all the connectivity information is displayed, users would be unlikely to be able to navigate effectively in a spaghetti-like visual representation.

In the next section, we will address criteria that might be useful in determining the information important for visual navigation, and which should therefore be extracted and preserved in the visual representations, whereas redundant information may be filtered out to increase the clarity and simplicity of the visual environment.

5.2.2 Explicit and Implicit Structures

When users navigate through a visually represented world, the strategies and behavioural patterns of their visual navigation will inevitably be affected by a perceived structure, or metaphor, in association with the environment. There are many options for the underlying structuring metaphor. One could choose an existing hierarchical logical structure to organise and represent the environment. The structuring metaphor may associate information with a geographical backdrop, as seen in a geographical information system (GIS).

However, an explicit organising structure may not always come naturally with a given data set, or the existing structure may simply be inappropriate to the specific tasks in hand. What are the methods available for us to derive an appropriate structure? How can we connect such derived structures with the cognitive map in the user's mind?

Recent studies have shown that browsing through a table of contents is preferable over more analytical methods, such as query formulation. Chimera and Shneiderman (1994) examined three generally used interface methods for browsing hierarchically organised online information, including stable, expand/contract and multipane tables of contents.

The major drawback to a stable interface is that users have difficulty in perceiving the entire hierarchical organisation of the text at a glimpse. They must perform a considerable amount of scrolling with a stable interface, and can get lost in a large document. The expand/contract and multipane interfaces are designed to overcome this problem, by displaying the high-level information contiguously and giving users the choice of viewing specific section and subsection levels on demand. The motivation is to provide a balance of local detail and global context (Furnas, 1986). Not surprisingly, Chimera and Shneiderman's experiments confirmed the superiority of dynamic visual representations to static ones. Their findings also highlighted the role of structures in guiding people in visual navigating in a large database or information space.

5.2.3 Landmarks

Predominant landmarks in the virtual environment represent the results of a search using LSI as the search engine. The 20 documents that have the highest document-query relevance scores are displayed in the scene. These hit documents are marked by cylinder spikes arising from the document spheres, and the height of a spike is proportional to the document-query relevance estimated by the LSI-based search engine. Documents with the highest search bars are most likely to meet the needs of the search, and should be checked first.

Figure 5.3 shows a scene based on a search of conversation analysis and related concepts. Users can click on a document sphere and read its content in the split screen; moreover, the associative network representation of the semantic space allows users to explore documents that are not returned as hit documents themselves, but which may fall into the neighbourhood of a hit document. This expansion can be seen as a special type of query expansion.

The pop-up menu in the scene shows eight different viewpoints for users to choose. These viewpoints are provided to facilitate users' navigation in the virtual world, as it may not be a trivial task to move around using the keyboard and the traditional mouse. By choosing one of these viewpoints, users can examine the virtual world from a different perspective more easily. Figure 5.4 shows the same virtual world from a different viewpoint – Landscape South.

5.2.4 Route Knowledge

Links preserved by the Pathfinder network are explicitly displayed, a route from one paper to another having the strongest strength. The presence of a route in the virtual environment suggests to the user that papers on the route between two relevant papers may be worth browsing.

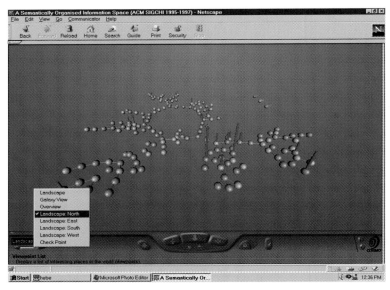

Figure 5.3   Choosing a viewpoint in the virtual space (Landscape North).

Papers from different years are coloured accordingly: papers from CHI95 are red; from CHI96 green, and from CHI97 blue. This colouring scheme can be used for detecting emerging trends in research questions and application domains, addressed by papers in consecutive years of conferences. For example, if we see a

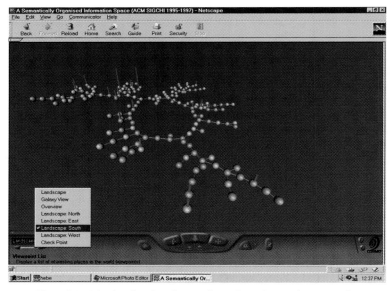

Figure 5.4   Viewing the virtual space from viewpoint Landscape South.

group of papers gathered together in blue (i.e., papers from the latest conference), it suggests that new topics have been introduced into the conference series. If a cluster of papers in the network have every colour but blue, this suggests that the particular topic area has not been addressed by recent papers in the conference.

The complexity of node placement relies on the number of pairwise similarity measures to be taken into account. Pathfinder networks tend to have fewer links, because of the triangle inequality condition. Links violating this condition were removed from the final network. Minimum spanning tree solutions may reduce the number of links even further. General aesthetic layout criteria include minimising the number of links crossing and overlapping, symmetrical displays and closeness of related nodes (see Chapter 3). Although the spring-embedder algorithm does not explicitly support the detection of symmetries, it turns out that in many cases the resulting layout demonstrates a significant degree of symmetrical arrangement.

5.2.5 Survey Knowledge

Figure 5.5 is a screenshot of a new version of the virtual environment (not included in these studies), which visualises the search process so that users can visually navigate through the semantic space and locate the information they need. This screenshot was generated from a search query, including visualsation and navigation, to the same semantic space. The results of the search were superimposed over the global semantic space. As shown in Fig. 5.5, there are three major clusters of documents that should be inspected during information foraging. Users may explore the neighbouring nodes of these clusters to find more documents relevant to a given topic. Information retrieval becomes a visual inspection of spatial representations of a semantic structure.

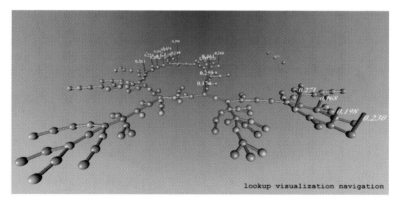

Figure 5.5 Superimposing the results of a search over the global semantic map (search query: *visualisation, navigation*).

5.3 Study I: Spatial Ability

The first study focuses on correlation relationships between spatial ability and visual navigation. An earlier version of the spatial user interface is used in this study, which is rendered in VRML 1.0. (the second and third studies use VRML 2.0 and Cosmo Player 2.0). Live3D is used as the VRML viewer plug-in to Netscape Navigator. This study is the first step in searching for connections between visual navigation tasks and spatial abilities.

5.3.1 Procedure

Eleven subjects participated in the study (three females and eight males). Nine of the subjects were enrolled on an M.Sc. course in Information Systems, one subject was a first year Ph.D. candidate, and one was a final year honours degree student.

A demographic questionnaire was given to these subjects in order to elicit some general information about their experiences in graphical user interface and hypertext systems, especially the Web. On average, these subjects had used computers for three years or longer, and the WWW for less than six months. They normally use the Internet more than four times a week. The most common activities were using e-mail and browsing the WWW.

Subjects used only one user interface in this study – a spatial user interface based on a semantic space derived from 169 papers published in three recent ACM SIGCHI conference proceedings – CHI 95,[3] CHI 96,[4] and CHI 97.[5] The semantic space was constructed in a virtual reality scene according to inter-document similarities, using latent semantic indexing, and the structure was simplified by Pathfinder network scaling, to ensure that articles on similar topics could be grouped together whenever possible.

Since latent semantic indexing is essentially a dimension-reduction process, a link between a pair of articles is determined by an overall similarity. However, this strategy may encounter problems in certain applications. For example, it is probably not suitable for users who want to identify links according to relationships of a particular type. This is a recognised problem in the literature of information retrieval and information visualisation, as, for example, the design of Cat-a-Cone (Hearst and Karadi, 1997).

In this study, the user interface was based on the Netscape Navigator 3.0 browser and its Live3D VRML 1.0 plug-in viewer. The screen was split into two frames. As usual, the virtual world was displayed in the left-hand side frame, while the right-hand side frame displayed the abstract of a paper selected from the virtual world. The initials of authors of each paper were used as the label, next to the document sphere. If the mouse cursor was on a sphere, the title of the paper would pop up next to it. If the user clicked on the sphere, the abstract would appear in the right-hand side frame.

---

[3]http://www.acm.org/sigchi/chi95/proceedings/
[4]http://www.acm.org/sigchi/chi96/proceedings/
[5]http://www.acm.org/sigchi/chi97/proceedings/

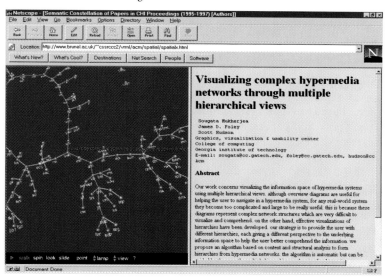

Figure 5.6 The user interface of CHI Proceedings (Study I).

Users could manipulate the virtual world in a number of ways. They could *walk* towards the visualisation model, by moving their mouse cursor forward. The most important design rationale of the virtual space is to allow users to have greater control over the amount of information displayed in the frame. If users wanted to have an overview of the entire space, they could walk backwards until the entire structure was visible. If they wanted to examine local details, they could walk up closer to an area so that they could see labels clearly in that area.

The actual abstracts of these papers are stored on a Web server at the Brunel University. The experiment was conducted on a PC with 233MHz CPU and 32Mb RAM, with a 17-inch display monitor. All the movements on the computer screen were videotaped for subsequent examination and analysis.

The study included pre-test and post-test phases. In the pre-test, spatial ability scores were collected from a standard paper folding test (Eckstrom *et al.*, 1976), in which subjects were asked to answer multiple-choice questions about the consequence of punching a hole in a paper folded in a particular way. An overall spatial ability score on this test ranged from 0 to 20. The average of the spatial ability scores in our study was 10, with a standard deviation of 3.91.

A short demonstration was given to subjects on how to use the Live3D VRML viewer. They were then asked to complete two major tasks (named Task 1 and Task 2), and two minor tasks. Ten minutes were allowed for each major task, and three minutes for each minor task. After completion of these tasks, they were asked to complete a post-test questionnaire concerning usability and user satisfaction.

The two major tasks required subjects to find papers related to particular topics. Once they had found a relevant paper, they were instructed to save the abstract of the paper to a local directory on their PC. In Task 1, subjects were instructed to find as many papers as they could about a topic, whereas in Task 2, they were told to find only five papers on a different topic.

For scoring user performance on Tasks 1 and 2, a relevance judgement was derived as follows. First, we generated a list of papers based on a full-text search for a task's topic across the entire collection of 169 papers. Then, irrelevant papers were removed from the list and additional relevant papers were added to the list, based on the first author's own judgement. This process led to three types of relevant papers, according to how one may determine whether they are relevant. One can determine the highly related papers directly from their titles. For the intermediately relevant papers, one may have to read the papers' abstracts and keywords. For the difficult determinations, one may need to explore the content more deeply. For example, if the user looks for papers on 'visualisation', it is likely that they will retrieve papers 1 and 2 below easily, just by reading the titles, but the relevance of paper 3 is less obvious:

Paper 1. Tilebars: visualization of term distribution information in full-text information access.

Paper 2. Visualizing complex hypermedia networks through multiple hierarchical views.

Paper 3. An organic user interface for searching citation links.

There were 24 relevant papers for Task 1, and 18 for Task 2 in the semantic space of 169 papers.

Following Task 1, there was a brief spatial memory test. Subjects were asked to sketch the shape of the visualised semantic space as best as they could from memory. This test was designed to find out what subjects could remember, after having searched through the semantically designed user interface. Studies have shown that the more information processing resources that are applied to study materials, the better those materials are recalled (Craik and Lockhart, 1972). We expected subjects to be engaged in this information visualisation deeply enough for memory performance for the structure of the space to be high. Details from these sketches should highlight what subjects learned about the structure of the semantic space, and how deeply the information they worked with was encoded in memory.

A categorisation and an abstraction task followed Task 2. Subjects were asked to name clusters of papers in the visualised semantic space. We intended to use this task to find out whether subjects could summarise groups of papers associated with distinctive structural patterns, and what naming schemes they would use. These data points will be used in future designs based on these materials, with the hope that the added semantic structure (e.g., labels, landmarks, and signs) will benefit ease of interaction with the user interface.

Task performance scores were measured in terms of the number of times a subject selected to read the abstract of a paper, the number of abstracts she saved for each task, and the number of saved abstracts relevant to the study topics, as per their instructions. The entire session lasted approximately 30 minutes.

5.3.2 Results

Correlations were computed between task performance and spatial ability scores, as were correlation coefficients between spatial ability and general user satisfaction scores. The search strategies of subjects who had the highest/lowest performance scores were examined from the videotape, in order to identify usability issues, and strategies relevant to future user interface designs of this genre.

5.3.2.1 Task Performance

Task performance scores were split into two groups, according to spatial ability scores. Group A refers to subjects with higher spatial ability scores, and Group B refers to subjects who have scored lower in the paper-folding test. On average, Group A saved more abstracts than Group B in both Task 1 (Mean = 7.4 and 3.2, respectively) and Task 2 (Mean = 4.6 and 3.8, respectively). According to our relevance judgement, Group A also found more relevant abstracts than Group B (Mean = 3.6 and 1.8, respectively for the sums of Task 1 and 2).

Recall was positively correlated with spatial ability, based on the paper folding scores in both Task 1 and Task 2 ($r = 0.42$ and 0.37, respectively). Precision was strongly negatively correlated with spatial ability in Task 1, and to a lesser degree in Task 2 ($r = -0.53$ and -0.18, respectively).

The total number of abstracts viewed by each individual was not correlated with spatial ability in Task 1 ($r = 0.07$), but it was negatively correlated with spatial ability in Task 2 ($r = -0.43$). The number of abstracts regarded as relevant by each individual was positively correlated with spatial ability in both Task 1 and Task 2 ($r = 0.45$ and 0.27, respectively).

5.3.2.2 Navigation Strategies

In order to analyse navigational patterns in further detail, we superimposed the frequencies of accessing papers that are judged relevant in Task 1, according to a relevance judgement described above, over the visualised semantic structure (see Fig. 5.7). Relevant papers are marked as boxes, and the number of dots beside each box indicates how many different individuals successfully found that target in Task 1.

Task performance scores suggest that subjects did reasonably well if relevant papers were located in structurally significant areas of the user interface. However, if they were located on the outskirts of the structure in the user interface, subjects were less successful. In addition, subjects seemed to be affected by the varying visibility of topical keywords (i.e., whether a search word appeared in the title, or was hidden in the abstract, or a complete vocabulary mismatch) across the semantic space. This could be a serious issue if one cannot easily recognise the relevance of a paper, especially when they are located in a key position, such as a gateway or a branching point. These positions, or hotspots, were typically examined by subjects in their first few moves; the navigation route

Figure 5.7   The locations of search targets in Task 1 (Chen and Czerwinski, 1997).

would be different if one failed to recognise a relevant paper because of looking
for it elsewhere, instead of exploring targets locally.

To understand how users actually navigated through the semantic space, we
reviewed the videotapes of subjects who have the highest and lowest task

Table 5.1 Task performance statistics and correlation
with spatial ability

Tasks	Mean	SD	Correlation (r-value) with spatial ability
Task 1			
Recall	0.13	0.09	0.42
Precision	0.64	0.35	−0.53
Abstracts viewed	15.30	5.95	0.07
Abstracts saved	5.30	4.00	0.45
Task 2			
Recall	0.13	0.07	0.37
Precision	0.79	0.32	−0.18
Abstracts viewed	14.60	11.26	−0.43
Abstracts saved	4.20	3.71	0.27

performance scores. The findings were informative. First, regardless of task performance, most of the subjects regarded the central circle structure as a natural starting point. They tended to aim at the central circle as an initial user interface action, and zoom into the virtual world in order to bring this circular area into focus. The outskirts of the central circle tended to be ignored during the initial search. Next, subjects would check a number of positions on the circle, especially points connecting to branches. Over time, they would gradually expand their search space outwards, to reach nodes farther away from the central area. One example of a good strategy was sampling a single node in each cluster, and then moving on to other clusters quickly during the initial stage. This strategy minimised the likelihood of becoming lost in a local minimum.

It is interesting to note that sometimes, even when a subject actually hit a target, she would initially ignore it. However, when she came back to the same target after saving several other targets, she saved the previously ignored or unrecognised target immediately. This suggests that subjects raised and lowered their acceptance thresholds as they gained experience within the information space.

Some subjects hopped from one cluster to another in long jumps, whereas others carefully examined each node along a path, according to the virtual semantic structure. Subjects who made longer jumps apparently realised that they might be able to rely on the structural patterns to help with their navigation. Navigational patterns also highlighted the special role of distinctive structural patterns such as circles, stars, and long spikes, as we expected from earlier research (Chen, 1998a, b). The video needs to be analysed more thoroughly in order to gather more detailed data about navigation strategies.

5.3.2.3 Spatial Memory

The spatial memory test provided an alternative viewpoint to look at the interaction between visualised semantic structures and individuals' understanding of how the semantic space is organised. By identifying what subjects learned about the structure, and how their remembered user interface details vary from one area to another, we were able to understand more about various characteristics of our visual semantic structure. Figure 5.8 shows the sketches of the semantic space from four subjects chosen randomly. These sketches not only show that the subjects have focused on different areas in the semantic space, but also that they can remember the semantic structures inherent in the user interface quite vividly. These figures are partially related to the differences in interactions between subjects' navigation strategies and their emerging cognitive maps. One interesting question that awaits future research is whether subjects' maps would converge over repeated exposure and use of the information space.

Most subjects clearly remembered the shape of the central circle. In (a), the subject highlighted the central circle and three sub-areas around the circle. The video analysis confirmed that these had been the most often visited areas in his search. In (b), the subject was able to remember more details about the branches surrounding the central circle. In addition, he added some strokes inside the

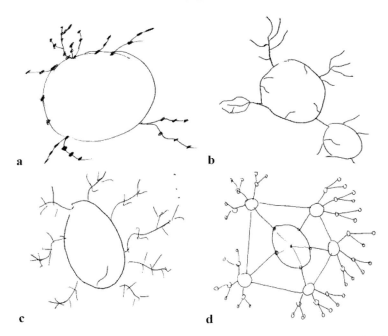

Figure 5.8   Subjects' sketches of the semantic information space searched during the study (Chen and Czerwinski, 1997).

circle, although they were not as accurate as other structural patterns in his sketch. In (c), the subject had focused on the central circle and sub-structures within the circle. He vaguely indicated the existence of some branches outside the circle, but accurately outlined the shape of the branch inside the circle. In fact, the video shows that his initial search focused on the circle and the branch inside the circle, before he switched to a finer-sift search mode. Another related factor could be that at one point he found a relevant paper, saved it, and adjusted the view to search more carefully in the local area. In this view, the inside-circle branch happened to be in the centre of the screen for about two minutes. In (d), the sketch becomes more conceptual. The subject had probably focused on the outskirts of the semantic space, because the outskirts of the sketch are more accurate than is the depiction of the central area. It is also interesting to note that nodes are different in their size, and that there is a sense of symmetry, which is generally regarded as a desirable feature in graph drawing. Subjects who sketched (a) and (b) achieved higher recall in task performance, whereas subjects who sketched (c) and (d) had higher precision scores. While this provides a clue to how subjects' spatial memory may be influenced by this information visualisation, as well as their individual differences in ability and strategy, further analysis needs to be carried out to arrive at meaningful implications for 3D user interface design.

5.3.2.4 Categorisation and Abstraction

The categorisation and abstraction task was designed to help us understand how individuals would refer to distinctive structural patterns, and which features associated with these patterns are likely to be most useful in design.

Seven subjects were able to give names to structural patterns without checking further details. However, some subjects found this task very difficult, and could not complete it. Some wanted to check particular spheres again before they could confidently provide a name for the given structures. One subject named the central circle as a 'General Issues' area, and another one as the 'M25' – a motorway around Greater London. These names could make sense as personal landmarks. For example, the shape of the central circle is similar to a ring motorway in a road atlas. One subject named a cluster as 'Virtual Reality'– apparently because he remembered some virtual reality papers in that area. (Note that 'virtual reality' was not even a task topic). From this preliminary report, it is clear that subjects were capable of assigning meaningful interpretations and labels to the semantically-driven user interface in this study.

5.3.2.5 User Satisfaction

A standard post-test questionnaire was used to assess usability issues and user satisfaction. There were three blocks of questions and multiple-choice statements about overall satisfaction, usability issues and user interface design. We also examined correlation coefficients between spatial ability and answers to the post-test questionnaire.

In general, user satisfaction ratings suggested areas of the user interface that worked well, and areas where software could be improved. Correlation with spatial ability was not generally predictive of satisfaction with the interface.

The majority of the subjects liked the system, (on average mean = 3.36, SD = 1.02). To a lesser extent, they wanted to recommend this system to others, and said they would use it on a regular basis (see Table 5.2). In addition, spatial ability was negatively correlated with the 'I would use it on a regular basis' statement ($r = -0.22$).

Eight people (73%) liked the visualisation idea for organising papers. Nine subjects (82%) thought the user interface was imaginative, but 36% felt that it was confusing, and 19% thought it lacked predictability. None of the users rated the user interface as boring.

Table 5.2 Global appeal ratings for the user interface (r-value: correlation with spatial ability pre-test scores)

Global appeal (all ratings are on a 1–5 Likert scale, with 1 = negative and 5 = positive).	Mean	SD	r-value
I liked it.	3.36	1.02	0.03
I would recommend this software to others.	2.82	1.54	0.00
I would use this software on a regular basis.	2.27	1.56	−0.22

Table 5.3 Design satisfaction ratings for the user interface (r-value: correlation with spatial ability pre-test scores)

Design	Yes (%)	r-Value
imaginative	82	−0.08
fun	55	−0.07
original	36	−0.28
confusing	36	0.34
intuitive	36	0.00
not my type of program	18	0.51
predictable	9	−0.34
boring	0	0.00

The following four usability related scores were slightly below average. During the post-test interview, a number of possible reasons were identified for this, such as being unfamiliar with manipulating a VRML world, the incorporation of unlabelled structures, and a lack of understanding of clustering models in general. These issues will be discussed further in following sections.

Online appeal factor ratings were mixed, although some subjects liked the unique user interface design. In particular, simplicity, ability to zoom and walk around topics, and navigating in topical clusters were among the named favourite features. On the other hand, average ratings were low in the areas of customisability, community and familiarity. Obviously these are areas in which the authors will need to put serious efforts into redesigning the user interface. Spatial correlation coefficients appear to be very complex. No distinctive patterns of how spatial abilities might influence the online appeal of a 3D world have been identified in the initial analysis of the data.

When asked 'Who would use this software?', a number of possible applications were mentioned, including researchers who want to have an overview of topics, or people who want to use it as a personalised digital library.

5.3.3 Reflection

This study has produced an interesting but complex set of findings, and a large amount of data yet to be fully analysed. Based on initial results, we have

Table 5.4 Usability satisfaction ratings for the user interface

Usability	Mean	SD	Spatial correlation
When I started, the purpose of the software was clear.	2.82	1.72	−0.19
It was easy to get where I wanted to go.	2.45	1.44	0.11
When I started, I knew what I could do.	2.36	1.63	−0.13
Each area of the software was clearly marked to indicate my location.	2.18	1.60	−0.40

Table 5.5 Satisfaction ratings for the online appeal of the user interface (r-value: correlation with spatial ability pre-test score)

Online Appeal	Mean	SD	r-Value
This software feels unique (or different).	4.45	0.52	0.34
This software is mentally challenging.	3.64	0.92	0.11
This software has appealing graphics.	3.45	1.13	0.23
This software is responsive (not too slow).	3.36	1.50	0.16
This software provides valuable information.	3.27	1.74	−0.02
This software is easy to use.	2.82	1.72	−0.20
This software uses cutting edge technology.	2.73	1.62	0.03
This software provides a detailed environment to interact with.	2.64	1.63	−0.02
This software is timely.	2.55	1.63	0.24
This software is personalised or customisable.	2.18	1.72	0.52
This software provides a shared experience (or community).	1.91	1.75	0.16
This software feels familiar.	1.82	1.54	−0.33

identified significant implications for system design, usability evaluation and user behavioural modelling, to be incorporated into the next versions of the system. An in-depth observation of individuals' navigation strategies should be of interest to the design and evaluation of other spatial semantic space systems in the HCI community.

An important issue in previous studies of hypertext information retrieval is how efficiently one can locate a primary target in hyperspace, and how that influences subsequent browsing. In this study, subjects relied heavily on popping up title information to assess the relevance of papers, certainly during the initial stages of search in the virtual world. Subjects confirmed in post-test interviews that it would have been much more helpful if they could have had some means of quickly narrowing down their search space. One natural solution to this problem could be to provide index search facilities to locate a highly probable paper with which to start their navigation through the space.

As an initial step in this direction, Fig. 5.9 is a screen shot of how the hits of a search could be superimposed on the overall semantic structure. With this improvement, it is hoped that users will be able to choose their starting point for navigating more easily. A number of users have requested cluster labelling as another improvement to the user interface. Further empirical studies are needed to refine the system in the near future. It will be very interesting to analyse how the user-driven search enhancements will affect how individuals navigate and search through the virtual environment.

In this study, several subjects commented on the need for more accurate user interface controls, so that the manipulation of the VRML world would be easier. For example, they would have liked to specify the degree of zooming accurately, instead of having to use the walk control. A few subjects had problems with losing control of the VRML world while navigating. Once this occurred, they had to reset the viewpoint to its initial position. An application-specific dashboard might be useful in these instances. Some subjects over-shot their target in the virtual world, so that the virtual world was then behind the viewpoint. From our

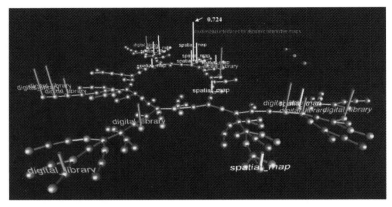

Figure 5.9   An initial prototype which superimposes search hits onto the overall semantic structure of the user interface (Chen and Czerwinski, 1997).

observations, it proved difficult for users to get the appropriate viewpoint back if they were new to using the Live3D viewer, and was disconcerting to the user. Therefore, it might be prudent to avoid dramatic shifts in the point of view of a virtual world for novice users, at least in this type of system.

5.3.4 Search Strategies

A number of interesting search strategies were captured by the videotapes. Many subjects directed their initial focus towards the central circle in the visualisation model. We found that each task session started with a pre-search stage, where subjects would adjust the visualisation model to a comfortable position for starting navigation. It turned out to be a common choice for many subjects to devote all of the screen real estate to the display of the central circle before they started to examine titles and/or abstracts of papers. Branching points, where two branches were connected, were also found to be strategically significant in our initial analyses. Subjects often checked the title of a paper at such positions. Subjects were able to jump across a considerable distance from these branching points, which confirms our speculation that distinctive structural patterns do have a special place in guiding visual navigation.

An understanding of the organisational principle seems to be reflected in the search strategies subjects used in this study. For instance, one successful search strategy was to focus on the central ring initially, and then sample documents outward from the ring. In this way, subjects were able to make optimal use of the clustering organisation inherent in the user interface. Figure 5.10 shows the first few moves in the virtual environment of a particularly effective subject. The large shaded area denotes where he had subsequently focused his search in this area, and was able to retrieve several targets successfully. Note that this subject achieved the highest task performance scores for both tasks, but did not have the highest spatial ability score in the paper-folding pre-test.

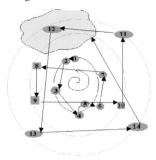

Figure 5.10 One subject's initial moves while searching the semantic space (Chen and Czerwinski, 1997).

People with lower spatial ability scores may develop good strategies, if they understand how the structure is organised, but this may take time. Some people only realised that they could benefit from the structure during the second half of their session. On the other hand, others thought that the idea was simple enough to understand straightaway, but exhibited difficulty in manipulating the virtual world in the Live3D viewer. Therefore, more research needs to be carried out to look at the long-term benefits of using this kind of visualisations in information retrieval tasks, as well as examining better user interface controls and 3D input devices.

The spatial memory test also highlighted the need for reinforcing strategically significant points, or structural hotspots, as well as larger structural patterns in the virtual environment. Strong stimuli (e.g, landmarks or signs) should be recommended, to reinforce users' cognitive map of the virtual space. For example, an animation of how papers were organised would help users to understand the nature of the organisation. This notion awaits further user interface design work.

5.3.5 Incremental Learning

A somewhat surprising behaviour was observed when a few subjects encountered a paper that was indeed judged to be relevant according to our list of correct papers. Sometimes, subjects carried on their search as if they didn't notice the relevance of a paper. However, when they came back to the same paper, after successfully finding a few other papers, they saved it without hesitation. Reasons behind this phenomenon are still not clear because it happened to several subjects. One possible explanation is that these were subtle papers and saving relevant papers on the same task topic helped them to make up their mind. Papers that they found between their first encounter and the second encounter might fill in some conceptual gap. This consideration led us to the triangle inequality assumption in Pathfinder network scaling. If we use this assumption, we can conjecture a model as follows to explain this behaviour. To an individual user, the semantic similarity between the task topic and a subtle paper is not clear initially. If she found another paper obviously related to the topic and somehow related to the first paper as well, she was able to associate the task topic with the first paper. Based on this argument, one would expect that since the explicit links in the visualisation model were derived as a Pathfinder network (see Chen, 1997 for details of the modelling), users would be able to identify such implicit connections more easily. However, this is a complex issue that is beyond the scope of this study.

5.3.6 Spatial Ability

Correlation between spatial ability and user behaviour was computed for a number of different tasks, as well as preference data. Although we found that recall was positively correlated with spatial ability, as were a number of other measures, the overall impact of spatial ability was not straightforward. Sometimes the direction of the correlation was unexpected. A few aspects of the design of this study could be improved in future research, to help clarify the impact that spatial ability might have on the usability of such information visualisations. For example, the entire task session was very limited in terms of time, especially for subjects who had not used the VRML viewer prior to the test session. The sample size should be increased to minimise variability in the data resulting from extreme combinations of spatial ability and experience with computers.

On the other hand, the spatial memory test and the categorisation task turned out to be very informative. The videotape coding provided an effective way of understanding users' navigation strategies. We recommend usability studies on visualisation-based information systems to include such tasks.

5.4 Study II: Associative Memory and Visual Memory

The second study aims to explore the relationship between two cognitive factors, associative memory and visual memory, and visual navigation performance in a semantically organised virtual environment. The analysis will focus on corresponding correlation coefficients.

5.4.1 Procedure

Ten subjects (six males and four females) participated in this study. The age of the participants ranged from 25 to 40, and all were computer-literate. Their experiences with virtual environments were diverse.

The user interface was the same as that used in Study I. In order to minimise the network disturbances, local copies of the abstracts of these papers are stored on a web server at Brunel University. The experiment was conducted on a Windows NT 4.0 with 233 MHz CPU and 32 Mb RAM, with a 17-inch display monitor. In Study II, instead of using Live3D, Cosmo Player 2.0 was used as the VRML plug-in viewer with the Netscape Communicator 4.05.

As in Study I, Study II included pre-test and post-test phases. In the pre-test, associative memory scores (MA-1) and visual memory scores (MV-1) were obtained one day before search sessions, based on the factor-referenced tests in Eckstrom *et al.*, (1976). All subjects performed the test under the neutral mood.

A brief tutorial was given to subjects about the basic controls of the Cosmo Player 2.0 before the search. Subjects were given two search topics. They were told to find as many relevant papers as they could for the first topic within 15 minutes. For the second topic, they were told to stop once they found five relevant papers. Following the design of our earlier study of spatial ability and visual navigation (Chen and Czerwinski, 1997), subjects were asked to sketch the spatial layout of the search space at the end of the first search sub-session. When the second topic was completed, subjects were asked to name the cluster of papers in the semantic space. This was designed to find out what subjects could remember after having searched through the spatial user interface. Subjects were instructed to save the abstracts of relevant papers into a dedicated local directory on the computer.

Qualitative and quantitative performance measures were collected during the test session. The recall and precision scores were based on the results of a search using the underlying latent semantic indexing techniques. We used the keywords appearing in the task descriptions to formulate the search. The top 20 papers returned by the LSI were regarded as the short-listed documents for the given topics. Because the semantic space was generated on the basis of the LSI modelling, it is reasonable to use the results of LSI on the same document collection to measure the relevance. Correlations were computed between task performances and subjects' memory scores and, in addition, usability and user satisfaction rating were analysed.

5.4.2 Results

The number of abstracts saved by each individual was positively correlated with memory associated test in Task 1. As predicted, subjects with better memory performed better tasks. However, the number of abstracts saved by each individual was negatively correlated with both memory tests in Task 2. The possible reason for this could be that in Task 2 it was difficult to search for a specific topic. Subjects would need to explore the content of the paper more deeply, especially those without background in this area The use of more general content papers could solve this problem. Table 5.6 lists Pearson's correlation coefficients regarding the two memory factors. Associative memory was strongly correlated with the mean recall scores of Task 1 ($r = 0.855$, $p = 0.003$), whereas

Table 5.6 Pearson's correlation coefficients between memories and task scores

Memory tests	Associative memory		Visual memory	
	MA-1		MV-1	
Performance scores	Pearson	Sig. (1-tailed)	Pearson	Sig. (1-tailed)
Task 1 (mean scores)	0.855	0.003	0.180	$p = 0.335$
Task 2 (mean scores)	−0.575	0.068	−0.649	$p = 0.041$

visual memory was negatively correlated with the mean recall scores of Task 2 (r = −0.649, p = 0.041).

All the subjects included a central circle in their sketches. However, the detailed structures vary. Figure 5.11 includes four sketches of the spatial layout of the underlying search space, made by subjects who had the highest performance scores, as well as the ones who had lowest performance scores.

In sketch (a), the subject was able to remember most details about the surrounding branches and strokes inside the central circle. The details were the most accurate, and the highest scores in both recall and precision were achieved by this subject. The sketch in (b) was very interesting: most links were omitted, but it still gave an accurate outline of the structure. This sketch shows the branches that he visited several times in greater detail. In sketch (c), although the overall recall was not accurate, the subject depicted the branches that he searched, especially the branch that he started with. Finally, in sketch (d), the structure was coarse. This subject had the lowest recall score for the first topic. These sketches may provide an explanation of how the spatial memory of users may be influenced, not only by what is available from a virtual environment, but also by individual differences in terms of their cognitive abilities and task-related strategies.

The categorisation and abstraction task was designed to help us understand the nature of clusters of papers, as perceived by individuals through the spatial metaphor. Some subjects wanted to check each cluster again before they could provide a name. Some named a cluster after something that was familiar to them, or something that was easy to memorise, for example, a comet, the head of a dolphin, or the western frontier. Some subjects actually used a content-based naming scheme, including visualisation, user interfaces, and interaction

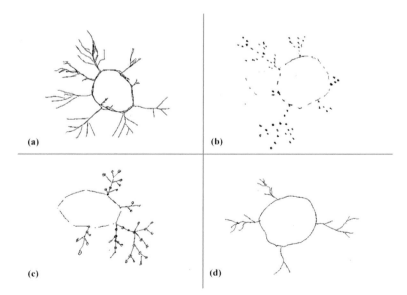

Figure 5.11   Sketches of the spatial layout of the semantic space searched.

techniques. Various names were given to the central circular structure: 'the mothership's orbit', 'the universe', and 'the main ring'.

A general questionnaire assessed the usability of the spatial user interface and user satisfaction. There were three parts, concerning the overall satisfaction, subjective usability ratings, and design preferences. The majority of the subjects would recommend this system to others (mean = 3.30). Correlations with MA1 and MV1 were not statistically significant.

Most of the subjects thought that the user interface was original, intuitive, imaginative and fun. Some found that it lacked predictability. Few found it to be confusing or boring.

Many subjects agreed that the purpose of the software was clear. However, the scores to the other three usability questions were slightly below the average (see Table 5.4). These results suggest that subjects might need to be more familiar with manipulating a virtual world. The last statement, 'each area was clearly marked to indicate my location', has the lowest mean, which is not surprising, as the representation of the spatial model in the virtual environment remained unchanged during a search session. 'Users need to know their location in the virtual world' was the message that came over strongly, in this and other experiments.

The majority of subjects agreed that the spatial user interface was unique, easy to use, and incorporated a sense of sharing. Many subjects liked the unique interface design (mean = 4.20, SD = 0.63). Subjects did not feel familiar with the user interface.

In this study, users searched through a semantic space, rendered as a virtual world. With little knowledge about the underlying computational model of the user interface, users adopted a brute-force search strategy. They relied heavily on

Table 5.7 Global appeal of the user interface

Global appeal (all ratings are on a 1–5 Likert scale, with 1 = negative and 5 = positive)	Mean	SD	MA-1	MV-1
I would recommend this software to others.	3.30	1.49	0.144	0.252
I like it.	2.90	1.20	0.243	0.463
I would use this software on a regular basis	2.78	1.56	0.177	0.254

Table 5.8 Design satisfaction ratings for the user interface

Design satisfaction	Mean	SD	MA-1	MV-1
Original	4.00	1.07	0.290	−0.038
Intuitive	3.50	1.35	0.272	0.208
Imaginative	3.40	0.84	−0.296	0.199
Fun	3.20	1.55	−0.006	0.249
Predictable	2.80	1.55	0.220	0.350
Confusing	2.20	1.62	−0.103	0.034
Not my type of program	2.00	1.83	−0.329	0.237
Boring	1.40	1.17	−0.044	−0.063

Table 5.9 Usability satisfaction ratings for the user interface

Usability	Mean	SD
When I started, the purpose of the software was clear.	3.80	1.03
When I started, I knew what I could do.	2.90	1.29
It was easy to get to where I wanted to go.	2.80	1.03
Each area of the software was clearly marked to indicate my location.	2.20	0.79

Table 5.10 Satisfaction rating for the online appeal of the user interface

Online appeal	Mean	SD
This software feels unique (or different).	4.20	0.63
This software provides a shared experience (or community).	4.00	0.89
This software is responsive (not too slow).	3.50	1.18
This software is mentally challenging.	3.44	1.01
This software has appealing graphics.	3.33	1.22
This software provides a detailed environment with which to interact.	3.30	1.49
This software provides valuable information.	3.25	1.39
This software is easy to use.	3.20	1.14
This software feels familiar.	2.20	1.75

rolling their mouse over the spheres in the virtual world, and bringing up the titles for initial inspection. Subjects commented that the spatial interface should help them to locate where they were, or where they have been. We predicted that people with better memory abilities would navigate the virtual world more effectively and efficiently. As predicted, we found a strong positive correlation between associative memory scores and performance scores for Task 1 (Pearson's $r = 0.855$, $p = 0.003$). On the other hand, visual memory scores were negatively correlated with the scores for Task 2 (Pearson's $r = -0.649$, $p = 0.041$). In addition, it is clear that if users understand more about how the semantic space is generated, they may develop more effective search strategies.

5.5 Study III: Associative Memory and Spatial Ability

The third study was an experimental study, which aimed to further explore the relationships between individual differences and search performance. Spatial ability (VZ-2) and associative memory (MA-1) were considered.

5.5.1 Procedure

In the pre-test, spatial ability scores (VZ-2) and associative memory scores were obtained from standard tests in Eckstrom *et al.*, (1976).

Within-subject design was used, where subjects were asked to find as many papers as they could in relation to four topics. Two user interfaces were used in each session: one was with the spatial version, and the other was with a textual version. Each subject was scheduled according to a Latin-Square design. In the spatial version, the search facility was only available within each node content window, whereas in the textual version, one could search keywords in either the table of contents window or the node content window. Twelve subjects participated in the experiment. Each session included a pre-test sub-session, in which spatial ability scores (VZ-2) and associative memory scores (MA-1) were obtained. Subjects also completed a pre-test questionnaire about their experiences in online search and VRML-based user interfaces. Subjects were asked to search with one user interface on two topics, and then switched over to the other user interface for the remaining two topics. Ten minutes were allowed for each topic. At the end of each topical search, subjects were asked to complete a brief questionnaire about their knowledge of the topic they had just searched. Finally, after subjects had completed search tasks for all four topics, they filled in a post-test questionnaire regarding the overall experience of using the two interfaces.

Among the 12 subjects, five of them were Ph.D. students or researchers, five were academic staff in our department, and two were administrative staff. The average age was 33, with five years of experience in online search. Most subjects had experience in searching on the WWW. Few people had used VRML-based virtual worlds before the experiment.

The spatial user interface in the experiment consisted of a split screen layout; the left-hand side window displayed the virtual reality model of the semantic space, whereas the right-hand side window displayed the content of the document that the user selected in the semantic space. As the user's mouse rolled over a sphere in the spatial display, the title of the associated paper was displayed at the bottom line of the browser. Once a sphere was clicked, its content appeared in the right-hand side window. The content of a node included the title of the corresponding paper, the authors and their affiliations, the abstract, and a list of keywords. Subjects could use these cues to decide whether or not they should include a particular paper in their answers.

They were instructed to save relevant papers for each topic into a dedicated file directory on the local computer. As most of these subjects were not familiar with the four search topics, the relevance of a document was judged by pooled answers among subjects. If two or more subjects selected a document as an answer to a given topic, then it would be included in the set of documents relevant to this topic. The recall and precision were subsequently based on the standard definition.

In the data analysis, we particularly concentrated on the relationships between individual differences and the search performance scores, including correlation coefficients between spatial ability scores with recall and precision, and associative memory scores with recall and precision. The effects of the form of user interfaces, spatial versus textual, on these measures, were also analysed. Spearman's correlation coefficients were computed between subjective ratings, and both spatial ability and associative memory scores. Unless stated otherwise, all the statistical significance was one-tailed at the conventional 0.05 level. Higher spatial ability scores and higher associative memory scores were associated with the positive direction.

5.5.2 Results

The mean usability ratings on the spatial and textual user interfaces are shown in Fig. 5.12. According to this sample of users, most of them gave higher ratings to the textual user interface on questions such as 'easy to learn' and 'easy to use'. On the other hand, the average scores of the textual user interface and that of the spatial one, were about the same on the question of the overall usefulness in the search.

Spearman's correlation coefficients reveal that associative memory and the usefulness rating on the textual user interface was negatively correlated (Spearman's $r = -0.597$, $p = 0.020$), which suggests that a user with a good associative memory is more likely to favour the spatial user interface, rather than the textual one. In this sample of users, their spatial ability scores and associative memory scores were positively correlated (Pearson's $r = 0.581$, $p = 0.024$).

Table 5.11 is a summary correlation coefficient matrix. Our focus is on the relationships between individual difference measures and the task performance measures. As shown in the table, precision with the spatial user interface and associative memory were negatively correlated (Pearson's $r = -0.544$, $p = 0.034$), whereas the precision with the textual user interface was negatively correlated with spatial ability (Pearson's $r = -0.553$, $p = 0.031$). Both correlations are statistically significant, and the magnitudes can be regarded as medium or large.

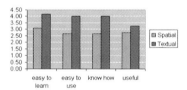

Figure 5.12   The mean usability ratings of the spatial and textual user interfaces ($N = 12$).

Table 5.11 A summary correlation coefficient matrix

Individual differences ($N = 12$)		Spatial ability (VZ-2)		Associative memory (MA-1)	
		r	Sig.	r	Sig.
Spatial UI					
	Recall	−0.126	0.348	0.042	0.449
	Precision	−0.397	0.100	−0.544	0.034
Textual UI					
	Recall	−0.192	0.275	−0.282	0.187
	Precision	−0.553	0.031	−0.459	0.066

In general, subjects performed slightly better on the textual interface than the spatial one. General factorial analysis and linear regression analysis were used to analyse the multivariate effects on the overall information foraging performance. Spatial ability scores (VZ-2) and associative memory scores (MA-1) were used as covariants in these models. A dummy variable S was also assigned, to indicate whether the spatial user interface was used before the textual one.

A great effect of associative memory on precision was found in an ANOVA analysis ($F(1, 10) = 6.69$, $p = 0.027$), which explains 40% of the variance. However, the main effect of associative memory on recall was not statistically significant ($F(1, 10) = 0.672$, $p = 0.431$).

Stepwise linear regression analysis yielded a single predictor model for both precision and recall. Associative memory explained more than 70% of the variance ($R^2 = 0.731$, Adj. $R^2 = 0.707$). Spatial ability (VZ-2) and the dummy variable S were excluded from the model. Similarly, associative memory remained the best predictor for recall, explaining 59% of the variance according to the adjusted R^2.

In summary, associative memory appears to be a good predictor of information foraging performance with the spatial user interface, whereas spatial ability seems to be overshadowed by the cognitive factor of memory.

5.6 Summary

The main results of these studies are summarised as follows. In the first study, a strong correlation was found between spatial ability and how accurately a spatial structure is memorised. The study focused on the overall searching strategies in visual navigation; for example, whether subjects took advantage of document clusters.

In the second study, the relationships between two cognitive factors, associative memory (MA-1) and visual memory (MV-1), and information foraging performance were analysed. Ten subjects searched for two topics, relying on the strong spatial metaphor of the underlying semantic structure. A strong positive correlation was found between associative memory and overall recall.

In the third study, the same spatial user interface and a textual user interface were used in a within-subject experimental design, used by twelve subjects, with special reference to spatial ability (VZ-2) and associative memory (MA-1). Each subject searched four topics, using both user interfaces according to a Latin-Square design. Precision with the spatial user interface was negatively correlated with associative memory, whereas precision with the textual user interface was negatively correlated with spatial ability.

Associative memory appears to be a good predictor of information foraging performance: it typically explains 60–70% of variance in overall recall and precision. In addition, subjects with a good associative memory are more likely to prefer the spatial interface to the textual one, even though on average the performance with the textual one is slightly better than with the spatial interface.

Having analysed several relationships involving individual differences and information foraging performance, we found that associative memory seems to be a good predictor of information foraging performance within our semantically organised spatial environment; typically explaining between 60–70% of the variance in recall and precision. We also found that individuals with good associative memory are more likely to prefer the spatial user interface to the textual one. The conclusion that more attention should be paid to the role of associative memory in the design, use, and evaluation of virtual environments for visual navigation and information foraging purposes. For example, we expect that enhancing visual cues in the virtual environment may compensate for differences in associative memory, making it easier for users to identify and locate local structures in the global semantic space.

Our analysis did not reveal a strong impact of spatial ability on users' performance. Nevertheless, a negative correlation was found between spatial ability and precision with the textual interface. The implications of this negative correlation demand further investigation.

These two studies also reveal the weaknesses of using measures such as recall and precision, given that the underlying semantic space is organised according to a particular indexing mechanism, in this case latent semantic indexing. More appropriate measures need to be developed and adapted for the study of human factors in virtual environments, which may lead to insights into why good spatial ability appeared to be associated with a poor precision score. Subjects' sketches in the second study were particularly informative. Not only can a sketched spatial layout reflect the spatial attention of individuals, it may also reflect the mental map that individuals developed with reference to the shape of the virtual environment.

We have briefly discussed three types of metaphors for the design and use of an information space: spatial navigation, semantic navigation, and social navigation. In these two studies, the focus of our work was on the spatial and semantic metaphors of navigation. Social interaction in virtual environments is a topic beyond the scope of this chapter, but it is an integral part of interacting with a virtual environment. Although in both studies, the virtual world was used in a single user mode, what are the implications if individuals find themselves sharing the semantic space? Our initial experience with the multiuser version suggests the fundamental question: 'Can we achieve a synergy of cognitive and social dimensions in a virtual environment?', because if we can find a synergy of the two dimensions, social interaction may provide an alternative means of resolving individual differences in virtual environments.

Bibliography

Anderson, J (1980). *Cognitive Psychology and Its Implications*. Freeman (San Francisco).

Benyon, DR (1993). Accommodating individual differences through an adaptive user interface. In: M Schneider-Hufschmidt, T Kühme, and U Malinowski (eds.), *Adaptive User Interfaces – Results and Prospects* . Elsevier (Amsterdam).

Benyon, DR, and Murray, DM (1993). Adaptive systems: From intelligent tutoring to autonomous agents. *Knowledge-based Systems, 6*(3).

Benyon, D, and Höök, K (1997). *Navigation in information spaces: Supporting the individual*. Proceedings of Human-Computer Interaction: INTERACT 97, Chapman and Hall, pp. 39–46.

Boyd, C, and Darken, R (1996). *Psychological issues of virtual environment interfaces*. Proceedings of CHI 96, ACM Press, pp. 426.

Campagnoni, F, and Ehrlich, K (1989). Information retrieval using a hypertext-based help system. *ACM Transactions on Information Systems, 7:*271–91.

Carroll, JB (1974). *Psychometric tests as cognitive tasks: A new structure of intellect.* Educational Testing Service (Princeton, USA), pp. 74–6.

Carroll, JB (1993). *Human Cognitive Abilities: A Survey of Factor Analytical Studies.* CUP (Cambridge, UK).

Chen, C. (1998a). Bridging the gap: The use of Pathfinder networks in visual navigation. *Journal of Visual Languages and Computing, 9*(3):267–86.

Chen, C. (1998b). Generalised Similarity Analysis and Pathfinder Network Scaling. *Interacting with Computers, 10*(2):107–28.

Chen, C, and Rada, R (1996). Interacting with hypertext: A meta-analysis of experimental studies. *Human-Computer Interaction, 11*(2):125–56.

Chen, C, and Czerwinski, M (1997). Spatial ability and visual navigation: An empirical study. *New Review of Hypermedia and Multimedia, 3*:67–89.

Chen, C, and Czerwinski, M (1998). From latent semantics to spatial hypertext: An integrated approach. Proceedings of the Ninth ACM Conference on Hypertext and Hypermedia (Hypertext 98) (Pittsburgh, PA., June 1998), ACM Press, pp. 77–86.

Chen, C, Czerwinski, M, and Macredie, R (forthcoming). Individual differences in virtual environments: An Introduction. *Journal of the American Society for Information Science*(Special Issue).

Chimera, R, and Shneiderman, B (1994). An exploratory evaluation of three interfaces for browsing large hierarchical tables of contents. *ACM Transactions on Information Systems, 12*(4):383–406.

Craik, FIM, and Lockhart, RS (1972). Levels of processing: A framework for memory research. *Journal of Verbal Learning and Verbal Behavior, 11*:671–84.

Dahlbäck, N, Höök, K, and Sjölinder, M (1996). *Spatial cognition in the mind and in the world: The case of hypermedia navigation.* Proceedings of the Eighteenth Annual Meeting of the Cognitive Science Society (University of California, San Diego, July 1996).

Darken, RP, and Sibert, JL (1996). *Wayfinding strategies and behaviors in large virtual worlds.* Proceedings of CHI 96.

Deerwester, S, Dumais, ST, Landauer, TK, Furnas, GW, and Harshman, RA (1990). Indexing by Latent Semantic Analysis. *Journal of the American Society for Information Science, 41*(6):391–407.

Dillon, A, and Watson, C (1996). User analysis in HCI: The historical lessons from individual differences research. *International Journal of Human-Computer Studies, 45*(6):619–637.

Dillon, A, McKnight, C, and Richardson, J (1990). Navigating in hypertext: A critical review of the concept. In: EAD Diaper (ed.), *Human-Computer Interaction – INTERACT 90*, Elsevier (Amsterdam), pp. 587–92.

Dourish, P, and Chalmers, M (1994). *Running out of space: Models of information navigation.* Proceedings of HCI 94.

Eckstrom, RB, French, JW, Harman, HH, and Derman, D (1976). *Kit of factor-referenced cognitive tests.*Educational Testing Service (Princeton, USA).

Edwards, D, and Hardman, L (1989). Lost in hyperspace: Cognitive mapping and navigation in a hypertext environment. In: R McAleese (ed.), *Hypertext: Theory into practice.* Intellect Books (Oxford, UK).

Egan, D (1988). Individual differences in Human-Computer Interaction. In: M Helander (ed.), *Handbook of Human-Computer Interaction.* Elsevier (Amsterdam), pp. 543–68.

Eisenberg, M, Nishioka, A, and Schreiner, ME (1997). *Helping users think in three dimensions: steps toward incorporating spatial cognition in user modelling.* Proceedings of the 1997 International Conference on Intelligent User Interfaces (IUI 97), pp. 113–120.

Furnas, GW (1986). *Generalized fisheye views.* Proceedings of CHI 86. ACM Press, pp. 16–23.

Hearst, M, and Karadi, C (1997). *Cat-a-Cone: An interactive interface for specifying searches and viewing retrieval results using a large category hierarchy.* Proceedings of the Twentieth Annual International ACM/SIGIR Conference (Philadelphia, PA, July 1997), ACM Press.

Herndon, KP, Dam, A v, and Gleicher, M (1994). The challenges of 3D interaction: A CHI 94 Workshop. *SIGCHI Bulletin, 26*(4):36–43.

Höök, K, Dahlbäck, N, and Sjölinder, M (1996). Individual differences and navigation in hypermedia. Proceedings of ECCE-8 (http://www.cs.vu.nl/~eace/).

Kline, P (1994). Review of Carroll's human cognitive abilities. *Applied Cognitive Psychology, 14*:387–99.

Lokuge, I, Gilbert, SA, and Richards, W (1996). Structuring information with mental models: A tour of Boston. Proceedings of CHI 96, ACM Press.

Pirolli, P, and Card, SK (1995). Information foraging in information access environments. Proceedings of the Conference on Human Factors in Computing (CHI 95) (Denver, CO), ACM Press, pp. 51–8.

Schvaneveldt, RW, Durso, FT, and Dearholt, DW (1989). Network structures in proximity data. In: G Bower (ed.), *The Psychology of Learning and Motivation, 24.* Academic Press, pp. 249–284.

Streeter, LDV, and Wonsiewicz, S (1985). How to tell people where to go: Comparing navigational aids. *International Journal of Man-Machine Studies, 22*:549–62.

Sutcliffe, A, and Patel, U (1996). 3D or not 3D: Is it nobler in the mind? In: MA Sasse, RJ Cunningham, and RL Winder (eds.), *People and Computers XI.* Springer-Verlag (London, UK), pp. 79–94.

Tolman, EC (1948). Cognitive maps in rats and men. *Psychological Review, 55*:189–208.

Veerasamy, A, and Belkin, NJ (1996). *Evaluation of a tool for visualization of information retrieval results.* Proceedings of SIGIR 96 (Zurich, Switzerland). ACM Press, pp. 85–92.

Vicente, KJ, and Williges, RC (1988). Accommodating individual differences in searching a hierarchical file system. *International Journal of Man-Machine Studies, 29*:647–68.

Chapter 6
Virtual Environments

What is a virtual environment? To start with, it can be designed for a single user, or multiple users. For a single user virtual environment, the design may focus on the use of a metaphor, the construction of the environment, and how a single user can interact with the virtual environment. On the other hand, for a multiple user virtual environment, the focus may be devoted to the support of communication and social interaction. Another aspect of a virtual environment is its role in providing resources for people to access computer networks.

Sometimes researchers distinguish collaborative virtual environments (CVEs) from general multi-user virtual environments, or distributed virtual environments, in order to emphasise the nature of the social activities to be supported. Sophisticated virtual environments may utilise advanced telecommunication technologies, as well as multimedia techniques, for example, 3D graphics, high-quality audio and video. Alternatively, a virtual environment can be built on text-based communication tools.

Virtual environments not only provide a rich medium for applying information visualisation techniques, as well as other techniques, but also a far-reaching context that stimulates the development of new visualisation techniques. To answer the question 'What is a virtual environment?', one should focus on the activities a virtual environment would enable people to perform and take part in, and, only in this context, the purposes that various enabling techniques serve.

In this chapter, we include a number of examples of popular and much-populated virtual environments, ranging from text-based chat rooms to multimedia, multiuser, and virtual reality-enriched cyber-cities and cyberspaces. The aim is to illustrate two major aspects of a virtual environment: construction and interaction. The construction of such an environment is concerned with design and organisational principles. The interaction model addresses how participants of a virtual environment can interact with each other, as well as with various objects arranged in the environment.

We first focus on the role of spatial metaphors in the construction of virtual environments. A fruitful perspective is to examine the interplay between information visualisation and virtual environments (Fig. 6.1). The construction of a virtual environment can benefit greatly from information visualisation designs. Information visualisation, by setting itself in a context of a virtual environment, can gain many more insights into the nature of visualisation and how it might meet people's needs. The concept of information workspaces has been introduced by Card *et al.* (1996), Rao *et al.* (1995), and Robertson *et al.*

Figure 6.1 The integral role of information visualisation techniques in the design of virtual environments.

(1991). The primary design principle of an information workspace is that users should be able to access a wide variety of information visualisation tools to meet the varied needs arising in their working environments.

Some challenging criticisms of the use of spatial metaphors are also included in this chapter. We will extend the analysis of the role of spatial metaphors in framing the behaviour of participants in a virtual environment, by examining the relationships between spatial configurations and the structure of discourse and other social activities.

6.1 Informal Communication and Mutual Awareness

Informal communication has been regarded as an important element of collaborative work (Kraut *et al.*, 1988; Whittaker *et al.*, 1994). Kraut *et al.* (1990) have shown that informal communication tends to be brief, frequent, and unplanned, and that physical proximity is a good predictor of scientific collaboration. Whittaker *et al.* (1994) analysed informal communication in the workplace, in order to find out what is needed for distributed collaborative systems to support such interactions.

Gaver *et al.* (1995) specifically identified limitations on the ability of media spaces to support informal shared awareness. For example, there are discontinuities, or seams, between local and remote scenes in a media space. Based on ethnographic findings, Benford *et al.* (1997) developed a support structure in a collaborative virtual environment, using a task-driven approach.

Much attention has been given to the notion of proximity and its role in mediating informal communication. Proximity is fundamental to structuring and visualising a semantic space for informal communication and social construction of knowledge.

6.1.1 From Proximity to Mutual Awareness

When people are near to each other in the physical world, they may become interested in knowing what others are doing. As the distance between them becomes less, they may start to talk to each other. Proximity-triggered communication mechanisms are essentially based on a similar scenario. They have been adapted in distributed computer environments to deal with the need for mutual awareness and direct communication. Relevant empirical data are yet to be available for us to understand fully the underlying mechanisms that transform the need of mutual awareness into direct interaction and how we can effectively support such transitions in distributed collaborative systems.

A well-known example of a proximity-driven communication triggering mechanism is from SEPIA, a cooperative hypermedia authoring environment (Haake and Wilson, 1992). SEPIA uses three modes to model the degree of interdependency among the participants of a collaborative system. In the independent mode, participants behave as if they are the only user on the system, in the loosely-coupled mode (LC), participants start to maintain mutual awareness to a certain extent, and in the tightly-coupled mode (TC), where participants are fully engaged in interaction with each other.

SEPIA aims to track and facilitate interactions among co-authors. The proximity between co-authors is measured in terms of the distance between their positions in SEPIA's activity spaces. If one user opens a composite node that is currently being used by someone, then these two users will enter a loosely-coupled mode from an independent one. In this case, communication patterns would be strongly shaped by the underlying structure of the activity spaces.

A proximity-triggering mechanism is based on the closeness between people to initiate communication, whereas a problem-drive mechanism, such as Montage (Tang et al., 1994), allows people to communicate as and when a problem arises. Incorporating the two approaches could provide a viable solution for a more flexible environment, that accommodates informal and formal communication with mutual initiation. We are interested in the discourse structure in a virtual environment, based on a semantically enriched spatial model, and the factors that trigger various transitions.

6.1.2 Spatial Metaphors

Spatial metaphors have been increasingly popular in the design of collaborative systems over the past few years. The following description from Tolva (1996) reflects how natural a spatial metaphor can be when describing our way of thinking:

> 'the model of the intersecting sheets of paper – parallel, interpenetrating planes connected by zero-length "worm holes" – is one way of visualizing link-rich text. Physicists call such a thing "multiply connected surfaces"; we call it hypertext.'

> (Tolva, 1996, p. 67)

Kaplan and Moulthrop (1994) have explored some trends in hypermedia towards modelling hypermedia as extended or global spaces. In this approach, nodes and links acquire meaning in relation to the space in which they are deployed. As echoed in the title of their article, 'Where no mind has gone before: ontological design for virtual spaces', they pointed out that familiar metaphors drawn from physics, architecture, and everyday experience have only limited descriptive or explanatory value for this type of space.

The notion of virtual spaces shifts the focus from an external to an internal perspective, and highlights the need for a more sophisticated approach to hyperspace. A hyperspace is more than an architectural model of an information space – it must have its own semantics.

Kaplan and Moulthrop also considered an analogy between the semantic space of hypermedia and the interstellar spaces in science fiction:

'To imagine journeys beyond the solar system, science fiction writers have to invent methods of faster-than-light travel. These inventions often involve discontinuities in the space-time continuum: wormholes, trans-dimensional portals, or the solution most familiar to addicts of American TV, the "warp field effect", in which vessels bend or fold space around themselves. . . . We are concerned here only with the analogy between Roddenberry's famous "final frontier" and another imaginary space, the semantic domain in hypermedia. Both are in a crucial sense elastic – spaces in which dimensional properties like distance and contiguity can be easily annulled.'

Kaplan and Moulthrop highlight the distinctive difference between navigating floating vessels and traveling through spaces in a starship. The spacecraft of Star Trek and other starships move by distorting the space–time continuum. Instead of propelling through a medium, like aircraft or boats, they warp or wrap space around themselves, or teleport themselves. Similar ideas are found in ancient Chinese classic novels: zero-time travel was described as if one can shrink the large distance so that the destination comes to meet the starting point.

Dillon *et al.* (1993) suggest that the precise nature of the representation is less important to workers in the field of interactive technology than the insights any theory or model of navigation provides. They propose that landmarks, routes and surveys should be considered as instantiation of basic knowledge in the design of electronic information spaces. They call for better spatial metrics and metaphors for hypermedia. Kaplan and Moulthrop emphasise that on the one hand, semantic and architectonic spaces cannot be perfectly reconciled, but on the other hand, we should aim for systems that accommodate the two in harmony as well as possible, given the contingent nature of any such harmony.

The appeal of a spatial model is rooted in its simple and intuitive association with our experience in the physical world. Conference rooms, virtual hallways, and virtual cities are examples of the impact of architectural and urban design on electronic worlds. Users feel familiar and comfortable with systems based on such spatial models. From the point of view of a designer, it is a natural choice to build an electronic environment similar to the real world, so that users can easily adopt and transform their interactive behaviour, styles, and patterns, from the physical world into virtual ones.

The use of spatial models in the design of previous collaborative virtual environments has been criticised as over-simplifying the issue of structuring interactive behaviour (Harrison and Dourish, 1996). A natural, stimulating, and collaborative environment needs more than a spatial model alone can adequately provide. People need resources from which they can derive a sense of *context*, to adapt and organise their course of action and conversation.

The development of collaborative virtual environments can be seen as a process of internalising resources in a working environment into an electronic world. Such electronic worlds are designed to support mutual awareness, informal communication, and many other features, and to improve the accessibility of resources which may influence the way people adapt their behaviour in a new environment.

The use of spatial models in previous collaborative virtual environments has been criticised as over-simplifying the issue of structuring, or framing, interactive behaviour. Harrison and Dourish (1996) examined the notions of space and spatial organisation of virtual environments. They called for a re-examination of the role of spatial models in facilitating and structuring social interaction. In fact, they highlighted the critical distinction between space and place, by arguing that it is the notion of place, rather than that of space, which actually frames interactive behaviour.

According to Harrison and Dourish, (1996), designers are looking for a critical property that can facilitate and shape interactive behaviour in a distributed working environment. This critical property, called appropriate behavioural framing, will provide users with a reference framework within which to judge the appropriateness of their behaviour. Harrison and Dourish argued that spatial models are simply not enough for people to adapt their behaviour accordingly. Rather, it is a sense of place and shared understanding about behaviour and action in a specific culture that shapes the way we interact and communicate (Harrison and Dourish, 1996).

Activity theory, rooted in the work of Vygotsky (1962), has attracted much attention from HCI, CSCW, and Information Science. According to activity theory, human cognition is an adaptation to ecological and social environments. More importantly, it is mediated by cultural signs, including languages and tools. Knowledge organisation, information structure, co-operation patterns, language, and communication forms are interrelated with the work of specific communities of people. The individual's information needs, knowledge, and subjective relevance criteria should be seen in a larger context (Hjorland, 1997).

Research in virtual environments, especially textual virtual environments such as MOOs, has addressed the question of how a virtual environment as a medium shapes conversations (Erickson, 1997; Toomey *et al.*, 1998). For example, Erickson (1997) analysed how people communicate in Café Utne, one of the busiest Web conferencing communities on the Internet. Café Utne is built on a metaphor of a place where people come, and find conversations concerning their interests. Erickson found that the social pressures for participation, often found in face-to-face participation, are missing in the virtual discourse medium. He concluded that mutual awareness would be an important factor that may shape the discourse in such virtual environments (Erickson, 1997).

In this chapter, we describe a novel approach to the design of a 3-dimensional virtual environment. We will focus on the role of an enriched spatial metaphor, in which the underlying semantics of a subject domain are reflected through the structure of the virtual environment. We show that this approach offers a framework that naturally unifies spatial models, semantic structures, and social interactive behaviour within the virtual environment. By offering users a wider range of choices in sharing and experiencing this semantically organised virtual place, this approach has both theoretical and practical implications for bringing media spaces and collaborative virtual environments closer.

6.1.3 Structuration

The experience from earlier media spaces suggests that a media space evolves as it is used by people. In Gidden's theory (Giddens, 1984), this process is called structuration. We will discuss further the role of a context in understanding interactive behaviour.

6.1.4 Gidden's Theory

The theory of structuration (Giddens, 1984) focuses on the interdependent relationship between human action and social structure. Structures are composed of *rules* and *resources*. These rules and resources provide contextual constraints that individuals draw upon when acting and interacting. The interplay between structure and action produces and reproduces social systems. To some extent, this is what has been experienced in the evolution of media spaces, such as the Palo Alta-Portland link (Bly *et al.*, 1993).

Interactionism emphasises the *social* impact on the creation and the interpretation of meanings, in contrast to *objective* meanings of reality (Kling, 1980) upheld by system rationalists. The nature of the collaboration, according to interactionism, is that people are establishing a mutual understanding of meanings and processes to be dealt with in a particular context. Individuals' views of the world are situational in nature. The term 'infrastructure' refers to resources, procedures, and institutionalised values for providing these supporting resources, including organisational plans, definitions of roles, and documentation.

6.1.5 Collaborative Virtual Environments

According to Benford *et al.* (1997), 'collaborative virtual environments aim to provide support for co-operation by placing users within a shared virtual space that affords particular forms of co-operation'. It becomes possible, in such environments, to study interrelationships between documents, mutual awareness, co-ordination, and co-operation. In VR-VIBE (Benford *et al.*, 1995), the semantic documents are visualised with reference to users' queries, or 'points of interest' (POIs), such that the spatial position of a document icon reflects the relevance of a document to different queries.

Media spaces are distributed electronic environments designed for supporting both the social and task-oriented aspects of collaborative work. The principal design rationale is 'that work is fundamentally social' (Bly *et al.*, 1993). For geographically distributed groups, it is particularly important not to overlook the role of informal interaction (Bly *et al.*, 1993).

We are interested in a semantically organised virtual space, and how such spatial organisation shapes the cognition, interpretation, and the interaction of users. We also need to compare our approach with the valuable lessons learned from the use of previous media spaces, and how people work in distributed groups. We would like to explore how information visualisation and semantic space modelling techniques can be utilised in the design of new media spaces, and more generally, whether media spaces and collaborative virtual environments work in harmony, in order to augment our working environments more effectively.

MASSIVE (Greenhalgh and Benford, 1995) is a well-known virtual space for distributed multi-user interaction. It uses a spatial model of interaction. Participants' awareness of each other, and opportunities for interaction, are supported through spatial extensions of their presence – 'aura', attention – 'focus', and influence – 'nimbus'. These mechanisms have been designed using real-world patterns of awareness and interaction in these virtual spaces.

MASSIVE is a collaborative virtual environment designed for teleconferencing (Greenhalgh and Benford, 1995). Multiple users may use the system simultaneously to communicate using arbitrary combinations of media, especially audio, graphics, and text, over computer networks. The MASSIVE system is built on a spatial model, incorporating a fundamental concept of awareness. Users' positions and orientations with reference to other users are represented on the basis of this spatial model.

The ultimate goal of a media space is to help people to transcend the limits of the physical world, and work harmoniously and productively. Informal communication has been recognised as one of the most crucial elements in successful collaborative work. A challenging issue in the design of collaborative environments that support informal communication has been to facilitate seamless transitions from accessing information individually to engaging social interaction. The use of spatial models in previous collaborative virtual environments has been criticised as over-simplifying the issue of structuring interactive behaviour. In this chapter, we describe a novel approach to the design of a 3-dimensional virtual environment, focusing on the role of an enriched spatial metaphor, in which the underlying semantics of a subject domain are reflected through the structure of the virtual environment. We show that this approach offers a framework that naturally unifies spatial models, semantic structures, and social interactive behaviour within the virtual environment. By offering users a wider range of choices in sharing and experiencing this semantically organised virtual place, this approach has both theoretical and practical implications on the design of media spaces.

The Distributed Interactive Virtual Environment (DIVE) is an Internet-based multi-user VR system (Carlsson and Hagsand, 1993). DIVE supports the development of virtual environments, user interfaces and applications, based on shared 3D synthetic environments. It is especially tuned to multi-user applications, where several networked participants interact over a network.

Participants navigate in 3D space, and interact with other users and applications. It is integrated with the WWW. DIVE reads and exports VRML 1.0 and several other 3D formats, and its applications and activities include virtual battlefields, spatial models of interaction, virtual agents, real-world robot control, and multi-modal interaction.

6.2 Information Spaces and Social Spaces

Virtual environments incorporate a broad range of information and communication systems for both individual and social use. These systems are often characterised by the use of virtual reality, multimedia, 3-dimensional graphics, computer networks, and various communication facilities. Virtual environments can be categorised along two dimensions concerning the role of a spatial

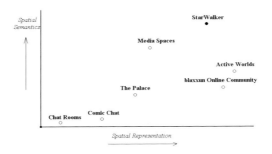

Figure 6.2   The role of a spatial metaphor.

metaphor: spatial representation and spatial semantics. Spatial representation refers to the use of textual, graphical, multimedia, or virtual reality. Spatial semantics refers to the extent to which the meaning of spatial configuration is related to the information needs of users (see Fig. 6.2).

Figure 6.2 illustrates the tension between spatial configurations and the semantics of such configurations in several representative virtual environments. For example, in traditional chat rooms, little spatial configuration is involved. As a result, its rating on the semantic dimension is low. The Palace, inherits the meaning of places in the physical world, using photo-realistic images to convey its spatial organisation, such as a bar or the beach. The design and use of these virtual environments will be described further. Although media spaces and collaborative virtual environments had little overlap in terms of their evolution until recently, they do have some profound connections. In fact, they can be seen as two different approaches to the same problem: to facilitate informal collaboration between people separated by geographical distance. Therefore, media spaces are considered to be of considerable significance to the design of new virtual environments.

6.2.1 Media Spaces

Pioneering media spaces are typically equipped with video and audio channels connecting groups of people across geographically separated sites. Media spaces integrate video, audio, and computer media to help individuals and groups to work together, despite being spatially and temporally distributed (Mantei *et al.*, 1991). Famous media spaces include Xerox's Palo Alto-Portland link (Bly *et al.*, 1993), CAVECAT (Mantei *et al.*, 1991), and Virtual Windows (Gaver *et al.*, 1995).

The evolution of a media space has been characterised by the interplay between the design and how people actually use it. A variety of metaphors have been used in the design to help users to interact and communicate. For example, in order to provide a sense of proximity for distributed groups, Tang *et al.* (1994) developed a media space called Montage, where people can make momentary, reciprocal 'glances' among networked workstations. This is a lightweight approach: when people have encountered problems, they can quickly and easily find out whether colleagues who might be able to help are available.

Bly *et al.* (1993) have grouped distinguishing characteristics of media space design into three major points of reference: spatial, object, and figural. The notion of media space is associated with a mapping from abstract electronic space to abstract physical space. Spatial models and metaphors have been increasingly popular in collaborative systems. Many media-space systems are designed to reflect the structure of the physical world. Offices, hallways, conference rooms, and design studios have frequently appeared in media spaces and collaborative virtual environments using spatial metaphors.

Media spaces and collaborative virtual environments have some subtle but fundamental differences. For example, media spaces normally involve both real and virtual worlds, known as hybrid spaces (Harrison and Dourish, 1996), whereas a virtual environment gives users the freedom to do things that might be impossible in a real world setting. The power of information visualisation techniques can largely strengthen and augment users' abilities.

6.2.2 Active Worlds

Active Worlds,[1] presented by the Circle of Fire, is a generic platform for creating and exploring virtual worlds. Registered users can build their own properties as well as visit gardens, parks, and houses built by others. There are hundreds of virtual worlds in Active Worlds, ranging from the Yellowstone National Park to Mars, and the system is featured in Damer's book on avatars (1998). Figure 6.3 shows a scene from Active Worlds. People's avatars gathered around the ground zero – the entry point to the virtual world, and users can chat with other visitors to the virtual world using a textual chat dialogue window.

Figure 6.3   A naturalistic landscape in Active Worlds (The Circle of Fire).

[1]http://www.activeworlds.com/

Figure 6.4   Online Communities (the Black Sun Interactive).

6.2.3 Online Communities

A rival virtual world platform is provided by *blaxxun interactive*. Its online community[2] accommodates 3D interactive VRML worlds, based on a client-server architecture on the Internet. The online community client browser is a VRML plug-in for both Netscape and Internet Explorer. *blaxxun*'s VRML browser is one of the few VRML browsers that work with both VRML 2.0 and 1.0 worlds. The *blaxxun* community server allows users to build and support their own 3D interactive VRML worlds. One major advantage of using VRML in online community is that it allows users to integrate existing VRML worlds into a multi-user virtual environment. Chat is supported by textual dialogue windows on the client browser.

The spatial metaphor is often intended to resemble the physical world. Figure 6.4 is a screenshot of a scene near to the ground zero, i.e. the entry point, of the Activity World. This virtual world is organised on an abstract spatial model. However, chatting and dialoguing in this type of virtual world did not seem to develop into deeper and more engaging conversations, despite the fact that engaging conversations do arise in chat rooms. Can we facilitate and promote the transition from an informal chat to a productive conversation through the design of a virtual environment?

6.2.4 The Palace

The Palace[3] is one of the earliest graphic online environments. It uses photo-realistic images as the background to chat rooms, known as palaces, which take the form of environments such as a bar, a beach, or a museum. Users can create their own multimedia palaces, as well as explore existing ones. Visitors to a

[2]http://www.blaxxun.com/community/
[3]http://www.thepalace.com/

Figure 6.5   A meeting place in The Palace.

palace are represented as graphic characters, known as avatars. They are visible to everyone in the same palace. The Palace supports text-based chats. Figure 6.5 is a screenshot of The Palace. Some people use photographs as their avatars, while others use comic figures. Temporary visitors have the simplest avatars. Speakers' words appear in a talk balloon next to their avatars. Avatars can move around within chat rooms on a 2-dimensional plane (Fig. 6.6).

Figure 6.7 shows a scene from The Palace, at a place called Memorial Park. CC entered the Memorial Park. Zoe arrived later and said hello to CC.

The Palace uses scenery photographs as the background of a virtual place. QuickTime VR (Chen, 1995) is an interesting work done at Apple, which

Figure 6.6   Floating in Harry's Bar (The Palace).

Figure 6.7   Visiting the Memorial Park at The Palace.

Figure 6.8   Greetings in the Memorial Park at The Palace.

provides an image-based virtual environment. The scene is based on images of a place in the real world.

There are Web sites where users can choose their own avatars.[4] Similar to conventional search engines, the query to the avatar database specifies which avatars one would need. The result is a group of avatars that match the initial requirements.

---

[4]http://www.avnet.co.uk/devalin/guild/index.html

6.2.5 Gopher VR

Gopher VR – a spatial interface to GopherSpace – was developed to create a publicly accessible 3D space (McCahill and Erickson, 1995). Thomas Erickson's publication list[5] includes additional interesting articles about the design of Gopher VR.

The design of Gopher VR focuses particularly on the design issues raised by 3D spatial interfaces. Most 3D spatial interfaces to information spaces are in research laboratories. Gopher VR aims to enable a broad range of people to access a large public information space. Two potential advantages of 3D interfaces are specifically pursued in the design of Gopher VR: compact and natural 3D representations of high dimensional information and meta-information, and, in the long run, use of the information space as a social space, with 3D serving as a natural framework for supporting social interaction (Erickson, 1993).

The design of Gopher VR is also driven by problems identified with the existing Gopher user interface. Erickson lists the following problems in (McCahill and Erickson, 1995):

The 'Lost-in-Space' problem: users may feel lost in their navigation, and have difficulty remembering where they found an interesting article. The 'lost-in-hyperspace' problem is well known in hypermedia. This problem is due in part to the absence of any global representation of the information structure, and in part to the path followed by a user often being invisible for them to trace back. Users need an overview of Gopher Space, within which they can see their locations and the paths they have followed.

The grouping problem: within a directory, it is difficult to show relationships between items represented in a linear list. A similar problem is seen in the lists of results generated by search engines. The results are typically sorted by document-query relevance, but the user interface does not convey their relative relevance effectively. Ideally, both relevance to the search query and 'closeness' to other documents should be clear to the user at a glance.

The browsing problem: it is difficult to browse, because the names of documents reflect so little of their content. The user has to open the document – often a time consuming process in itself – and read the document. Users need to see more information about the content of a document, without there being so much that they are unable to compare different documents.

In addition to solving these problems, there are a number of intriguing prospects which a new interface should consider:

Interaction traces: users browsing a large information space could benefit from the activities of previous visitors. For example, users are often interested in knowing about the relative popularity of documents, as judged by the frequency with which they are viewed or copied. The idea behind interaction traces is to reflect this in the visual appearance of the document's icon. Researchers have explored ways in which visible representations of computational objects can reflect the ways in which users have interacted with them, for example, 'read wear' and 'edit wear' (Hill *et al.*, 1992; Hill *et al.*, 1995).

---

[5]http://www.pliant.org/personal/Tom_Erickson/TomsPubs.html

Providing a sense of place by customisation: Gopher Space is generic: any gopher directory looks like all the others, regardless of where it is or what it contains. Gopher VR wants to reflect its contents, and something about those who construct it and maintain it. As information spaces develop their own sense of place, it seems likely that users will begin to recognise places and regions; and, while users may still get lost, they may begin to develop a sense for where they're lost (McCahill and Erickson, 1995).

Transforming information spaces into social spaces: the most natural way for obtaining information is to ask someone else. In fact, sometimes people search for documents so that they can find out about their authors, to whom they then direct their queries (Erickson and Salomon, 1991). Much information access is part of a larger, often collaborative task: people seek information because they are trying to solve a problem, test a theory, understand a concept, or communicate their understanding to others. All this suggests that information access should not be isolated from other activities.

The increasing popularity of MUDs for supporting conversation, teaching, and other group activities, demonstrates that virtual spaces – even those that are purely textual – can serve as frameworks for a broad range of collaborative activities (Curtis and Nichols, 1993; Dieberger, 1997; Erickson, 1993, 1996; 1997). The design of Gopher VR is to explore expanding Gopher Space into a social space supporting a broad range of activities that complement information browsing and access.

Figure 6.9 shows the results of a search as a spiral in Gopher VR. The spiral has a family resemblance to the circular arrangement: it defines an enclosed area with a centre point. Furthermore, the open and dynamic shape of the spiral reflects the transitory nature of most queries. A spiral provides a natural ordering of search results. The more relevant the documents, the closer they are to the root of the spiral. A search that returns a large number of very relevant documents will have a tightly coiled spiral, whereas one with few relevant items will have a very loose spiral.

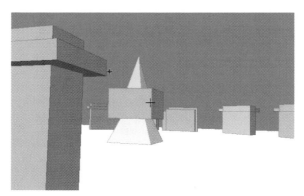

Figure 6.9   GopherVR: The approach to the new neighbourhood allows the user to get a sense of the overall arrangement in the neighbourhood. (Reprinted with permission of Thomas Erickson).

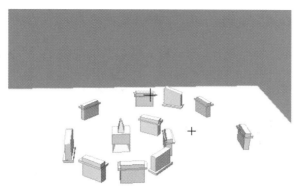

Figure 6.10   Search results are displayed in a spiral pattern in GopherVR. (Reprinted with permission of Thomas Erickson).

6.2.6 VR-VIBE

VR-VIBE was developed at Nottingham University, UK (Benford *et al.*, 1995). It was designed to support the co-operative browsing and filtering of large document stores. VR-VIBE extends an information visualisation system – VIBE – into three dimensions. The essence of VR-VIBE is that multiple users can explore the results of applying several simultaneous queries to a corpus of documents. Co-operative browsing is supported by directly embodying users, and providing them with the ability to interact over live audio connections, and to attach brief textual annotations to individual documents.

Users specify keywords that they wish to use to generate the visualisation, and place these keywords in 3D-space. Representations of the documents are then displayed in the space, according to how relevant each document is to each of the keywords. The relevance is based on a simple keyword-matching model. The position of a document to a given keyword is proportional to the relative importance of the keyword to the document (see Fig. 6.11).

VR-VIBE was used in an example of searching a CSCW bibliography of 1581 entries and five keywords; some other users browsing the information space were also visible. Only documents with sufficiently high relevance ratings are displayed; less relevant documents are not displayed.

6.3 The *StarWalker* Virtual Environment

The StarWalker virtual environment is designed to maximise the role of implicit semantic structures in the structuration process of social activities within a virtual environment (Chen *et al.*, 1999). The principle design rationale is that if the virtual environment can reflect the underlying semantic structure of an abstract information space, then users may develop more engaging social interactions.

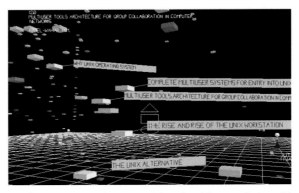

Figure 6.11   3D information space in VR-VIBE (reprinted by permission of Steve Benford).

As noted by Harrison and Dourish in (1996), what distinguishes a space and a place is whether people can derive various contextual cues from the resources available. The appropriateness of interactive behaviour in a particular multi-user virtual environment is subject to the interpretation of individual participants. Such interpretation may be regarded as a type of social construction of knowledge (Hjorland, 1997). It is such collective sense-making that actually transforms a space into a place. Dieberger (1997) referred to the construction of such a sense of a place and how it shapes the behaviour of users in a MOO[6] environment as social connotation.

6.3.1 The Background

StarWalker is a multiple user, domain-specific, three-dimensional virtual environment. People can meet and talk in this virtual environment, with direct reference to the scholarly literature of a specific subject domain. Users can explore domain-specific knowledge structures as a virtual reality world.

The first prototype of the StarWalker virtual environment is based on the semantic space extracted from the ACM SIGCHI conference proceedings (1995–1997). More recently, spatial models of other semantic spaces have been generated and become available for the StarWalker virtual environment, for example, the ACM Hypertext conference proceedings (1987–1998) (Chen, 1999; Chen and Carr, 1999; Chen and Czerwinski, 1998).

The StarWalker virtual environment is based on a client-server architecture, to maintain communication and coordination among multiple users. The design emphasises that a virtual environment must integrate semantic, spatial, and social structures in order to foster social interaction in a scholarly environment.

The distribution of red vertical search bars will converge into a smaller and smaller area if the search query becomes more and more approximate to the entire vocabulary used in the modelling process of the semantic space (Fig. 6.12).

---

[6]MOO: Multiuser Object-Oriented.

Figure 6.12   A single-user virtual world in which results of a search are displayed dynamically over a global structure.

6.3.2 Construction

A key element of the StarWalker virtual environment is the visualisation of an abstract information space. The visualisation highlights the underlying semantic structure associated with the information space, derived using latent semantic indexing and Pathfinder techniques (see Figs. 6.22 and 6.23).

This unique approach is a natural integration of latent semantic indexing (LSI) and Pathfinder network scaling (Chen, 1998a, b; Chen and Czerwinski, 1998). The latent semantic space is modelled and simplified as a Pathfinder network. The resultant Pathfinder network becomes the blueprint of a virtual reality scene in VRML. These virtual reality models can be integrated into the design of a user interface, accessible through our familiar Web browsers. As with other virtual worlds, users are able to explore the information space in a variety of intuitive ways, such as walking, flying, and rotating.

A significant part of the work is a combination of the visualisation of an abstract information space with a multi-user chat environment. The combined virtual environment presents a new metaphor of social interaction. Multiple users can explore the same semantic space. Furthermore, the spatial and semantic implications of the new metaphor provide a concrete test bed in which one can observe and make sense of the dynamics of social interaction, especially social navigation. Users can not only see how others navigate in a three-dimensional virtual world, but also talk to them, using multi-user chat facilities.

The diagram in Fig. 6.13 illustrates the overall architecture of the StarWalker virtual environment. Not surprisingly, the Web is the major source of data. Domain specific corpuses are selected from the ACM Digital Library, which contains more than 15,000 scientific articles published by the ACM. In particular, our focus is on two subject domains: human-computer interaction (HCI) and hypertext. Two examples demonstrate how the underlying structures can be derived and represented as the backbone of the StarWalker virtual environment.

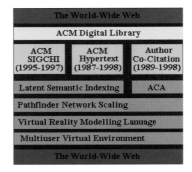

Figure 6.13   The architecture of the StarWalker virtual environment.

The first example derives content-based information structures. These structures are extracted using latent semantic indexing and Pathfinder network scaling techniques. The result is a network of documents linked according to the strongest semantic relationships. The second example derives reference-based information structures. Author co-citation analysis generates the strengths between each pair of authors who have published in the field. Pathfinder network scaling is also used in generating a network of authors. These associative networks are rendered in VRML, which are then embedded as a part of a multi-user virtual environment, so that it can be accessed from the WWW.

Currently, the initial prototype of the StarWalker virtual environment relies on the blaxxun's online community client-server architecture. Users with the blaxxun's online community client browser, freely available from http://www.blaxxun.com/, are able to access the StarWalker virtual environment on the Internet (Fig. 6.16). The blaxxun online community client browser supports a text-based chat facility, along with a virtual reality scene written in VRML. Many of these virtual worlds are seamlessly integrated with the World-Wide Web (WWW). Virtual worlds provide a convenient gateway to access documents on the Web. The user can 'beam' to an avatar, and invite the other person for a private chat. Of course, one may simply watch how other people (in their avatars) travel through semantic space and how they interact with each other.

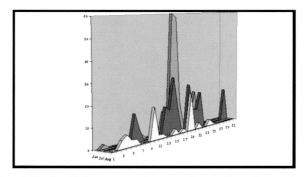

Figure 6.14   StarWalker accessed by external users (June–August, 1998).

Figure 6.15 blaxxun interactives provide various avatars for visitors to choose.

Figure 6.14 shows the access to StarWalker from external users in three consecutive months. Access patterns appear to be clustered, which is probably due to the snowball effect – people tend to visit a virtual world if they can see a crowd already there. A thorough analysis of access logs may reveal predominant patterns of its use in further detail.

Figure 6.16 is a screenshot of the StarWalker client user interface. The semantic model in the background is based on a semantic space derived from the

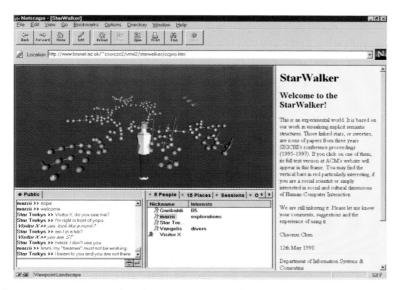

Figure 6.16 Users can explore the semantic space and interact with others in StarWalker.

ACM SIGCHI proceedings. On arrival, users will see the landscape scene in front of them. The night sky colour implies that this is an unlimited space – users can go wherever they like.

The underlying semantic structure is rendered as a star constellation. It is tempting for users to question the nature of the model, the meaning of the links, and why they are placed in a shared virtual environment. In fact, these have been the most frequently asked questions when a new visitor arrives in the StarWalker. Do these questions lead to more specific questions about the spatial model and, more importantly, the underlying subject domain. The design of StarWalker aims to provide a virtual environment where conversations and other social interaction can be triggered by the semantic implication of a spatial metaphor.

In fact, visitors frequently asked about the semantic structure embedded in the StarWalker virtual environment, instead of the overall spatial metaphor. In our experience, StarWalker has given users a strong feeling that it is considerably different from other virtual worlds that they have visited – most of them are based on buildings, cities, and other familiar landscapes.

The StarWalker virtual environment introduces new social structures appropriate to a specific online community. The design principle is that if a virtual environment reflects the knowledge structure of a subject domain, it will shape the structure of social interaction to a considerable extent. A particularly interesting area is the development of semantically organised virtual environments where people can not only chat, but also develop deep conversations about specific subjects.

6.3.3 The User Interface

Users visiting the StarWalker virtual environment are able to perform the following tasks:

- talk in public or private,
- walk or fly through the virtual world,
- beam to other avatars,
- reposition to a pre-defined viewpoint in the virtual world,
- view the full text version of a paper in HTML,
- move to other virtual worlds,
- search (restricted access at the moment).

Upon entering the virtual world, the visitor will see a landscape view of the semantic structure (see Fig. 6.17). There are seven viewpoints currently available for users to change their perspectives, including an overview, several landscape views from various directions, and a galaxy view to reinforce the new paradigm of interaction.

Users are able to watch the movement of the avatars of other users. Because the topology is semantically significant, the movement of avatars may also be meaningful. In Fig. 6.18, we can see an avatar, a car, approaching the area with a number of landmark poles. Such awareness could be useful; for example, the person is probably interested in topics discussed by papers in that area.

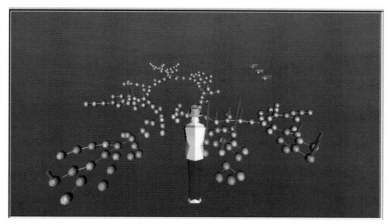

Figure 6.17   This is the scene at the entry point to the virtual environment.

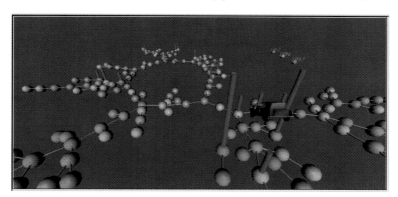

Figure 6.18   A visitor, with an avatar of a car, flying through the virtual galaxy.

6.3.4 Social Navigation

We have all seen crowds of people gathered at scenery viewpoints, around popular exhibits in a museum, or in front of a classic painting in a gallery. Such clustering behaviour of like-minded people is a common source of reference for judging the value of a place or a point of interest. Social navigation is a counterpart of such referencing strategies and searching heuristics in abstract information spaces. Social navigation has drawn the attention of researchers from a diverse range of interests (Dieberger, 1997; Dourish and Chalmers, 1994; Erickson, 1996, 1997; Harrison and Dourish, 1996; Jeffrey and Mark, 1998; Pedersen and Sokoler, 1997).

To make social navigation possible, one needs not only a virtual place where people can meet and talk, but also a virtual place that has meanings and values, so that people can associate themselves with various places accordingly. In StarWalker, since the latent semantic structure is reflected in the spatial configuration of the virtual environment, the positioning, movement, and

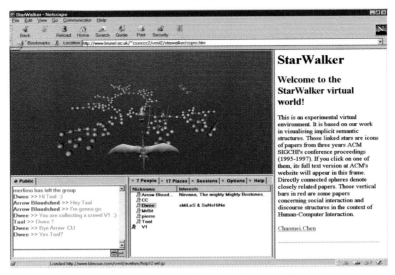

Figure 6.19 Seven people visiting the StarWalker.

groupings of avatars in such space becomes significant and meaningful to the peer participants at the time. Mutual awareness in such environments becomes semantically interpretable. Browsing semantics of concurrent users become visible and meaningful.

The trajectory of an avatar can reflect the nature of interaction between a user and the virtual environment. It is interesting to see that the movement of avatars seems to be associated with the landmarks in the scene, i.e. the vertical red poles, which may lead to more chances for avatars to *meet* each other.

Figures 6.20–6.22 are three consecutive snapshots taken from the StarWalker client screen. Upon arrival, the user will face the landscape model. Going forward is a natural step: it brings the user closer to the model. Therefore, avatars seem to

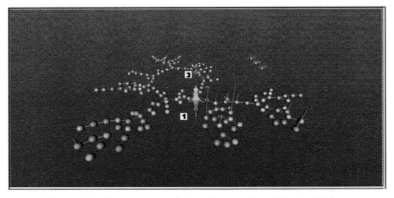

Figure 6.20 Two avatars exploring the central circle in StarWalker.

Figure 6.21 More avatars arrive in StarWalker.

follow an invisible avenue. In the second snapshot, more avatars arrive in StarWalker, and their positions clearly reflect their initial choice. In the third snapshot, avatars spread out to explore various locations, but mainly around the areas with distinctive landmarks – the red, spiky search bars.

Embedding information visualisation into an organising spatial model introduces a number of advantages that enrich the virtual environment. New types of interactive behaviour become appropriate and meaningful. For example, in Fig. 6.23, the spatial model visualises the semantic space, based on all the papers published in the proceedings of ACM conferences on Hypertext between 1987 and 1998.

This semantic world not only provides a valuable gateway to access a large amount of scholarly articles in the same subject domain, but also presents users with an initial cognitive map that they can extend, modify, and transform, as they learn more about the subject domain. In other words, the semantic world is more than a tool for information retrieval, it can support learning and knowledge management.

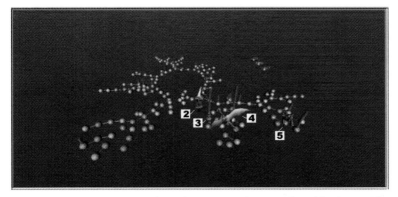

Figure 6.22 Positioning, movement, and social groupings of avatars, shaped by the spatial-semantic backdrop within StarWalker.

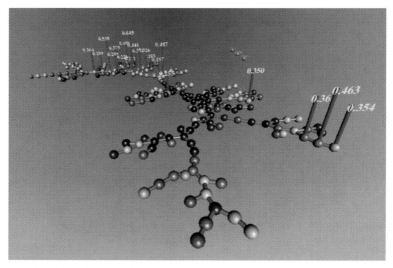

Figure 6.23 Spatial and temporal dimensions of StarWalker in the atlas of ACM Hypertext Conference Literature (1987–1998).

In the spatial model shown in Fig. 6.23, the global latent semantic structure is derived from LSI and Pathfinder, as described earlier. It is superimposed by the result of a search in LSI, using the terms 'spatial', 'visualisation', and 'map'. This single scene includes papers published over nine conferences in the series. They are colour encoded: darker ones indicate papers published in the earlier years of the series, and lighter ones from more recent conferences. In this domain map, one can examine how emerging themes are related to classic ones over a decade-long span. For example, in Fig. 6.23, we can see two major clusters regarding research in spatial hypertext and visualisation: one cluster of papers may represent a computational approach to the broad theme, and the other cluster represents the user-centred approach. Both approaches use spatial metaphors, but the underlying methodologies and interpretations of resultant spatial models are different. By examining these types of patterns, collaboratively as well as individually, we may use collaborative virtual environments such as StarWalker as a forum to stimulate and foster social interaction at a deeper level.

It is significant that a virtual environment should enable users to adapt the virtual space according to their own interests. Users should be able to personalise a sub-space, and re-structure it to meet their own needs. For example, researchers can use their own publications to extract related papers in the shared environment. The persistent nature of StarWalker allows people to access such resources as an integral part of their distributed collaborative environment. In this way, a media space and a collaborative virtual environment can be merged and integrated. Users can explore and share their interpretation of knowledge structures more effectively.

6.4 Social Interaction in StarWalker

In order to find out special characteristics of social interaction in the virtual world of StarWalker, we include the following examples of virtual meetings on topics specifically related to the design of StarWalker to topics inspired by the metaphor of the StarWalker. In this chapter, we focus on two aspects of social interaction within the virtual world:

- the dynamics of the discourse;
- a mutual coupling between the discourse and the spatial structure of the virtual world.

The analysis of the dynamics of the discourse is largely based on the interaction process analysis (IPA), which tracks down transitions between task-oriented and socioemotional episodes in face-to-face meetings of small groups. We need to find out how conversations in a virtual world such as StarWalker differ from conversations in the real world, or in other virtual worlds. If the IPM model can characterise the discourse of an engaging and balanced conversation, then a balanced discourse structure of a virtual meeting may lead to insights into how engaging conversations differ from casual and passing conversations. Furthermore, we would like to find out how conversations are related to the spatial structure of the virtual world, in particular, the influence of the constellation metaphor on perspectives that people choose to adopt in their conversations.

6.4.1 Contextualisation Cues and Mutual Coupling

Several methodologies from sociology, anthropology, and linguistics are potentially useful for exploring the structure of social interaction, and how it reflects the influence of a meaningful context. Two concepts are particularly concerned with structures of social contexts: the concept of *contextualisation cues* from linguistics (Gumperz, 1982) and the concept of *frames* from sociology (Goffman, 1974). The following review is partially based on (Drew and Heritage, 1992).

Sociolinguistics had initially treated context in terms of the social attributes speakers bring to talk – for example, age, class, ethnicity, gender, geographical region, and other relationships. Studies of data from natural settings have shown that the relevance of these attributes depended upon the particular setting in which the talk occurred, and also upon the particular speech activities or tasks speakers were engaged in within those settings.

The dynamic nature of social contexts and the importance of linguistic details in evoking them, have been studied in Gumperz (1982). He shows that any aspect of linguistic behaviour may function as a contextualisation cue, including lexical, phonological, and syntactic choices, together with the use of particular codes, dialects, or styles. These contextualisation cues indicate which aspects of the social context are relevant in interpreting what a speaker means. By indicating significant aspects of the social context, contextualisation cues enable people to make inferences about each other's communicative intentions and goals.

The notion of contextualisation cues offered an important analytical way to grasp the relationship between language use and speakers' orientations to context and inference making. There is a significant similarity between the linguistic concept of contextualisation cues as outlined by Gumperz (1982), and the sociological concept of frames developed by Goffman (1974). The notion of frames focuses on the definition which participants give to their current social activity – to what is going on, what the situation is, and the roles which the participants adopt within it. These concepts both relate specific linguistic options to the social activity in which language is being engaged.

Conversation analysis (CA) is one of the most influential analytical tools in the study of talk-in-context (Drew and Heritage, 1992). It focuses on the contextual sensitivity of language use in everyday conversations. CA has been frequently used in the study of ordinary talk between people in a wide variety of social relations and contexts. The combination of virtual environments and online discussion facilities in our approach enables researchers to study discourse structures in a new environment. We will analyse dialogues in our virtual environment using a number of analytical techniques, including conversation analysis.

The organisation principle of our shared three-dimensional semantic space is based on an enriched spatial model. The intention is to provide additional resources that stimulate participants to question, interpret, and discuss the meaning of the underlying spatial metaphor. The spatial model therefore invites people to discuss their own understanding of the semantic structure, and of the implications of the presence of such a structure on the appropriateness of interactive behaviour and discourse structures.

6.4.2 Social Episodes

The study of social episodes has been strongly influenced by the landmark work of Forgas over the last two decades, notably Forgas (1979) and Forgas *et al.*, (1984). The strong influence is reflected in more recent studies of social episodes and social cognition, such as Rooney and Schmelkin (1996). A distinguishing significance of the work of Forgas is that it has established an effective way of studying a wide variety of aspects of the so-called social episodes, based on multidimensional scaling techniques. A key focus of such analytical studies is on what people perceive, and how they interpret what they see of complex social, cultural, and ecological activities.

The reasons for introducing the study of social episodes here are twofold. First, social episodes are traditionally studied in real-world behaviour settings. We knew little about social episodes in a virtual environment until relatively recently, despite the fact that many virtual environments are based on real-world settings and scenarios. There is a wide spectrum of virtual environments in which the dynamics and structures of social episodes are likely to be different, but associated with what people do in the real world. The study of social episodes, therefore, is a potentially valuable source of knowledge for the design of virtual environments, and for the understanding of social interaction in new settings.

The second reason is the need for effective analytical and modelling methodologies that are easy to understand and which can be adopted by researchers and practitioners who might not have experiences in social psychology. There are some intrinsic connections between techniques in the multidimensional scaling family and the visualisation techniques that we have described earlier in this book.

The term 'social episodes' is used in a number of different senses in many areas of social science, such as sociology, social psychology and linguistics. What is common among these difference uses is that 'episode' always refers to a unit of social interaction. Similar concepts of a unit of social interaction include a 'situation', an 'encounter', or even a 'performance'. Episodes are the smaller building blocks of larger and more complex social situations. A dinner party, as a social situation, can be divided into a number of social episodes, such as arrival and greetings, drink and chat before dinner, and the dinner (Argyle, 1976). The problem with such perspectives is that situations and episodes may not always be clearly distinguished consistently.

Alternatively, the term 'episode' is also regarded as a generic label of goal-directed recurring interaction sequences with a culturally determined meaning. It is argued that the study of formal, explicitly regulated, episodes may provide the clue to the understanding of naturalistic episodes.

In the study of social episodes, environments are distinguished as macro- and micro-environments. In a macro-environment, the scene is usually landscape, streets, and whole institutions, whereas a micro-environment typically involves a room, the equipment of a room, or a shop. Canter and his colleagues explored the relationship between the person and the environment in a series of studies (Canter et al., 1974; Canter et al., 1985). The study of social episodes in a virtual environment seems likely to be a fruitful area of research, which may lead to useful insights into the role of abstract information spaces in stimulating and fostering social interaction.

6.4.3 Meeting With a Domain Expert

The first analysis of discourse structures is based on a virtual meeting between the first author and a domain expert in distributed virtual environment systems. The domain expert was invited to join the session from a remote site. The meeting lasted about an hour and half in a private mode – other visitors to the virtual world could not take part in the meeting. The analysis focuses on the following two questions:

1. How did the discourse proceed alternatively between task-oriented and socioemotional episodes in the virtual meeting?
2. Were these changes triggered by the spatial structure of the virtual world?

In the following transcript, speaker A denotes the author, and speaker B denotes the domain expert.

6.4.4 Co-ordinated Movements

As noted in Bowers et al., (1997), users in embodied virtual environments were found to co-ordinate their avatars so that they could see each other in the conversation. Similar movements and adjustments were also found in our virtual meeting: the two users moved about their avatars until they could see each other:

A: Hello?
B: Hi there – where did you go?
A: I was facing the world.
B: Ah – so its probably behind me now?

This episode suggests that there is a strong connection between users and the positions of their avatars in the virtual world. In many virtual worlds, it is common to see the following dialogue:

A: Is there any way to beam to an object here?
B: No – you would have to set a viewpoint in the VRML world.

Users in the virtual world are able to seek instant help from each other.

6.4.5 Transitions Between Episodes

According to Bales' IPA model, a face-to-face small group meeting tends to switch between task-oriented episodes and socioemotional ones. In several cases, a transition from a task-oriented episode to a socioemotional one can be clearly identified.

A: I probably should set a meeting point in the central circle.
B: Yes and some images for the sides, top and bottom to help orientation.
A: Good points.
B: I wrote about that in my paper for the VR journal.
A: I saw your ad for a Ph.D. a while ago – very interesting.
B: Thanks – we've found a student too.

The focus of the conversation smoothly drifts from specific design options to a wider, social, and institutional point of view. The following socioemotional episode highlights a photo-taking event in the virtual world, and a consequence of the overlapped 'talk' towards the end.

A: Can you move to the highest red bar?
B: I'll try . . .
A: I'd like to take a photo of you in the virtual world.
B: Okay, I'm next to one of the tall, red bars.
A: See you now.
B: I'm saying 'cheese'.
A: Click.
B: I hope you got my good side.
A: The scale of the world looks too big.
B: I need to take some pictures too, for a poster session.

A: The radius of a sphere is 4 meters . . .
B: Also, is the data spread in the vertical plane?
A: Okay, where do want me to stand?
B: For the photo – its in a different world.
B: I might ask you to volunteer another time.

Two strands emerged after the 'photo' was taken in the virtual world. (Line 8) – speaker A started to talk about technical details of the design; (Line 9) – indicating a transition back to a task-oriented episode, while speaker B continued the original theme about taking pictures in virtual worlds (Line 10). The development of parallel strands is mainly due to the delay in receiving the text from the remote server. This is a known problem with textual-based virtual worlds. Higher-quality audio and video communication channels help to alleviate this, such as NetMeeting and CuSeeMe. The snapshot in the virtual meeting is shown in Fig. 6.24, in which speaker B was standing at the foot of a very tall red pole.

The next episode is an example of a *Social–Task* transition, which was proceeded by talks about research systems and their developers. A task-oriented episode was clearly marked by a specific technical question from speaker B as follows:

A: Yes, I am not good at people's names.
B: Okay, can you tell me what the semantic relationship is between the balls in the scene?

This question contains three definite references to the spatial structure visualised in the virtual world: *the* semantic relationship, *the* balls, and *the* scene. The scene and the visualised structure were shared between the two speakers within the virtual world. A similar question would have been much longer and more complex, if the spatial structure was not available to the speakers. The virtual

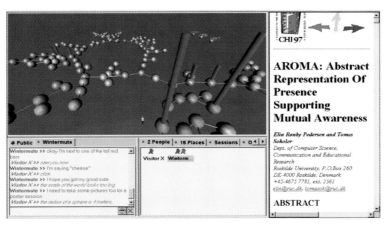

Figure 6.24   The snapshot taken in the virtual meeting. Speaker B was standing by a red vertical pole.

world therefore provides visual contextualisation cues that can help speakers to understand and interpret their context.

6.4.6 Chat in StarWalker

The second analysis focuses on casual talks in the virtual world of StarWalker. In these cases, users have a diverse range of backgrounds and interests. It has been noted that people do experience engaging conversations in primitive virtual worlds (Damer, 1998). The aim of the preliminary analysis is to find out to what extent the content of a conversation is triggered and shaped by the spatial structure.

The analysis particularly focuses on the following questions:

1. Why do people visit the StarWalker virtual world?
2. What do they talk about in StarWalker?
3. What do they think of the overall organisation of the StarWalker virtual world?
4. What is the most interesting feature to them?
5. What do they think of the semantic network?

Most visitors have been regular users of the blaxxun's online communities. They tend to be interested in meeting people, and curious to explore a new virtual world (Figs 6.25 and 6.26). The following examples partially explain why they came:

- Hello . . . don't remember seeing this world before . . .
- I saw it on the list and never been here.
- StarWalker sounded interesting.

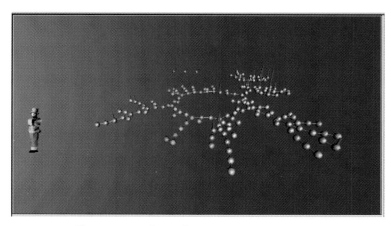

Figure 6.25   Exploring the virtual space on your own.

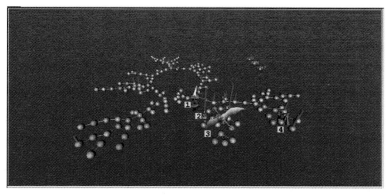

Figure 6.26   Social navigation may become possible, as avatars gather in StarWalker.

The spatial metaphor of StarWalker evoked several episodes with the familiar question-and-answer pattern. The following example, in which A and C have not previously met, is a typical example:

C:	As I look at this it looks more like a star map.
A:	Yeah?
A:	It would be nice if each node had music . . .
C:	Yes, if you put our galaxy center in the center. . . . . well, you know.
A:	Do you know where I can get a gif for that?
C:	Well, you really can't get one of our galaxy.
A:	Hi, MAD660.
C:	Mankind has not been that far yet.
MAD660:	For what?
C:	Foto of our galaxy.
C:	?
A:	To get a glimpse of our galaxy.
C:	We can only view the edge.
A:	As a backdrop of this world?
C:	Oh, cool.
C:	Go to nasa.gov.
C:	Hubble ST (space telescope) has all kinds of good stuff.

In many virtual worlds, people often feel free to ask for help. Such requests were quite common in StarWalker, with users asking, for example, how to configure preferences of a browser plug-in, and how to open audio channels along with the built-in textual interface.

Users also talked a lot about the spatial layout and its meaning. Many people thought the semantic model was a molecule. One visitor said, 'Ahaa, I see now. It is the DNA for me as an avatar and the vr-universe!' Some users thought it was a star map, others thought it was to do with Star Trek or spaceships.

It is clear from the transcripts that StarWalker gave users a strong feeling that it is considerably different from other virtual worlds they had visited. Most of them are based on buildings, cities, and other familiar landscapes. Note, in the following example, that visitor OML referred to the place as an inner space.

OML: I saw it on the list and never been here.
OML: StarWalker sounded interesting.
OML: But instead of going to outer space I came into inner space.

Here is another interesting example. One visitor asked if this place was only for 'trekkies'. Looking at this example again, users were concerned whether their social behaviour would fit the constraints implied by the StarWalker spatial metaphor.

Marzii: Only trekkies allowed?
Star Trekys: Depends, Mar.
Marzii: (De)pends on what?
Star Trekys: Are you a trekkie?
Star Trekys: Treky.
Marzii: Not a trekky – more like an observer.
Star Trekys: You are here right?
Marzii: Correct.
Star Trekys: Since you are, you must be allowed.
Star Trekys: Or you couldn't be here.
Marzii smiles at Star Trekys.
Marzii: Aha – logic.

The unique feature of the StarWalker virtual world was a recurring subject in dialogues in StarWalker. One user said:

● 'I have not seen any multiuser environment this abstract before . . .'
● 'I always thought the communities look too much like the "real" world . . .'

Much of the conversation in the public session was related to the semantic or spatial organisation of the StarWalker. In parallel, participants' interests were discussed in an informative way. In contrast to the invited meeting with the domain expert, the overall spatial metaphor played an important role in maintaining an interesting and considerably focused conversation between two people who had never met each other before.

6.4.7 Dynamics of Social Interaction

In this chapter, we have introduced a novel approach to the development and study of virtual environments, based on a notion of structural duality and a semantically enriched spatial metaphor in StarWalker. Users clearly noticed the uniqueness of StarWalker in terms of its spatial metaphor, and the semantics conveyed through the virtual environment as a whole. Will they interact and communicate differently with each other in StarWalker?

We have analysed conversations from StarWalker in an attempt to identify links between social interaction and the contextual role of the spatialised semantic space. Our initial experiences suggested that StarWalker provides a flexible platform for shared intellectual work in specific subject domains, as well as for social interaction in general. Based on our experiences with StarWalker in the past few months, we can draw the following conclusions:

- Incorporating information visualisation components into a virtual environment leads to a flexible virtual environment, not only for social interaction, but also for shared intellectual work.
- The notion of social navigation fits the new metaphor very well; the combination of spatial, semantic, and social navigation results in a coherent and intuitive means of interaction.
- The concept of structural duality turns out to be a thought-provoking way of approaching a better understanding of social dynamics in virtual environments. It has the potential of functioning as a reference framework to unify inter-disciplinary approaches addressing some challenging issues raised in computer mediated social interaction, and collaborative work.

StarWalker demonstrates a generic approach to the development of virtual environments, with potential applications in areas such as shared digital libraries, collaborative learning, and virtual conferences for special interest groups and virtual communities.

Who will benefit from this type of virtual environment? Given that the semantic space is restricted to a specific subject domain, researchers, practitioners, and students are likely to benefit most. Special interest groups and virtual communities may also use virtual environments similar to StarWalker to create a persistent place to meet and collaborate.

The preliminary results of this investigation into the relationship between discourse and the contextual role of the visualised semantic space, indicate that the virtual environment may accommodate more focused and deeper social interaction than that fostered by general-purpose virtual worlds currently available on the Internet.

6.5 Conclusions

In this chapter, we have introduced a number of virtual environments and the design rationale underlying them. We have focused on the role of information visualisation techniques in the development of dynamic and evolving virtual environments, and have emphasised the notion of social navigation as one of the most fundamental organisational principles for a virtual environment.

We have described a novel approach to the development of semantically organised virtual environments, illustrating the design rationale and theoretical issues through the experimental virtual environment of StarWalker, and have also focused on how semantically-enriched spatial models mediate the interactive behaviour of users in a domain-specific context.

Our experience with StarWalker is encouraging – many visitors to the virtual environment have shown interest in the organisation principle, and some engaging conversations have taken place. This approach can be incorporated with techniques developed in media spaces. The enriched spatial model may play a significant role in attracting people to visit, to interact, and to adapt it into their distributed working environments.

Pioneering media spaces and collaborative virtual environments have resulted in invaluable experiences and lessons. Information visualisation, which has played a crucial part in our approach, is rapidly emerging as a new discipline, and we need to tackle many challenging issues as we start to deal with social and ecological dynamics, as well as cognitive and individual differences in a wider context.

6.5.1 Challenging Issues

Introducing information visualisation into the design of multi-user virtual environments has profound and far-reaching implications to both fields of study. Virtual environments will be enriched by the incorporation of information visualisation components, by becoming more interactive and intuitive, to fulfil the mission of providing a medium for social interaction across geographical distance. At the same time, virtual environments play a contextual role in highlighting the usefulness of information visualisation techniques, and in giving more insights into visual navigation in a wider context, such as information foraging.

There seem to be two broad avenues to pursue: individual differences, and social dynamics in semantically organised virtual environments. In fact, these avenues may lead to two new frontiers in the research of information visualisation and virtual environments, given their theoretical and methodological roots in multiple disciplines – psychology, HCI, sociolinguistics, ethnomethodology and computer-supported cooperative work. Chief among the issues we have identified for further study is the problem of accommodating both social interaction and individual requirements within the same virtual environment. Will it be a fruitful route to pursue the convergence of information visualisation and virtual environments at a deeper level?

6.5.2 Future Work

The design and initial use of StarWalker has led to theoretical, empirical and engineering issues regarding the development and use of virtual environments for social interaction. It would seem sensible to review discourse analysis techniques more critically in further studies. IPA, for example, distinguishes only task and social-emotional discourse, and yet even in the small examples discussed here, it is clear that situated social action often falls outside these categories. The nature of a dialogue must be understood in its context. Further work on social episode and work domain analysis could strengthen the study of the relationships between situational context and dialogue structure.

A recurring theme in our journey throughout the chapters has been the interplay and convergence between information visualisation and virtual environments. Both of the fields are inter-disciplinary in nature. Fostering focused social interaction provides a good point for us to articulate various theories and methods into a cohesive whole, and also provides a test bed for the development of an integrative paradigm to advance information visualisation and virtual environments. The ultimate goal of these studies is to augment reality and make our social and intellectual interaction more efficient, natural, and enjoyable.

Note

The current prototype of StarWalker is accessible on the WWW using blaxxun's online community client browser:
http://www.brunel.ac.uk/~cssrccc2/vrml2/starwalker/.

Bibliography

Argyle, M (1976). Personality and social behaviour. In: Harre R (ed.), *Personality*, Blackwell (Oxford).

Benford, S, Snowdon, D, Colebourne, A, O'Brien, J, and Rodden, T (1997). *Informing the design of collaborative virtual environments*. Proceedings of the international ACM SIGGROUP conference on Supporting group work: the integration challenge (GROUP 97), pp. 71–80.

Benford, S, Snowdon, D, Greenhalgh, C, Ingram, R, Knox, I, and Brown, C (1995). VR-VIBE: A virtual environment for co-operative information retrieval. *Computer Graphics Forum, 14*(3):C349–C360.

Bly, SA, Harrison, SR, and Irwin, S (1993). Media spaces: bringing people together in a video, audio, and computing environment. *Communications of the ACM, 36*(1):28–46.

Bowers, J, Pycock, J, and O'Brien, J (1997). *Talk and embodiment in collaborative virtual environments*. Proceedings of CHI97, ACM Press. Available: http://www.acm.org/sigchi/chi97/proceedings/jb_txt.htm.

Canter, D, Rivers, R, and Storrs, G (1985). Characterizing user navigation through complex data structures. *Behaviour and Information Technology, 4*(2):93–102.

Canter, D, West, S, and Wools, R (1974). Judgments of people and their rooms. *British Journal of Social and Clinical Psychology, 13*:113–18.

Card, SK, Robertson, GG, and York, W (1996). *The WebBook and the Web Forager: An Information workspace for the World-Wide Web*. Proceedings of the ACM Conference on Human Factors in Computing Systems (CHI 96) (Vancouver, Canada, April 1996), ACM Press. Available: http://www.acm.org/sigchi/chi96/proceedings/papers/Card/skc1txt.html.

Carlsson, C, and Hagsand, O (1993). DIVE: A platform for multi-user virtual environments. *Computer Graphics, 17*(6):663–9.

Chen, C (1998a). Bridging the gap: The use of Pathfinder networks in visual navigation. *Journal of Visual Languages and Computing, 9*(3):267–86.

Chen, C (1998b). Generalised Similarity Analysis and Pathfinder Network Scaling. *Interacting with Computers, 10*(2):107–28.

Chen, C (1999). Visualising semantic spaces and author co-citation networks in digital libraries. *Information Processing and Management*, 35(3), 401–419.

Chen, C, and Carr, L (1999). *Trailblazing the literature of hypertext: Author co-citation analysis (1989–1998)*. Proceedings of the Tenth ACM Conference on Hypertext (Hypertext 99) (Germany), ACM Press, pp. 51–60.

Chen, C, and Czerwinski, M (1998). *From latent semantics to spatial hypertext: an integrated approach*. Proceedings of the Ninth ACM Conference on Hypertext and Hypermedia (Hypertext 98) (Pittsburgh, USA, June 1998), ACM Press, pp. 77–86.

Chen, C, Thomas, L, and Chennawasin, C (1999). Representing the semantics of virtual spaces. IEEE Multimedia, 6(2) (April–June 1999).

Chen, SE (1995). *QuickTime˙VR: An image-based approach to virtual environment navigation*. Proceedings of the Twenty-second Annual ACM Conference on Computer Graphics (SIGGRAPH 95), pp. 29–38.

Curtis, P, and Nichols, DA (1993). *MUDs grow up: Social virtual reality in the real world*, Xerox PARC.

Damer, B (1998). *Avatars! Exploring and Building Virtual Worlds on the Internet*, Peachpit Press (Berkeley, USA).

Dieberger, A (1997). Supporting social navigation on the World-Wide Web. *International Journal of Human-Computer Studies*, 46:805–25.

Dillon, A, McKnight, C, and Richardson, J (1993). Space – The final chapter or why physical representations are not semantic intentions. In: McKnight C, Dillon A,and Richardson J (eds.), *Hypertext: A Psychological Perspective*, Ellis Horwood, pp. 169–91.

Dourish, P, and Chalmers, M (1994). *Running out of space: Models of information navigation.* Proceedings of HCI 94 . Available: ftp://parcftp.xerox.com/pub/europarc/jpd/hci94-navigation.ps.

Drew, P, and Heritage, J (eds.) (1992). *Talk at Work: Interaction in Institutional Settings.* CUP (Cambridge, UK).

Erickson, T (1993). *From interface to interplace: The spatial environment as a medium for interaction.* Proceedings of the European Conference on Spatial Information Theory, Springer-Verlag, pp. 391–405. Available: http://www.pliant.org/personal/Tom_Erickson/Interplace.html.

Erickson, T (1996). The World-Web Web as social hypertext. *Communications of the ACM, 39*(1):15–17.

Erickson, T (1997). *Social interaction on the net: Virtual community as participatory genre.* Proceedings of the Thirtieth Hawaii International Conference on Systems Science (Hawaii), IEEE Computer Society Press, pp. 23–30. Available: http://www.pliant.org/personal/Tom_Erickson/VC_as_Genre.html.

Erickson, T, and Salomon, G (1991). *Designing a desktop information system: Observations and issues.* Proceedings of CHI 91 , ACM Press.

Forgas, JP (1979). *Social Episodes: The Study of Interaction Routines*, Vol. 17, Academic Press (London).

Forgas, JP, Bower, GH, and Krantz, SE (1984). The influence of mood on perceptions of social interactions. *Journal of Experimental Social Psychology, 20*(6):497–513.

Gaver, WW, Smets, G, and Overbeeke, K (1995). *A Virtual Window on media space.* Proceedings of CHI 95, ACM Press, pp. 257–64.

Giddens, A (1984). *The Constitution of Society: Outline of the Theory of Structuration*, Chicago, Polity Press (Chicago).

Goffman, E (1974). *Frame Analysis*, Harper and Row (New York).

Greenhalgh, C, and Benford, S (1995). MASSIVE: A virtual reality system for tele-conferencing. *ACM Transactions on Computer Human Interaction, 2*(3):239–61.

Gumperz, J (1982). *Discourse Strategies*, CUP (Cambridge, UK).

Haake, J, and Wilson, B (1992). *Supporting collaborative writing of hyperdocuments in SEPIA.* Proceedings of Hypertext 92, ACM Press, pp. 138–46.

Harrison, S, and Dourish, P (1996). *Re-place-ing space: The roles of place and space in collaborative systems.* Proceedings of CSCW 96, ACM Press, pp. 67–76.

Hill, WC, Hollan, JD, Wroblewski, D, and McCandless, T (1992). *Edit wear and read wear.* Proceedings of CHI 92 Conference on Human Factors in Computing Systems (Monterey, USA, May 1992), ACM Press, pp. 3–9.

Hill, W, Stead, L, Rosenstein, M, and Furnas, G (1995). *Recommending and evaluating choices in a virtual community of use.* Proceedings of CHI 95, ACM Press.

Hjorland, B (1997). *Information Seeking and Subject Representation: An Activity-Theoretical Approach to Information Science*, Greenwood Press (Westport, USA).

Jeffrey, P, and Mark, G (1998). *Constructing social spaces in virtual environments: A study of navigation and interaction.* Proceedings of Workshop on Personalised and Social Navigation in Information Space (Stockholm, March 1998), pp. 24–38. Available: http://www.sics.se/humle/projects/persona/web/workshop/proceedings.html.

Kaplan, N, and Moulthrop, S (1994). *Where no mind has gone before: ontological design for virtual spaces.* Proceedings of ECHT 94, pp. 206–16.

Kling, R (1980). Social analyses of computing: Theoretical perspectives in recent empirical research. *ACM Computing Serveys, 12*(1):61–110.

Kraut, R, Egido, C, and Galegher, J (1988). *Patterns of contact and communications in scientific research collaboration.* Proceedings of CSCW 88 (September 1988), ACM Press, pp. 1–12.

Kraut, R, Egido, C, and Galegher, J (1990). Patterns of contact and communication in scientific research collaboration. In: Galegher, J, Kraut, R, and Egido, C (eds.), *Intellectual Teamwork*, Lawrence Erlbaum (Hillsdale, USA), pp. 149–73.

Mantei, MM, Baecker, RM, Sellen, AJ, Buxton, WAS, Milligan, T, and Wellman, B (1991). *Experiences in the use of a media space.* Proceedings of CHI 91, ACM Press, pp. 203–8.

McCahill, M, and Erickson, T (1995). *Design for a 3-D spatial user interface for internet gopher.* Proceedings of the World Conference on Educational Multimedia and Hypermedia (ED-MEDIA 95) (Graz, Austria). Available: http://www.pliant.org/personal/Tom_Erickson/GopherVR.html.

Pedersen, ER, and Sokoler, T (1997). *AROMA: Abstract representation of presence supporting mutual awareness.* Proceedings of CHI 97 (Atlanta, March 1997), pp. 51–8.

Rao, R, Pedersen, JO, Hearst, MA, Mackinlay, JD, Card, SK, Masinter, L, *et al.* (1995). Rich interaction in the digital library. *Communications of the ACM, 38*(4):29–39.

Robertson, GG, Mackinlay, JD, and Card, SK (1991). *Cone trees: Animated 3D visualizations of hierarchical information.* Proceedings of CHI 97 (New Orleans, April/May 1991), pp. 189–94.

Rooney, SM, and Schmelkin, LP (1996). Social episode cognition. *Basic and Applied Social Psychology, 18*(1):97–110.

Tang, JC, Isaacs, EA, and Rua, M (1994). *Supporting distributed groups with a montage of lightweight interactions.* Proceedings of CSCW 94, ACM Press, pp. 23–34.

Tolva, J (1996). *Ut pictura hyperpoesis: Spatial form, visuality, and the digital word.* Proceedings of Hypertext 96 (Washington, DC), ACM Press, pp. 66–73.

Toomey, L, Adams, L, and Churchill, E (1998). *Meetings in a virtual space: Creating a digitial document.* Proceedings of the Thirty-first Annual Hawaii International Conference on System Sciences (Hawaii, HA), IEEE Computer Society, pp. 236–44.

Vygotsky, LS (1962). *Thought and Language,* MIT Press (Cambridge, USA).

Whittaker, S, Frohlich, D, and Daly-Jones, O (1994). *Informal workplace communication: what is it like and how might we support it?* Proceedings of CHI 94 (April 1994), ACM Press, pp. 131–7.

Appendix: List of Figures

Index